SEXUAL
SUICIDE

SEXUAL SUICIDE

George F. Gilder

Quadrangle/The New York Times Book Co.

SECOND PRINTING

Library of Congress Catalog Card Number: 73-79913
International Standard Book Number: 0-8129-0381-1
Jacket design and book design by James S. Ward, Inc.
Set in Linotype by Pyramid Composition
Production by Planned Production

Acknowledgments

Since this book was written among people who disagree with it—and since I often learned most from those who resisted most strongly—the author's claim of full responsibility for his conclusions will be received with unusual enthusiasm. In many instances I will be acknowledging those over whose protests, objections, and reproaches this book now reaches publication.

I was introduced to the subject by feminists so appealing and persuasive that it took me several enjoyable and edifying years to discover that they were wrong. In addition, my chief preparation in writing this book was immersion in feminist literature.

The best of all the some hundred books I read were by that somewhat ambivalent feminist, Margaret Mead, from whom I suspect I learned more than most of the feminists who quote her works. I feel *Male and Female* is the most important book published in the social sciences since World War II.

I am told that I am a sexist. I *do* believe that the differences between the sexes are our most precious heritage, even though they make women superior in the ways that matter most. The feminists refer often in their books to "human beings," but I do not care to meet one. I am only interested in men and women.

I first discovered this prejudice at a dinner party given by Peggy Dulaney, a longtime friend and an intelligent feminist, who is too generous to imagine that men are not her equal. Knowing her has offered me a continuous education in the superiority of women. But this prejudice would not have spurred me into writing a book without the discovery that even the moderate Republican ladies of the Ripon Society— and some of their powerful husbands—were sexual revolutionaries. It is Ripon Republicans of both sexes who are largely responsible for the Nixon administration's continuing commitment to job "targets" (i.e., quotas) for women—exemplified in what *The New York Times* has called the "shift of equal employment opportunity from . . . a predominantly 'black issue' to a woman's issue." As a Ripon member and editor of the *Forum*, I felt I should reject this betrayal of the civil rights movement.

Sally Stafford Nelson, of Baton Rouge, one of the leading feminists in Louisiana, provided me with both her library and the generous hospitality of her friends during the writing of much of this book. I hope she is treated clemently by her colleagues in the National Organization of Women—as well as by her male antagonists.

David and Peggy Rockefeller made completion of my writing possible by their encouragement and hospitality. The faith and kindness they have continually shown me—and the values of family and service they have embodied—are an enduring part of my life and an inspiration for this book.

Among those who read parts of the manuscript at various times and gave valuable criticism were Alison Clapp; Susan Arensberg of Alfred A. Knopf; Lee and Kate Auspitz of Harvard; Jeffrey Bell; and Irving Goldman and John Nields of Sarah Lawrence College. Professor Goldman's criticism of the anthropological sections was especially helpful, as was Alison Clapp's early aid in developing most of the thematic ideas.

A useful, generous, and tenacious combatant from the beginning has been Michael Brewer, over whose encouraging protests much of this book was written. I also should acknowlege the opportune enthusiasm and diligent, incisive editorial work of Nelson Aldrich Jr. of *Harper's*.

My family's help has been a vindication of my belief that it is the crucial institution of civilized society. This book is dedicated to my parents, who gave me their profound support. Walter and Cathy Palmer managed the manuscript and the author at their most ramshackle stages, making the book into something that could be submitted to a publisher. My sister Comfort Gordinier contributed several valuable ideas.

Rod and Mellie Gilder accommodated me and the book at several important and trying stages, read and offered close criticism for key chapters and thematic ideas, and in general gave me the benefit of their long experience in the teaching and practice of psychology and psychiatry.

I should acknowledge that the book would not be appearing now or in its present form without the continually wise and valuable counsel of Sidney Gruson of *The New York Times* or the resolve and decisiveness of Herbert Nagourney of Quadrangle. Together, moreover, they found me a perfect editor, Carol Southern, who delicately reshaped and socialized the manuscript and made me like it.

I would also like to pay tribute to Dr. Reese Alsop, the best writer in the family who introduced me to the world of writing; to Rosamond Gilder, who years ago showed me it is possible to use the word "brobdingnagian" with the same grace and propriety she uses all the others (it took me several years of sesquipedalian wrestling to get over it); and to William McCurdy, the best teacher at Harvard.

And finally a special tribute is due to Jane Stanton, who still lets me wear my track shoes in public.

George Gilder
Tyringham, Massachusetts
July 8, 1973

To my mother and Gilly.

Contents

Introduction

It is time to declare that sex is too important a subject to leave to the myopic crowd of happy hookers, Dr. Feelgoods, black panthers, white rats, answer men, evangelical lesbians, sensuous psychiatrists, retired baseball players, pornographers, dolphins, swinging priests, displaced revolutionaries, polymorphous perverts, and *Playboy* philosophers—all bouncing around on waterbeds and typewriters and television talk shows, making "freedom" ring the cash registers of the revolution.

Nothing is free, least of all sex, which is bound to our deepest sources of energy, identity, and emotion. Sex can be cheapened, of course, but then, inevitably, it becomes extremely costly to the society as a whole. For sex is the life force—and cohesive impulse—of a people, and their very character will be deeply affected by how sexuality is managed, sublimated, expressed, denied, and propagated. When sex is devalued, propagandized, and deformed, as at present, the quality of our lives declines and our social fabric deteriorates.

Even the attitude toward sex and sexuality as concepts illustrates the problem. The words no longer evoke an image of a broad pageant of relations and differences between the sexes, embracing every aspect of our lives. Instead "sex" and "sexuality" are assumed to refer chiefly to copulation, as if our sexual lives were restricted to the male limits—as if the experiences of maternity were not paramount sexual events. In fact, however, our whole lives are sexual. Sexual energy animates most of our activities and connects every individual to a family and a community. Sexuality is best examined not in terms of sexology, physiology, or psychology, but as a study encompassing all the ulterior life of our society.

Our current deformities make a familiar catalogue. This has been the decade when priests and homosexuals marry and politicians divorce; when *Playboy* philosophers in pulpits preach situational ethics ("if you itch, scratch") to dwindling audiences, who are already sore from scratching. It has been a period when all the technology of advertising and publicity has been applied to arousing sexual excitement, while nothing new at all has been offered for the relief of the man with his hand on the bottleneck; a period when every group of complainants and protesters, however well situated—from Ivy League students to suburban women—are decked out in the heroic vestments of the civil rights movement: "the [student] [woman] [junior professor] [professional baseball player] is the nigger of the world"; when the whole crowd is fitted with the Marxist trappings of a "new proletariat": Women, students, children of the world, unite; you have nothing to lose.

It has been a time when fashionable psychologists proclaim that all orifices were created equal ("I'm okay, you're okay"), and the "missionary position" (which we are all presumed to know means the man upstairs) is casually dismissed as the way squares peg round holes. It is a time of wife swapping, group swinging, and gay liberation; a time of dildoes in drugstore windows and perfume sprays in men's rooms; a time of oral sex and vaginal sundaes, with a Howard Johnson's array of flavors advertised in *McCall's.*

It is a time when few things are as they seem—and when appearances are propagated everywhere. In no realm are things less as they seem to the media—to the observer-kings of the American consciousness—than in sex. What is described as the sexual revolution is a terminal spinning, without traction: the sexual suicide society.

Among the popular books of the day is Dr. Phyllis Chesler's *Women and Madness*.[1] A professor of psychology and a poet, she believes that American society is driving women crazy by sexist discrimination and oppression. The only solution she offers is sexual suicide: the abolition of biological differences between men and women. "Science must be used," she says, "to either release women from biological reproduction—or to allow men to experience the process also" [*sic*].[2] At the end of her book is one of those analogies to Nazism. "How does the Nazi use of the human body for industrial purposes . . ." she asks, "differ from [the American system's] female—or male—prostitution?" Ms. Chesler's incredible book, a best seller, was celebrated on the front page of *The New York Times Book Review*.

Also well received was a tract for lesbianism called *Sappho Was a Right-on Woman*.[3] Again *The Times* led the way. In the past, it observed in its *Book Review,* lesbianism had been a burden for the women's movement. But this book would change all that. In particular it would help overcome, in the words of *The Times* review, "the nuclear family, that cradle of evil." [4] *The Times* did not explain why the nuclear family is a "cradle of evil." Perhaps it has something to do with Nazi Germany (though the Nazis also opposed the nuclear family and encouraged illegitimate births to counteract it.)

A typical scene—a cocktail party in a fashionable Massachusetts suburb. The young woman's voice shook with emotion: "I couldn't bring a child into the world. I just couldn't do it. It wouldn't be fair." No one in the room seemed surprised. A few nodded assent. It is a common refrain of educated young women—from age 15 on—in current-day America. *I have no interest in having children.*

A less fashionable revolutionary mecca—the singles bar. Depicted as a great sexual marketplace in newspaper and magazine accounts, and groovy indeed to the tourist's eye, it is deadly to those who seriously partake. Most of them are essentially unavailable on any profound level. The men are self-pitying, impotent with girls they like; or they are married and searching for an image of sexual bliss advertised in all the magazines as a province of shapely youth performing sexual exotica. The stable and serious girls rarely come back. And the serious men drink and banter. The Stones' "I Can't Get No Satisfaction," is the national anthem of the "love generation." Most of the single men fill their throbbing vanities with alcohol and go home to their swinging bachelor digs, perhaps to beat off to the Playmate of the Month, who by 1972—as an index of thrilling liberation—was beginning to display pubic hair.

Life as a swingle means, for all too many of its devotees, a succession of neurotic women and men of dubious emotional and physical health alternating with muckish evenings of pornography and television. The promiscuous revels of urban and college youth conveyed by the media are actually enjoyed by only a few erotic aristocrats and voyeurs. For the rest of us it is a sick joke, which makes us sickest if we are foolish enough to believe it and invest it with our money and aspirations.

The swinging existence—the *Playboy* ideal and image of youthful urbanity—is pursued chiefly by those who have no choice: various classes of neurotics and losers. But it is, nevertheless, maintained as the standard. Though it is hard to find people who are truly enjoying the culturally ordained images of carefree sex, few can assert a plausible alternative.

Try another famous center of liberation, the great Eastern University. Here differences between the sexes are systematically suppressed. In general, men and women go to classes together, few form families, birth control is ubiquitous. It is a perfect scene for sexual emancipation. And yet—birth control is repeatedly botched; pornography and masturbation are pervasive forms of sex; and impotence is the chief male complaint at the psychological clinic.[5] One discovers a widespread sense of pessimism and demoralization, a fascination with violence, revolution, drugs, and the occult—and a strangely desperate loneliness.

Promiscuity is tried and usually rejected. Monogamous relationships are intensely sought, but increasingly difficult to sustain. The revels of co-ed dormitories, on closer inspection, consist of marijuana reveries and traffic tie-ups at the door of the common bathroom. Otherwise what is really happening is a feverish, if often unsuccessful, pursuit of stable sexuality in a world of polygamous fantasies. The mass culture is increasingy promiscuous; thus marriage and procreative love are becoming a countercultural assertion. The remarkable fact is the tenacity of the quest for it.

Nonetheless, a kind of Gresham's law applies. Bad sex drives out the good, and the worst of all—philandering and homosexuality—are exalted. Gay liberation, pornographic glut, and one-night trysts are all indices of sexual frustration; all usually disclose a failure to achieve profound and loving sexuality. When a society deliberately affirms these failures—contemplates legislation of homosexual marriage, celebrates the women who denounce the family, and indulges pornography as a manifestation of sexual health and a release from repression—the culture is promoting a form of erotic suicide. For it is destroying the cultural preconditions of profound love and sexuality: the durable heterosexual relationships necessary to a community of emotional investments and continuities in which children can find a secure place.

The inflation and devaluation of sexual currency leads to a failure of marriage that subverts the entire society. The increasing incidence of divorce, desertion, illegitimacy, and venereal disease produces a chaotic biological arena. Anyone may be cut and slashed by the shards of broken families in the streets of our cities. When sex becomes a temporary release, to be prompted as well by one woman as by another, or by sex magazines; when sex becomes a kind of massage, which can be administered as well by a member of the same sex or by a machine for that matter—one's whole emotional existence is depleted. We can no longer fathom the depths of our biological beings, which are open only to loving sexual experience. Drugs and alcohol can substitute for erotic activity; and with a cheapened sexual currency, couples can no longer afford children emotionally. Babies come as mistakes, misconceived and misbegotten. They come back to get theirs later.

All these social problems are ultimately erotic. The frustration of the affluent young and their resort to drugs, the breakdown of the family among both the rich and poor, the rising rate of crime and violence—all the clichés of our social crisis spring from, or reflect and reinforce, a fundamental deformation of sexuality.

The chief perpetrators of these problems are men: [6] Men commit over 90 percent of major crimes of violence, 100 percent of the rapes, 95 percent of the burglaries. They comprise 94 percent of our drunken drivers, 70 percent of suicides, 91 percent of offenders against family and children.[7] More specifically, the chief perpetrators are *single* men. Single men comprise between 80 and 90 percent of most of the categories of social pathology, and on the average they make less money than any other group in the society—yes, less than single women or working women.[8] As any insurance actuary will tell you, single men are also less responsible about their bills, their driving, and other personal conduct. Together with the disintegration of the family, they constitute our leading social problem. For there has emerged no institution that can replace the family in turning children into civilized human beings or in retrieving the wreckage of our current disorder.

Yet what is our new leading social movement? It's Women's Liberation, with a whole array of nostrums designed to emancipate us. From what? From the very institution that is most indispensable to overcoming our present social crisis: the family. They want to make marriage more open, flexible, revokable, at a time when it is already opening up all over the country and spewing forth swarms of delinquents and neurotics, or swarms of middle-aged men and women looking for a sexual utopia that is advertised everywhere, delivered nowhere, but paid for through the nose (and other improbable erogenous zones). At a time when modernity is placing ever greater strains on the institutions of male socialization—our families, sports, men's organizations—the women's movement wants to weaken them further, make them optional, bisexual, androgynous. Most of the books of the feminists speak of the need to "humanize" (emasculate?) men.

Surely women's liberation is a most unpromising panacea. But the movement is working politically, because our sexuality is so confused, our masculinity so uncertain, and our families so beleaguered that no one knows what they are for or how they are sustained. Against a fetish of individualism and a spurious equality, against an economic emphasis on sexless efficiency, against an erotic hedonism that sees sex as a mere sensuality, against such ideological abstractions and glandular pulsations, our social fabric seems invisible. Like the Pentagon, our social science often reduces all phenomena to dollars and body counts. Sexuality, family unity, kinship, masculine solidarity, maternity, motivation, nurturing, all the rituals of personal identity and development, all the bonds of community, seem "sexist," "superstitious," "mystical," "inefficient," "discriminatory." And, of course, they are—and they are also indispensable to a civilized society.

So the way is opened for the feminists. The movement barges into all the private ceremonies, sexual mystiques, and religious devotions of the society as if they were optional indulgences rather than the definitive processes of our lives. In a world in which most men and women everywhere, throughout history, have spent most of their time and energy in elaborate rituals of differentiation, the feminists advance the preposterous idea that we are all just individual "human beings," only secondarily identified by sex or family. This assumption is statistically convenient. But it is a myth. And this myth makes the women unable to understand almost everything that happens in the society or to comprehend what is important in motivating men and women.

Perhaps the epitome of this attitude was the statement by *Esquire*'s house feminist, Nora Ephron, in a column on sex after liberation. "What will happen to sex after liberation?" she asks. "Frankly, I don't know. It is a great mystery to all of us." [9]

Since sex in all its dimensions is the single most important motivating force in human life, what happens to sex after liberation will largely determine what happens to everything else. But Ms. Ephron is honest and right. The liberationists have no idea where their program would take us. The movement is counseling us to walk off a cliff, in the evident wish that our society can be kept afloat on feminist hot air.

Demographers, historians, anthropologists, and zoologists have often observed that both human and animal societies sometimes reach a condition of demoralization in which they have difficulty reproducing themselves. The cause is a collapse of the future: a group no longer believes in a better world to come. The French aristocrats before the revolution, American Indians after the closing of the frontier, European towns faced with starvation and plague, tribes in the Pacific shaken by a Western intrusion on their religious rites—even animals moved to zoos or other alien conditions—all experienced a crisis of procreation.

We may soon be able to add to that somber list the American intelligentsia. Contrary to popular belief, many influential groups in this society are already failing to reproduce themselves, and the country as a whole is now at a level approaching zero population growth. Any increase of this trend would signify a serious national demoralization.[10]

In the most elemental sense, the sex drive is the survival instinct: the primal tie to the future. When people lose faith in themselves and their prospects, they also lose their procreative energy. They commit sexual suicide. They just cannot bear the idea of "bringing children into the world." Such people may indulge a lot in what they call sex. But it is a kind of aimless copulation having little to do with the deeper currents of sexuality and love that carry a community into the future.

Part One

Love and Family

1

The Balance of Potency

Much of the recent debate over our sexual relations has focused on the question of power. Elizabeth Janeway maintains that in the past women exercised power but that "now it has evaporated." [1] Kate Millett, on the other hand, believes that women have been oppressed throughout history.[2] Many feminists see a gain in female power in recent years. Others regard the gains as illusory. Only Midge Decter perceives that the women's liberation campaign itself is a response to anxieties over the increasing power and freedom of women.[3] In general, regardless of the assumptions about female power, men are said to dominate the society.

The liberationists have no trouble finding examples of male power. The President orders a fleet of bombers to devastate a foreign city. The Governor dispatches a battalion of the National Guard to pacify a campus. Muhammad Ali floors an opponent with a barrage of blows. Two policemen seize a prostitute and hurl her into the back of their car, while her customer walks away. A corporate entrepreneur buys a company and fires most of its workers. An obstetrician anesthetizes a woman and takes over the management of her childbirth. The sanitation workers strike and paralyze the city. A mugger snatches a purse. An assassin kills the President. An unknown assailant in an elevator gooses Susan Brownmiller.[4] The Supreme Court overthrows abortion laws. Several hundred thousand office managers dictate summarily to their secretaries.

Such a motley list could be extended indefinitely. One could devise a similar catalogue of female enactments, citing the occasional woman judge or policeman or karate champion or corporate executive. But the effort is frivolous, for men overwhelm women in visible and public exercise of power. One could more plausibly find statistics of ownership showing that women exceed men in total holdings (partly because women live to inherit the fortunes of men after their coronaries). One might also suggest that women account for most of our consumer spending. Such estimates are interesting, perhaps, but they lead only to an irresolvable debate about who actually makes familial decisions.

All such speculation about the power of the two sexes is of little significance to the lives and gratifications of real men and women. Most of the statistics of male power disregard the obvious fact that it is in large part exerted over other males. In any modern society very few men, and fewer women, exercise great public authority.

For most people, as Marx and others have observed, the one place they are least free, powerful, and individual is at work. Even the supposed titans of industry operate under severe marketplace constraints and psychological disciplines that cause them to labor some 70 hours a week. Few enjoy the kind of freedom that is fantasized by the movement or Herbert Marcuse. Leaving the great executives and entrepreneurs aside, most workers regard their jobs as bondage. When appraising the real power of the sexes, it is difficult to conceive of a measure less pertinent to the average man than the number of male Senators and millionaires. Most people enjoy their real gratifications not in the office or on the assembly line but in the domestic and sexual arenas, where female power is inevitably greatest.

The principal flaw of most of the literature of women's liberation is its incomprehension of the real power of women. Literally hundreds of tomes and pamphlets have been written on the need to establish "equality between the sexes." But since women are not presumed to have significant assets, the agenda always resembles an opening proposal in disarmament talks between the United States and the Soviet Union: Each side is willing to negotiate only about those "brutal weapons of aggression" in which the other side has the advantage. The feminist program thus usually consists of taking jobs and money away from men, while granting in return such uncoveted benefits as the right to cry.

It is on this issue of female power that Mrs. Janeway, the most sophisticated of the feminists, has a rare but disabling failure of perception. She sees that people behave as if women possessed important power. But it never occurs to her that women are actually powerful. Instead, in *Man's World, Woman's Place,* she asserts that female power is a "social myth." Then she labors for chapters to show that "social myths" are important enough to account for the pervasive male fear and respect of women.

It is a generous effort, since Mrs. Janeway could just as easily have dismissed these male fears as the typical sentiments, born of guilt, that most oppressors feel toward the oppressed. The usual feminist analogy is the slave owner's fearful attribution of great, mysterious sexual powers to the black male. But all these arguments of neurosis and myth fall before Occam's razor. The simplest explanation of male fear suffices: Women, in fact, possess enormous power over men. In a profound way, most women do not feel subordinate. For the conspicuous and calculable power of males is counterbalanced by a deep and inexorable power of women.

Sexual love, intercourse, marriage, conception of a child, childbearing, even breast-feeding are all critical experiences psychologically. They are times when our emotions are most intense, our lives most deeply changed, and society perpetuated in our own image. And they are all transactions of sexual differences.

The divisions are embodied in a number of roles. The central ones are mother and father, husband and wife. They form neat and apparently balanced pairs. But appearances are deceptive. In the most elemental sexual terms, there is little balance at all. In most of those key sexual events, the male role is trivial, even easily dispensable. Although the man is needed in intercourse, artificial insemination has already been used in hundreds of thousands of cases. Otherwise, the man is altogether unnecessary. It is the woman who conceives, bears, and suckles the child. Those activities which are most deeply sexual are mostly female; they comprise the mother's role, defined organically by her body.

The nominally equivalent role of father is in fact a product of marriage and other cultural contrivances. There is no biological need for the father to be anywhere around when the baby is born and nurtured. In many societies the father has no special responsibility to support the specific children he sires. In some societies, paternity is not even acknowledged. The idea that the father is inherently equal to the mother within the family, or that he will necessarily be inclined to remain with it, is nonsense.[5] In one way or another, the man must be made equal by society.

In discussing the erotic aspects of our lives, we must concern ourselves chiefly with women. Males are the sexual outsiders and inferiors. A far smaller portion of their bodies is directly erogenous. A far smaller portion of their lives is devoted to sexual activity. Their own distinctively sexual experience is limited to erection and ejaculation. Their rudimentary sexual drive leads only toward copulation. The male body offers no sexual fulfillment comparable to a woman's passage through months of pregnancy, to the tumult of childbirth, and on into the suckling of her baby. All are powerful and fulfilling sexual experiences completely foreclosed to men.

In very primitive societies, men have the compensation of physical strength. They can control women by force and are needed to protect them from other men. But this equalizer is relatively unimportant in a civilized society, where the use of force is largely restricted by law and custom. Here the men counterbalance female sexual superiority by playing a crucial role as provider and achiever. Money replaces muscle.

If women become equal in terms of money and achievement, there is only one way equality between the sexes can be maintained in a modern society. Women must be reduced to sexual parity. They must relinquish their sexual superiority, psychologically disconnect their wombs, and adopt the short-circuited copulatory sexuality of males. Women must renounce all the larger procreative dimensions of their sexual impulse.

As anyone can attest who has associated much with "liberationist" women, this is what they try to do. They are as dogged in denying that they have a maternal instinct as they are resolute in their insistence that many men do. But despite the feminist protestations, the man remains inferior in procreation: He cannot bear children. Any special access to the child must be granted to him by the woman. She must acknowledge the man's paternity. And only the woman can acquire sexual affirmation from feeding the infant at her breast.

Neither the primacy of the biological realm, nor the immense psychological role of the woman in it, is well understood in our rationalist age. Man's predicament begins in his earliest years. A male child is born, grows, and finds his being in relation to his own body and to the bodies of his parents, chiefly his mother. His later happiness is founded in part on a physiological memory. Originating perhaps in the womb itself, it extends through all his infant groping into the world at large, which begins, of course, in his mother's arms. In trusting her he learns to trust himself, and trusting himself he learns to bear the slow dissolution of the primary tie. He moves away into a new world, into a sometimes frightening psychic space between his parents; and he must then attach his evolving identity to a man, his father. From almost the start, the boy's sexual identity is dependent on acts of exploration and initiative.

Throughout the lives of men we find echoes of this image, of a boy stranded in transition from his first tie to a woman— whom he discovers to be different, and subtly dangerous to him—toward identification with a man, who will always deny him the closeness his mother once provided. At an early age he is, in a sense, set at large. Before he can return to a woman, he must assert his manhood in action. The Zulu warrior had to kill a man, the Mandan youth had to endure torture, the Irish peasant had to build a house, the American man must find a job. This is the classic myth and the mundane reality of masculinity.

Female histories are different. A girl's sexuality normally unfolds in an unbroken line, from a stage of utter dependency and identification with her mother through stages of gradual autonomy. Always, the focus of female identification is clear and stable.

The distinguished anthropologist Ashley Montagu has reported recent evidence that women treat girls and boys differently from the time of birth, fondling and caressing the girls more and making them feel more a part of their initial environment.[6] The mothers may unconsciously recognize that girls can enjoy a continuous evolution of identity with their mothers, while boys relatively soon must break this primary tie.

Of course, this analysis, essentially confirmed by the studies of Karen Horney [7] and Erik Erikson,[8] conflicts to some extent with the Freudian theory of penis envy and resulting female insecurity. But the pattern these earliest events might be expected to create—of a more stable and secure femininity and a more insecure and questing masculinity—is later enforced by the radically contrasting male and female experience of their sexuality.

Male sexual consciousness comes as an unprogrammed

drive. Nothing about the male body dictates any specific pattern beyond a repetitive release of sexual tension. Men must define and defend the larger dimensions of their sexuality by external activity.

The male sexual repertory, moreover, is very limited. Men have only one sex organ and one sex act: erection and ejaculation. Everything else is guided by culture and imagination. Other male roles—other styles of masculine identity—must be learned or created. In large part, they are a cultural invention, necessary to civilized life but ultimately fragile.

A woman is not so exclusively dependent on copulation for sexual identity. For her, intercourse is only one of many sex acts or experiences. Her sexual nature is reaffirmed monthly in menstruation; her breasts and her womb further symbolize a sex role that extends, at least as a potentiality, through pregnancy, childbirth, lactation, suckling, and long-term nurture. Rather than a brief performance, female sexuality is a long, unfolding process. Even if a woman does not in fact bear a child, she is continually reminded that she can, that she is capable of performing the crucial act in the perpetuation of the species. She can perform the only act that gives sex an unquestionable meaning, an incarnate result.

Thus, regardless of any anxieties she may have in relation to her sexual role and how to perform it, she at least knows that she has a role of unquestionable importance to herself and the community. Whatever else she may do or be, she can be sure of her essential female nature. Women take their sexual identity for granted and assume that except for some cultural peculiarity, men also might enjoy such sexual assurance. Women are puzzled by male unease, by men's continual attempts to prove their manhood or ritualistically affirm it. Judith Hole and Ellen Levine, in the *Rebirth of Feminism,* show typical female complacency when they call sexual identity "an almost immutable fact," like "the location of one's head." [9] Seymour Fisher's elaborate examination of female sexuality for the National Institute of Health confirms this greater security of women: "It was my conclusion, after reviewing all available studies," Fisher writes, "that the average woman is more 'at ease' with her own body than is the average man. . . . Her body 'makes sense' to her as one of the prime

means to become what she wants to become." [10] This assurance about sexual identity leads to a certain impatience with men.

Throughout the literature of feminism, in fact, there runs a puzzled complaint, "Why can't men *be* men, and just relax?" The reason is that, unlike femininity, relaxed masculinity is at bottom empty, a limp nullity. While the female body is full of internal potentiality, the male is internally barren (from the Old French *bar,* meaning man). Manhood at the most basic level can be validated and expressed only in action. For a man's body is full only of undefined energies. And all these energies need the guidance of culture. He is therefore deeply dependent on the structure of the society to define his role.

Nancy Chodorow ends her otherwise fine essay on "Being and Doing" by envisioning a world in which "male identity does not depend on men's proving themselves [by] doing." Like so many others in the movement, she wonders whether men can be "humanized." Chodorow laments that in our society men's "doing" is "a reaction to insecurity" rather than "a creative exercise of their humanity." [11]

She is essentially right. The male sexual predicament, like the female, is not the sort of arrangement that might have been invented by social engineers. It has a tragic quality that is difficult to adapt to egalitarian formulas. But the essential need to perform is alterable only in sexual suicide. There is no shortcut to human fulfillment for men—just the short circuit of impotence. Men can be creatively human only when they are confidently male and overcome their sexual insecurity by action. Nothing comes to them by waiting or "being." Even the degree of sexual confidence that most men *can* achieve in civilized society is dependent either on constant initiative or on culturally identifying and reserving certain roles and arenas as distinctively male.

Unlike a woman, a man has no civilized role or agenda inscribed in his body. While he can precipitate life in a woman, he can never create it in the sense that a mother does. The child can never be *his* unless a woman allows him to claim it with her or unless he so controls her and so restricts her sexual activity that he can be sure that the child is his. He cannot merely come back nine months later with grand claims. He must have a durable commitment.

Even then he must rely on the woman to bear and nurture the child, even to love it. His participation in the chain of nature, his access to social immortality, the very meaning of his potency, of his life energy, are all profoundly and inexorably contingent on a woman's durable love and on her sexual discipline.

These differences in sexual experience, of course, account for the Victorian "double standard," whereby chastity was required for women but some promiscuity was acceptable for men. One hesitates to say a good word for a pattern of behavior so discredited today—particularly since promiscuity is in general unfortunate and the pill has significantly changed the import of intercourse for women. Nonetheless, intercourse does play a role in the lives of males that is different from its role in the lives of females, and the difference is great enough to have moral consequences.

The chief difference is that, lacking the innate insecurity of males and possessing an unimpeachable sexual identity, women are not usually so reliant on intercourse. As Alfred Kinsey's colleague, Mary Jane Sherfey, observes in her liberationist book on female sexuality [12]—and as the Masters and Johnson experiments show—women can both enjoy sexual relations more profoundly and durably and forgo them more easily than can men. In those ways they are superior. Whatever other problems a woman may have, her identity *as a woman* is not so much at stake in intercourse. She has other specifically female experiences and does not have to perform intercourse in the same sense as her partner; she can relax and virtually always please her man.

The man, on the other hand, has only one sex act and is exposed to conspicuous failure in it. His erection is a mysterious endowment that he can never fully understand or control. If it goes, he often will not know exactly why, and there will be little he or his partner can do to retrieve it. His humiliation is inconsolable. Even if he succeeds in erection he still can fail to evoke orgasm—he can lose out to other men who can. And if he is impotent, it will subvert all the other aspects of his relationship and will undermine his entire personality. As Robert Musil has written, "the man's most masculine part is also the most easily intimidated." [13]

In general, therefore, the man is less secure than the woman because his sexuality is dependent on action, and he can act sexually only through a precarious process difficult to control. Fear of impotence is a paramount fact of male sexuality.

The women's literature, in its itch to disparage sexual differences, fails to comprehend these imperious facts of life, fails to understand that for men the desire for sex is not simply a quest for pleasure. It is an indispensable test of identity. And in itself it is always ultimately temporary and inadequate. Unless his maleness is confirmed by his culture, he must enact it repeatedly.

Thus there are times when sex may be psychologically obligatory for men. Particularly in a society where clear and affirmative masculine activities are scarce, men may feel a compulsive desire to perform their one unquestionably male role. It is only when men are engaged in a relentless round of masculine activities in the company of males—Marine Corps training is one example—that their sense of manhood allows them to avoid sex without great strain.

Most young men are subject to nearly unremitting sexual drives, involving their very identities as males. Unless they have an enduring relationship with a woman—a relationship that affords them sexual confidence—men will accept almost any convenient sexual offer. This drive arises early in their lives, and if it is not appeased by women, it is slaked by masturbation and pornography. It is not a drive induced chiefly by culture. Rural boys, conditioned to avoid sexual stimuli, avidly seek pornography when they scarcely know what it is—and when it is outlawed. The existence of a semi-illegal, multi-billion-dollar pornography market, almost entirely male oriented, bespeaks the difference in sexual character between men and women. One can be sure that if women passionately wanted pornography, it would be provided. The difference, as Midge Decter has written, to the guffaws of the liberationists, is that women lack the kind of importunate, undifferentiated lust that infects almost all men.[14]

Similarly, Fisher's empirical study of the female orgasm showed that in order to reach climax, women very often need a sense that their partners can be trusted not to leave them.[15]

This connection between orgasm and extended emotional ties is not present in males. Catherine Hahner of the New School for Social Research in New York confirms this difference and describes its current effect: "I'm convinced that women have a psychic predisposition toward monogamy, evolved through hundreds of thousands of years of responsibility for the survival of their offspring and dependence on a male provider. . . . But the male animal is not strictly monogamous. No primate is. . . . Our uteruses are telling us to stay home and make sure the children are fed and that we know who the father is, while the society [i.e., male propaganda] is telling us to get laid." [16]

This view, and Decter's, are strongly confirmed by a cross cultural study of 190 different societies made by Clellan S. Ford and Frank A. Beach.[17] Only in a very few, very primitive groups, do women equal males in promiscuity. Males almost everywhere show greater sexual aggressiveness, compulsiveness, and lack of selectivity. Over the whole range of human societies, men are overwhelmingly more prone to masturbation, homosexuality, voyeurism, gratuitous sexual aggression, and other shallow and indiscriminate erotic activity. In virtually every known society, sex is regarded either as a grant by the woman to the man, or as an object of male seizure. In most societies, the man has to pay for it with a gift or service. Although women are physiologically capable of greater orgasmic pleasure than men—and thus may avidly seek intercourse—they are also much better able to forego sex without psychological strain. In the United States the much greater mental health of single women than single men may be explained in part by this female strength. But greater sexual control and discretion are displayed by women in virtually every society throughout history and anthropology.

Of course, the girls of *Ms.,* on their procrustean beds, can simulate the shallow and compulsive male drive, particularly if they learn to detest their other female potentialities. But all the women's literature on the subject treats the woman's desire for promiscuity as an appetite for pleasure. Ms. Seaman, Ms. Sherfey, and the others describe the awesome possibilities of female orgasm—its luminosity and insatiability—and assert a woman's right to this pleasure. But however intensely pleasurable, intercourse for males is needed chiefly for identity affirmation, so that the men can know they are male, and for dispelling fears of impotence, homosexuality, and erotic suicide. In general, the sense of insecurity that impels the compulsive desire for promiscuity is a male phenomenon. In essence, the equivalent of nymphomania, a female aberration, is found in the healthiest of males.

This differing compulsiveness means that a woman's decision to pursue "illicit" sex ordinarily represents a more significant violation of love. It indicates a more deliberate repudiation of the values of ordered sexuality on which the social system depends. Thus, as a moral offense against the community, a woman's violation is more consequential than the man's temporary submission to his psychological and erotic demands. This is not to say that the woman is necessarily wrong in her decision; it is merely to say that one judges it differently. To uphold the double standard is merely to recognize the greater responsibility borne by women for the sexual prerequisites of civilized society. It is to acknowledge the much greater sexual power and responsibility inevitably exercised by women.

This difference also means that in most sexual encounters the woman has the superior position. The man is the petitioner; he bargains from the disadvantage. He can overcome his weakness only by aggressiveness. By controlling the situation, he can gain the sense of security that enables him to perform. Like a tightrope walker, he must usually keep moving. He can compensate for his greater need by a greater initiative. He can acquire the sense that he is preparing the woman and that he thus manages her readiness. In this way he escapes the extremely difficult challenge of performing on demand.

Aggressiveness on the part of the woman can jeopardize the whole process if it destroys the man's rhythm of control and enhances his insecurities. If conditions are right, he may succeed anyway. But the likelihood of impotence is increased. The key contingent variable in sex is the male erection, and it emerges from an internal psychochemistry of trust and confidence that is usually undermined by female activity. Germaine Greer's attempt to suggest that greater female aggressiveness will overcome male impotence reveals the complete failure to understand males that is omnipresent in her book.

The male responsibility for initiative derives from male sexual disadvantage. If women take the initiative, it compounds the disadvantage, disorienting the man and overburdening the woman. For she will still bear the greatest ultimate responsibilities. From her position of greater natural restraint and selectivity, she is the sexual judge and executive, finally appraising the offerings of males, favoring one and rejecting another, managing the sexual nature of the society.

The crucial process of civilization is the subordination of male sexual impulses and psychology to long-term horizons of female biology. If one compares female overall sexual behavior now with women's life in primitive societies, the difference is relatively small. It is male behavior that must be changed to create a civilized order. Modern society relies increasingly on predictable, regular, long-term human activities, corresponding to the female sexual patterns. It has little latitude for the pattern of impulsiveness, aggressiveness, and immediacy, arising from male insecurity without women—and further enhanced by hormonal activity.[18] This is the ultimate and growing source of female power in the modern world. Women domesticate and civilize male nature. They can destroy civilized male identity merely by giving up the role.

Female power, therefore, comes from what the woman can offer or withhold. She can grant to the man a sexual affirmation that he needs more than she does; she can offer him progeny otherwise permanently denied him; and she can give him a way of living happily and productively in a civilized society that is otherwise oppressive to male nature. In exchange modern man can give little beyond his external achievement and his reluctant faithfulness. It is on these terms of exchange that marriage—and male socialization—are based.

One problem today is that by giving up this power, many women are undermining their sisters who try to exercise it. When a great many women are willing to sleep around, granting sex on transitory male terms, it is more difficult for other women to insist on extended female terms. In addition, when there are many women easily available, men can more freely coax and bully reluctant ones into bed. In the United States, where the population of nubile young has been growing rapidly, the bargaining position of women has been somewhat further eroded by an excess of females of marriageable age. Because women marry younger than men—and the younger age groups are largest—there are marginally more eligible women. The current trend of growth in the nubile age groups will not be reversed until the 1980s.[19]

The women's liberation movement feeds on these conditions and worsens them for women. Many women join the movement after failing to induce men to enduring monogamy. They then disparage as unworkable the long horizons of female sexuality. But wherever male rhythms prevail long in modern society, the result is social disarray and individual unhappiness.

Such an image of woman's power—founded on common sense and observation rather than statistics of earning power—is regarded as a "myth" or "superstition" by Mrs. Janeway and the others. But one may argue that it is female power, organic and constitutional, that is real—holding sway over the deepest levels of consciousness, sources of happiness, and processes of social survival. Male dominance in the marketplace, on the other hand, is a social artifice maintained not for the dubious benefits it confers on men but for the indispensable benefits it offers the society: inducing men to support rather than disrupt the community. Conventional male power, in fact, might be considered more the ideological myth. It is designed to induce the majority of men to accept a bondage to the machine and the marketplace, to a large extent in the service of women and in the interests of civilization.

Any consideration of equality focusing on employment and income statistics, therefore, will miss the real sources of equilibrium between the sexes. These deeper female strengths and male weaknesses may be more important than any superficial male dominance because they control the ultimate motives and rewards of our existence. And in childbearing, every woman is capable of a feat of creativity and durable accomplishment—permanently and uniquely changing the face of the earth—that only the most extraordinary man can even pretend to duplicate in external activity.

Women control not the economy of the marketplace but the economy of eros: the life force in our society and our lives. What happens in the inner realm of women finally shapes what happens on our social surfaces, determining the level of happiness, energy, creativity, and solidarity in the nation.

These values are primary in any society. When they deteriorate, all the king's horses and all the king's men cannot put them back together again.

The Necessities of Love

Love is a desire for generation and birth in beauty.

Plato

It may seem unduly cynical to link love and marriage with the dismal science of economics. Love, it is our abiding faith, is the force that conquers all. And love from time to time does surmount very serious obstacles. In fact, love leavens the entire economy; it may well have been love—the desire of millions of men to gain the wherewithal for marriage—that precipitated the industrial revolution. It was love, in a similar way, that impelled many of the great migrations to the United States. The rule in Ireland that a man could not marry until he had bought or inherited a home brought hundreds of thousands of men to our nation's cities. Love conquers all when conditions are right.

But in many societies love rarely occurs at all, marriage is perfunctory, and men pursue other modes of gratification. In many parts of the world—and in some parts of the United States—love often arises between men and women but remains tragically unfulfilled because the economic conditions are wrong. Even where economic conditions are propitious, love may fail because cultural conditions are adverse.

It is thus less cynical than realistic to consider closely the economic, cultural, and sexual prerequisites of love. For there is reason to believe that we are currently undergoing a "crisis of eros" that is deeply affecting all our relationships. In terms of human happiness, it is likely that we have no problem more serious. But like all issues of sexuality, it reaches far beyond individual relationships. In fact, the great adaptability and resilience of love in millions of instances may lead us to deny the general crisis. Yet it is general conditions that create the long-term trends. And the trend seems to be against profound and enduring sexual ties.

It is fair to say that increasing numbers of Americans are profoundly confused about love. As usual, the women's movement is symptomatic. Although the feminists seem obsessed with the subject, they have no clear idea of what it is. They often avoid the problem of definition by deferring it to some postrevolutionary stage—to be achieved after the withering away of masculinity—when love will blossom between people who recognize each other as "human beings." In pursuit of this ideal, the women concern themselves a great deal with the question of how to "humanize" a man. But again, they are not hopeful of results until after the revolution. Until then, love between men and women may be regarded, in the words of one articulate feminist, as "both debilitating and counter-revolutionary." [1]

Germaine Greer, Elizabeth Janeway, Kate Millett, and Gloria Steinem all apparently agree with this formulation to some extent, since they depict almost all forms of love a woman might feel toward a man as degrading and infantile. Again, of course, they vaunt "love" between "human beings," whatever *they* are. The only hint they offer is that the man should display most of the qualities they find "degrading" when ascribed to women: tenderness, passivity, receptiveness, nurturance, delicacy. In other words, the man must not be "manly"—confident, aggressive, initiatory—although the woman should be . . . more or less . . . at least as far as one can tell, because the feminists are very vague about sex after liberation. As we've heard from Ms. Ephron, "It is a great mystery to all of us." [2]

This position can be derided, particularly by men unready to submit to processing or to plunge into "mystery." Many will understandably see the term "humanize" as a rather menacing euphemism for "emasculate." The women punctuate the threat with frightening claims of orgasmic "rights." The men feel they are expected to perform feats of sexual endurance and derring-do that would be hard work with a pneumatic drill. Since most males feel a tie between sexual ability and masculine identity, the apparent ideal of the effeminate superstud seems a morbid joke. Greer's recommendation to her educated sisters that they try virile lower-class men (for temporary relationships, of course) seems a dead giveaway of feminist hypocrisy.[3]

Nonetheless, the women do have a serious argument, which seems plausible to many people both disillusioned with love and excited by a sense of new possibilities of sexual freedom and variety. Although love, in its form of blissful monogamy, seems increasingly elusive, sex as a way of communicating warmth and exchanging pleasures seems increasingly available. It even appears that sex may be most exciting when it is spontaneous—exempt from the psychological complications of an enduring love.

The movement women, with the strong support of the pamphleteers and counselors of sex technique, go on to argue that sexual relations will be most gratifying if the conventional roles of the two sexes are not closely observed. They advise that the old "missionary position" be frequently abandoned (a male chauvinist relic, say the spokesmen of *Out From Under*). And they give the impression that ineffable pinnacles of pleasure are reachable if couples are just willing (as recommended by the new sex manuals) to overcome inhibitions and role stereotypes—leaving no erogenous zone unturned, or orifice unfathomed. The "tyranny of genital sex" is to be exuberantly overthrown, and oral and anal activity affirmed.

Of course, it is not expected that the entire *Kama-sutra* be conjugated every time. But the essential concept is sexual exchanges between two partners unbound by any clear image of sexual roles or by any single erotic pattern. Each partner is seen as communicating affection to the other by transmitting pleasure.

Since an individual can transact such pleasures with a variety of people—and since variety is refreshing—there is seen to be little physical or psychological reason for restricting sex to a single partner. Moreover, since sexual orgasm is regarded as the supreme human pleasure and is considered crucial to mental health, there seems little moral sanction for depriving those who have failed to find a long-term lover.

These attitudes are convenient for homosexuals. They have long since abandoned sexually determined roles and escaped from the "genital tyranny" of the "missionary position." The view that sex is best when the partners perform in psychologically similar, if versatile, ways leaves little grounds at all for objecting to homosexuality. If the homosexuals have problems, moreover, they can now be treated along with everyone else by Masters and Johnson, the prophets of the New Pleasures, who are not finicky about "the sexual tastes" of their patients.[4]

It would be a great mistake, however, to identify this fashionable concept of sex chiefly with feminism and homosexuality. For, ironically enough, it is also the essential sexual ideology of male chauvinism: the *Playboy* philosophy. Although the chauvinists may retain an image of male dominance, they are delighted with the prospect of female liberation. The prevailing motif of pornography is the same insatiable female, with her multiple serial orgasms, whom Mary Jane Sherfey discovered in the laboratories of Masters and Johnson, and who is celebrated monthly in the pages of *Ms.*

Like Germaine Greer and Shulamith Firestone, the *Playboy* philosophers want to abolish the "genital tyranny" and "finally and unanswerably break the connection between sexual intercourse and reproduction," from which so many complexes and inhibitions seem to flow. Like the feminist writers, the male chauvinists fantasize polymorphously aggressive women, free of inhibitions and fixations. And also like the feminists, the male chauvinists do not like to envisage their women dependent, or—God forbid—pregnant. *Playboy* is an eager supporter of both the equal rights amendment and abortion on demand.

In practice, this popular image of spontaneous and carefree "love between mature and equal human beings" is often workable. Carefree sexual activity—"without hangups"—often comes without "hangovers" too. Mutual needs are fulfilled lovingly, as long as is mutually desired, and the couple parts amicably. Each partner is defined as autonomous; neither, in theory, can be deeply hurt by the departure of the other. In a mature relationship between two adult human beings, no one is believed to suffer the mawkish toils of dependency. The two partners are free. They are liberated at once *from* expectations of lifelong enchantment, rarely fulfilled, and *for* deep physical gratifications more easily attainable. Thus, according to the theory, they will be happier and less vulnerable, dealing not with fantasies but with possibilities in the real world.

The feminists believe as well that the liberated couple can ultimately achieve a deeper and fuller love. When they are freed from their sex role stereotypes, they also can fulfill all their human emotional potentialities. The man does not have to worry about an image of initiative and aggressiveness, and he can enjoy receiving the ministrations of his partner. The woman feels free to act vigorously, exultantly. Each can ask the other to perform what were previously regarded as unconventional or "perverted" acts, without worrying about feelings of guilt or charges of kinkiness. The partners thus will reciprocate sexual services on an equal basis, each lovingly bringing the other to orgasm—each responding precisely to the individual sexual preferences of the other, rather than to some sexual stereotype of masculinity or femininity that many modern psychologists are said to regard as doubtful.

This view of the way to find both good sex and reasonably enduring love seems plausible to most sophisticated Americans. The feminists are no more daringly rebellious in their usual sexual imagery than is Hugh Hefner in his mock heroic battle against the dread forces of American puritanism (which usually produce several hate letters whenever he appears on network television). Nonetheless, the feminists, as well as the *Playboy* philosophers and the *Joy of Sex* technicians, are profoundly wrong—wrong about both love and sex. Like the musicologists who try to reduce Bach to algebra, they miss the point; collectively they are promoting in the United States an epidemic of erotic and social disorders.

They fail to understand the real sources of sexuality and love or the crucial role of sex both in individual personality and in civilization. They are thus subverting and stifling real sexuality and love, and are undermining civilized society. It is chiefly the common sense and conservative instincts of nonintellectual Americans that are retarding this fashionable movement of feminists, sexologists, male chauvinists, and pornographers, all of whom imagine themselves as conflicting forces but who can be seen objectively as collaborators in a Sexual Suicide Society.

These groups are unified in their desire to separate sexual activity as much as possible from procreation. This desire is hardly extraordinary. It is resisted only by the Catholic Church, and Norman Mailer,[5] among major American institutions; and in the general alarm about overpopulation, it gains the moral momentum of a veritable crusade and the financial support of the major foundations for scientific research. To a considerable extent, this effort is reasonable.

But the members of the sex coalition go well beyond a mere search for better contraceptives. They are not satisfied merely to control the biological tie between intercourse and childbirth. They also want to eliminate the psychological and symbolic connections. They may reluctantly acknowledge that in a sense procreation is the most important current role of intercourse—and certainly the key evolutionary purpose. They also may recognize its role in inducing males to join and support families. But they foresee a time when artificial means may be employed for human reproduction. By far the most frequent and durably important long-term use of sex, they would say, is the fulfillment of the physical and psychological need for orgasmic pleasure and the communication of affection. For these purposes, sex is most adaptable if it is not connected with procreation, if it is regarded as a completely separate mode of activity.

One effect of this concept of "companionate" or "affectionate" sex is to dethrone procreative genital intercourse as the normative form of sexual activity—the pattern toward which all other modes of sexual activity are seen to aspire and from which they flow. It is to deny that the sexual drive, whatever adaptations it may have, is fundamentally procreative—the product of millions of years of human evolution designed to perpetuate the species.

This ideology of nonprocreative sex is no trivial matter. We all know that in the age of the pill, every act does not have to intend children, if indeed it ever did. But we do not necessarily know that sexual pleasure is unrelated to the complex of drives and desires that evolved to reproduce the species in a loving and secure environment. Nor do we know that a complete break between procreative and erotic instincts will not ultimately undermine all forms of sexual pleasure.

Nonetheless, there is considerable evidence on the side of those whom we might term the separatists. The human being is the one animal that is apparently capable of sexual pleasure virtually at any time in the female cycle. Women actively seek and enjoy sex at times when they cannot conceive. Moreover, as the liberationists insist so much on reminding us, the woman's clitoris is an organ exclusively devoted to pleasure; it has no directly procreative function. As for the male, throughout human history he has often failed to show procreative instincts. At least he has not indicated any concern over what happens to his putative children. Nature has clearly provided both men and women with bodies and drives strongly demanding sexual activity regardless of the technical possibility of conceiving children in a given instance.

There is much evidence too in support of the separatists' theory that such autonomous sexual pleasure is good for its participants—affirming love, providing recreation, imparting a sense of wholeness and fulfillment—while procreative sex entails a number of severe social and psychological problems. Some women today report that their sexual desire even increases during those times in their cycles when conception is impossible (although Fox and Tiger offer contrary evidence).[6] Other women acknowledge that sex is very special when they want a child. But they say these pleasures are irrelevant to their drive for and enjoyment of sex in other circumstances. How, the separatist will ask, can one describe as fundamentally procreative a drive that is present and actionable in men and women under almost all biological conditions, a drive most intensely gratified in women through an organ that has no direct procreative purpose, and a drive that may increase in ardency specifically when conception is impossible?

One might further ask, Who cares? But as a matter of fact the feminists deeply care, and they are right in considering these questions to be crucial. For procreative genital intercourse stands at the crux of sexual differentiation. It provides both a practical agenda and symbolic pattern of male initiative and female receptivity, of male aggressiveness and female passivity. If it is the normative pinnacle of sexual relationships, "to which all other sexual energies aspire and from which they flow," then our sexual differences are of supreme importance; attempts to disparage them will founder on the irreducible realities of the sex act itself. To state the question directly: Does sex that is fully counter to the procreative pattern—that violates its genital focus and long-term horizons—ultimately reduce sexual energy and undermine love? Does the separatist ideal of polymorphous pleasures so fail to correspond with the inner syntax of sexuality that it strains the bonds of human personality, becoming disintegrative, not integrative, of body and mind and spirit? To answer these questions, one must explore the ties between sexual pleasure, procreation, and love.

Love performs its most indispensable role in inducing males to submit to female cycles of sexuality. In a civilized society men ultimately must overcome the limited male sexual rhythms of tension and release, erection and ejaculation, and adopt a sexual mode responsive to the extended female pattern —proceeding through pregnancy, childbirth, and nurture. By involving the long period of bearing and nurturing children, the female pattern entails a concern for the future, a sense of growth and evolution, a need for deferring gratifications, a desire for durable and secure relationships. The male pattern naturally focuses on actively wresting pleasures from the immediate environment. But in civilized societies, the majority of the men have come to recognize that it is the female time-orientation and the family that offer the highest rewards.

This recognition, the beginning of love, seems to be evoked by a man's desire, conscious or unconscious, to identify and keep his progeny. In a civilized society, he will not normally be able to claim his children if they are born to several mothers. He must choose a particular woman and submit to her sexual rhythms if he is to have offspring of his own. His love defines his choice. His need to choose evokes his love. His sexual drive lends energy to his love and his love gives shape, meaning, and continuity to his sexuality. When he selects a specific woman, he in essence defines himself both to himself and in society. Every sex act thereafter celebrates that definition and social engagement.

Without a durable relationship with a woman, a man's sexual life is a series of brief and temporary exchanges, impelled by a desire to affirm his most rudimentary masculinity. But with love, sex becomes refined by selectivity, and other dimensions of personality are engaged and developed. The man himself is refined, and his sexuality becomes not a mere impulse but a meaningful commitment in society, possibly to be fulfilled in the birth of specific children legally and recognizably his. His sex life then can be conceived and experienced as having specific long-term importance like a woman's.

The man thus can integrate his immediate physical sensations with his highest aspirations for meaning and community. The sex act itself can become a civilizing human affirmation, involving his entire personality and committing it, either in fact or in symbol, to a long-term engagement in a meaningful future.

All these aspects of love must be present for the highest erotic experience: choice, desire, and aspiration. Sexual desire alone fails to lead men to make durable choices; it fails to evoke aspirations for the future. Copulation itself is focused on the present. Choice is required and aspirations are evoked chiefly by the conscious or unconscious desire to have children with a specific partner. This is the key to love.

We must be clear on one point: The partners themselves are usually not conscious of the desire for children as their principal motive—and it may not be the immediate source. But the aspiration of lovers toward the future, the adoption of the long horizons of female sexuality, are all best explained— and best embodied—in children. Even if not articulated in this way, the sentiment of love can thus be considered the excited emotional anticipation of progeny, the instinctive apprehension of biological continuity, and the mystical intuition of social or genetic immortality.

Love thus is optimistic: an investment of faith in the future of the family, the society, and mankind. It is sexual energy that makes love so powerful; and it is love that makes sexual energy a vital force for psychological, ethical, and communal affirmation: for the long time horizons of civilization (and femininity) rather than the short-term horizons of primitive society (and masculinity). Love for women and children becomes love for the community that supports them and faith in the future in which one's offspring will live.

It is apparent that this kind of love can best be fulfilled in families, since by definition it aspires to create them. Similarly, it is clear that procreative intercourse is the form of sexual expression that is most affirmative of such love. It is also clear that other forms of love are displacements or elaborations of the fundamental procreative impulse. That is, even lovers who are not interested in procreation are enjoying instinctively and symbolically the sentiments of procreation. Older people —and couples who do not want children—may still be celebrating the faith in the future and the long commitment to the partner that derive from procreative instincts.

This concept of sexual love, symbolized in genital intercourse, again emphasizes the differences between the sexes. A man's love is focused on the symbols and associations of a women's mysterious procreative powers. He is attracted to her breasts and contours, her maternal sentiments, her tenderness, and her sense of long-term possibilities. The woman loves the man for his strength and protectiveness, for his temperamental qualities that provide an ability to support and protect her while she bears children—or while she surrenders to orgasmic ecstasy: and for his ability, at once, to control her in sexual intercourse and to submit to her long-term sexual patterns. –

Beyond these primal attractions, of course, both the woman and man will seek a partner with whom they can enjoy a long-term companionship. Thus the primal attraction of erotic differences will occur within a framework of cultural compatibilities. In a civilized society, both sexes will seek a partner whom they can envisage enjoying over time and who embodies those values they wish to transmit to their children. A procreative love will tend to seek out a partner with whom one can happily live, at least for the period in which the children are growing up.

But, in general, the prevalence of affirmative sexual love in a society will depend on the cultivation of the sexual differences symbolized in genital intercourse—and elaborated in all the temperamental differences deriving from divergent sexual roles. Again the man's identity is more precarious than the woman's. Being in part a cultural invention, masculinity is vulnerable to both cultural change and female attack and exposure. The feminists deride the male attempt to create "mysterious differences" in work or temperament that correspond to the woman's procreativity. But male effort to contrive seductive mysteries is an act of love, an effort to create a pattern of sexual distinctions that is affirmative of male identity and that fulfills the emotional and procreative needs of women.

If we agree that love can be usefully treated in these terms—as an aspiration for progeny—we can determine the forms of sexual expression that are most affirmative of it—and the forms that are most destructive. Clearly the most affirmative sex act in these terms is between two lovers attempting to conceive a baby. Other nonprocreative sexual experiences are affirmative, when they share the crucial characteristics of procreative intercourse—love for a partner of the opposite sex and a progress toward genital coition and orgasm. Under these conditions, a sex act will be a symbolic ritual enactment of procreative intercourse. It is thus an affirmation of love. It integrates the human sexual drive with a sense of meaning and community.

Other sexual activities may be considered affirmative, in a continuum, to the extent that they fit the normative pattern. Thus oral-genital sex with a person one loves may be better than with a person one does not. Oral contact may well be affirmative if it is designed to enhance desire for genital orgasm rather than substitute for it. Homosexuality is obviously a negative experience in these terms, although it may be mitigated to some inadequate degree when the relationship embodies futurity.

In terms of "sex role stereotypes," behavior that facilitates genital orgasm is clearly best. Thus the woman may be aggressive and the man passive only to the extent that the man's confidence and erectile potency is not jeopardized. The man must control his actions to enjoy intercourse most fully. To best serve his partner and not ejaculate prematurely, he must follow a gradual, managed trajectory to climax, while the woman will best enjoy herself and her partner if she loses control, if she completely relaxes, and allows climactic contractions to arise in her.

During most sexual encounters, moreover, a man can maintain erection for only a very limited period—and come to orgasm only a limited number of times—while a woman can have a relatively unlimited number of orgasms on a schedule contingent chiefly on the man's potency. No matter how excited the woman may be, intercourse is impossible if the man is not prepared. If the man's rhythm is disrupted, he may be impotent or premature, and the possibility for successful intercourse is greatly reduced. The man is the key variable. To give the woman control, though occasionally workable, is therefore contrary to the essential terms of genital intercourse. If one is doing sadomasochistic tricks, or messing around with vibrators, or even just probing for "little-known erogenous zones," of course, these rules do not apply. But in genital intercourse, they do: If the woman is to be fulfilled, the man must be in essential control.

This difference, stemming from the conditions of genital intercourse, tends to affirm what are so frequently dismissed as archaic stereotypes: the male initiatory and managerial, the woman, surrendering as well as she can to climactic abandon. This does not mean, obviously, that the woman cannot be vigorously active; it only means that her activity must not upset the fragile male sense that he is in command. In addition, it often means that if the female is aggressive, the man will have to be even more so in order for the sexual relationships to succeed.

This rather conventional theory of love and sexuality as procreative phenomena does not exclude the possibility that the sex drive might increase when a child is not wanted. Civilized sexual desire is conditioned by love. A sense that children could not be loved will inhibit sexual experience. Therefore a fear of unwanted children is a corollary of procreative love. The act of intercourse may still be a symbolic affirmation of the desire for children, an assertion of faith in the future. It may still correspond to the inner syntax of individual sexuality and identity.

There comes a point, however, when sex is no longer affirmative, when it tends to tear apart the armature of sexuality and identity and become subversive of civilized society. That point comes when as a practical matter the sex act does not express love, is not associated even unconsciously or symbolically with the procreative aspiration, and does not promote the subordination of primal male sexual impulses to long-term female patterns. Then the sex act becomes a temporary gratification that leads to emotional fragmentation in time rather than to a sense of continuity with nature and society.

If this kind of sex prevails, the male becomes dominant in the culture. If the women do not adapt to it, the community may endure along the usual matriarchal pattern, with the women maintaining families and other social continuities while the men roam in gangs or hunting parties. But in modern society, where there is little latitude for such diversionary male fulfillment, the men may impose their rhythms instead, and the women may well succumb to the short-term male pattern. They may deny their procreative natures and the associated long-term horizons, and proceed in the mode of primitive male sexuality. Under these conditions, a modern, civilized society will tend to disintegrate.

The women's movement, the *Playboy* chauvinists, the gay liberationists, the sexologists, and the pornographers all tend to indulge and promote such a disintegration. They all present alternatives to loving sexuality. The man and woman who are attempting to fulfill their sexual natures in an affirmative way are bombarded with contrary ideologies. The pornographer persistently and pervasively advertises the potential joys of promiscuity—of unknown but shapely bodies—continuously stimulates primitive male impulses, and subverts the attempt to maintain monogamous ties. The sex manuals present utopian images if the bliss that comes with an abandonment of "inhibitions" and "stereotypes" that may be important to affirmative sexuality. The woman's movement offers visions of a spurious sexual equality, in which women are to be considered erotically the same as men. The homosexuals romanticize a pattern in which ultimate sexual fulfillment is impossible and in which the temporary gratification is paramount. These forces together create an undertow that threatens to sweep out into a chaos of male rhythms the enduring structures of civilized sexuality.

Under these conditions, males find it increasingly difficult to observe long-term erotic horizons. Their sex lives become increasingly oriented toward the next conquest of a tempting body. And because their social and work motivations are so profoundly intertwined with their sexuality, they find their commitment to their jobs and communities also eroding. The emergence of impulsive male sexual patterns leads to adoption of a general pattern of hedonistic opportunism and impulsiveness. Where social pressures offer a plausible opportunity, the men will turn to short-circuit pursuits of crime and drugs. Other men may immerse themselves in the vicarious male rituals of T.V. football and violence, bombard their minds with the macho rhythms and incantations of high-volume rock or fuel their vanities with alcohol, immediate sex, and pornography. The commitment to work and community dissolves as the commitment to female sexual horizons declines.

This pattern profoundly skews all the structures of male

socialization. In a society where most of the men are following civilized sexual patterns and related long-term economic roles, strong pressures are imposed on the rest to go along. Men whose natural impulses are not subjected to the civilizing pressures of love and family may submit to the structures of motivation created by men who are socialized by women. The danger in modern society, promoted by the sexual separatists, is that the unsocialized men will become culturally dominant and it will be the civilized ones who have to resist the pressures of the society at large. A civilization dependent on long-term commitments and sexual patterns will be confronted by a powerful mass culture propagating a sexuality of immediate gratifications. A society profoundly dependent on monogamy will face a culture advertising promiscuity. We are close to that situation today.

The effect on men is more immediate and far-reaching because their identities and secondary sexual patterns are more dependent on culture. But ultimately the impact on women is just as tragic. Women face a cruel dilemma, exemplified in part by the current women's movement. They can respond to the increasing abdication of men from civilized social and sexual patterns by trying to play both key roles, sustaining long-term job commitments as well as familial responsibilities. The most talented and stable will succeed, thus perpetuating civilized behavior in the face of a hostile culture. Or women can choose careers alone, while either downplaying sex or partially adopting the male pattern. Or they can actively submit to male sexual impulses, abandoning their procreative horizons and attempting to enjoy themselves with whoever is around.

The women's movement displays all these tendencies: the women who work devotedly and then come home and care for their children, or if unmarried, try to persuade men to adopt feminine time-horizons and create a family; the women, often active in the movement, who focus on careers and adopt an opportunistic sexuality, only tentatively inclined to begin families; and the women who vigorously embrace a masculine mode, renounce their procreative possibilities, pursue promiscuous sexual circuits, and even display the entire syndrome of male insecurity, compulsiveness, and fantasies. The tragedy is that all three responses exacerbate the problem. Even the women who works to support her family, if she is whole-heartedly committed to her job, may facilitate the male abdication.

In the end, the sexuality of both men and women—and the spirit of the community—is reduced to the limited, barren, compulsive circuitry of uncivilized males. Confined in a shallow present, with little hope for the future or interest in the past, neither sex works or loves devotedly. While sex is given a steadily larger role, it loses contact with its procreative sources and becomes increasingly promiscuous and undifferentiated, homosexual, and pornographic. It becomes what in fact our current liberationists—male and female—already imagine it to be. It becomes in essence a form of sensuous massage.

Thus sex is losing its very character as sexuality. No longer governed by the normative syntax of procreative love—no longer responsive to the differing sexual configurations of mature men and women—erotic activity becomes a shapeless, dissolute, and destructive pursuit of ever more elusive pleasures by ever more drastic techniques. In the quest for a better orgasm or more intense titillation, a frustrated population goes on ever wilder goose chases in "little-known erogenous zones" —on ever more futile scavenger hunts for sexual exotica, picking up a whip here, an orgy there—but always returning to the increasingly barren and shapeless lump of their own sexuality. Such are the aporias of carnal knowledge—the dead ends of "spontaneity."

The fact is that there is no sexual gratification more durably intense than loving genital intercourse. The fact is that oral and anal novelties are only briefly titillating, a cul-de-sac. The fact is that there hasn't been a thrilling new erogenous zone discovered since de Sade. The fact is that promiscuity is ultimately a bore and pornography a stultification. The fact is that homosexuality, though related to the other separatist forms of sexuality, is worse, because it is usually a more irrevocable flight from identity and love. In addition, since it is not a sickness confined to a few congenital victims but an escape from sexual responsibility open to all, gay liberation and display is a threat to millions of young men who have precarious masculine identities. Moreover, the androgynous ideal of women's liberation—with its polymorphously copulating "human beings"—is a destructive fantasy. There are no human beings; there are just men and women, and when they deny their divergent sexuality, they reject the deepest sources of identity and love. They commit sexual suicide.

The Myths of Open Marriage

How but in custom and in ceremony
are innocence and beauty born.

Yeats
"A Prayer for My Daughter"

The widespread belief that monogamous marriage is obsolete is a grave portent for our society. Nonetheless, a virtual industry of popular literature has arisen to solemnly celebrate the decline of the institution. The most successful and symptomatic of the books is the best-selling *Open Marriage* by George and Nena O'Neill.[1] As a compendium of all the most fashionable ideas and prejudices of liberationist moderates, it is a most important book.

The significance of this and other recent books, apart from their huge popularity—their exact indulgence of sex consumer daydreams—is their total incomprehension of what marriage is, beyond the immediate interactions of the two partners. One has no sense of the institution's role in socializing men and children and contributing to a larger solidarity. One has no sense of its location within a specific economy and society. These books read as if marriage were purely a private contract, to be revised and reformed, opened and "peopleized" in any way necessary for the private growth and gratification of the partners.

In a sense, this view is very reassuring. Marriage offers so many secondary rewards—companionship, sexual pleasure, economy—that few people recognize its primary purposes or most profound motivations. The danger is that by excessive attention to the superficial needs of the partners, one may erode the internal structures and external functions of the institution.

Like much popular writing on sex, *Open Marriage* is essentially an essay in wish fulfillment. In florid language it tells you that all the burdens and responsibilities of orthodox marriage are dispensable. You can turn in your rigid old "closed couplehood" for an open "now" convertible, with a "dynamic framework" and no brakes. You can transcend "mere togetherness" and reach "the ultimate in cooperation . . . that creates, through expanding feedback and growth, a *synergic couple*" (their italics).[2] You can replace an "archaic, rigid, outmoded, oppressive, static, decaying, Victorian" institution with one that is "free, dynamic, honest, spontaneous, creative."

One could quote further from that "open, expanding energy system" of their rhetoric, but there is really no way to capture its full inspirational spirit. Let us simply say that it exceeds in lyrical intensity even the most hysterically romantic manual of the old Victorian marriage; it has more "high points" than the Alps, and more "dynamics" than an automobile ad.

Of course, if you are not ready for these "peak experiences," these "bursts of insight," these "super moments" that can be yours for only $6.95 (hardcover edition), the authors will understand. They are very tolerant people. They know you might prefer "to ignore the peaks [and] huddle in the narrow valleys" of "conditional and static trust, unequal status, limited love and a closed, self-limiting energy system, bondage." You may not be, when it comes down to it, a "now person." And that's all right, they think.

Nonetheless, the kind of advice that *Open Marriage* offers—as well as the book itself—is being promoted by women's magazines, marriage consultant services, perplexed preachers, and psychiatrists across the country. It is a phenomenon important to all of us, even if we "huddle" away in our "narrow valleys," because the future of our civilization is dependent to some considerable degree on the future of marriage. Whatever one may think of the book and its handsome authors, Professor O'Neill (a Ph.D. in anthropology) and his wife (a mere Ph.D. candidate but "altogether equal in personhood"), they are where it's at in contemporary marriage reform.

The book has its points. Except in the transcendent synergy stretches, it is often briskly written, seductively sensible, and nominally in favor of marriage. It contains cute games in which various relationships are described and you get to guess who has the open marriage. It is better at least than books like *Eve's New Rib,* by Robert Francoeur,[3] a theologian who looks with great hopefulness and sympathy on the new "horizons" of group sex, communalism, extracorporeal gestation, and polygamy. *Open Marriage* is devoted to the more plausible proposition that by increasing the autonomous growth of the two partners, one can relieve some of the strains on marriage caused by excessive and exclusive concern with togetherness and "couplehood."

Thus the O'Neills recommend greater emphasis on the individual's need for privacy and separate identity. Partners should be able to go out with other friends of both sexes when so inclined. If adultery should occur—what with "the nowness of self"—we should understand that it happens on occasion in almost every marriage system in the world. The O'Neills do not recommend it, but they indulge it "flexibly" when the open marriage reaches its more exalted stages. They contend that if there is sufficient trust between the partners, the deviations should not be seriously damaging to the marriage. In a coy passage toward the very end, they, oh so delicately, imply that a good mode of "transcendence" under these circumstances is to invite another couple over, if appropriate, and switch. ("Once you have achieved a true sharing within your marriage, there are no limits on its future development.")[4]

But one really should not focus on the group sex innuendoes ("sharing then becomes threefold, fourfold—not necessarily sexually, at all").[5] They are offered only as something of a grand prize for those who have followed the earlier prescriptions and reached the appropriate state of beatified "couple-power." The real question is whether their more mundane recommendations will improve marriages.

The O'Neills, groping into their dubious reserves of anthropological knowledge, assert that marriage has existed in almost every human society. We should not be alarmed, they say, that "the only people for whom the old-fashioned marriage [i.e., church, ceremony, etc.] now seems to hold a real mystique are homosexuals." [6] The institution will survive because it is based on "the innate human need for structure" and for "one-to-one intimacy." For evidence of the universality of marriage, they cite a statement by Bronislaw Malinowski made in debate in the early 1930s, and they point out that while there are now more divorces than ever, there are also more marriages.

They conclude that "in the here and now, marriage is still the choice of the majority for formalizing our most intimate one-to-one relationships and achieving growth through commitment, and it probably will remain so for several generations." [7] That this approach is taken seriously may be deduced from the increasing numbers of young people who clutter up their marriage ceremonies with commitments to "growth," "synergy," and "feedback." These rebels begin their lives together by reaching for the most honest and sacred language they know, and it turns out to be the idiom of a conglomerate board meeting.

Once established, marriage is seen by the O'Neills in much the same terms. Two equal, independent individuals maintain a "dynamic growth partnership." Rejecting the notion of complementary marriage connections, the O'Neills provide instead an ideal of perfect symmetry and reciprocity, with the roles both flexible and reversible. They categorically dismiss the notion of sex-specific functions and responsibilities. Unless the woman earns money (preferably as much as the husband) and the man keeps house (also on equal terms), the O'Neills fear that the two will have too little in common to "grow together." Imagination is not the strong point of the O'Neills: Though they deny it, when one actually scrutinizes their concept, equality turns out to mean sameness. The man earns money; so must the woman. The man philanders; so must his wife. The man initiates sex; so must she. The woman decorates the house, cooks a meal, or makes a bed; the man must eventually reciprocate.

Children, of course, are rather awkward in this scheme and the O'Neills would have as little to do with them as possible. They positively celebrate the childless marriage and declare that "the importance of motherhood has been inflated out of all proportion." "Motherhood," they grandly claim, "must be disentangled from the wife's role." It should be "optional" in an overpopulated world rather than "glorified." [8]

Open marriage thus begins to assume a rather rigid and burdensome structure of its own, governed by a tight calculus of reciprocity. The only time the O'Neills get tough is when faced with the possibility that some women might want to be equal without making money. Then they "do not hesitate to lay it on the line": ". . . only if you are materially rewarded for [your work] is it going to be taken seriously by others. Again this may sound harsh but in our culture that is the way things work." [9]

They approvingly quote Edith de Rham, "There is an aura of futility and condescension about dilettantism today, a sense of inadequacy in non-professional talent, because it merits no recognition and has no place in the modern world." [10]

The O'Neills add, "it may have its pleasures, but none of them make sufficient demands to bring about real growth." The home, as the O'Neills would have it from their upper-class pinnacle, is less edifying than any remunerative job; it "programs her for mediocrity and dulls her brain." [11] She had better get out into the world of business and the professions with all its "inspiring challenges" and "broadening vistas."

The O'Neills readily concede "that such completely equal sharing of family support is hardly possible for everyone until major societal change is effected in terms of family and child-rearing arrangements, and [until] all women are afforded the same opportunities in training and jobs as men." [12] They assume this change is occurring because of what they cutely call the ESE factor: the woman's new Educational, Sexual, and Economic freedoms. "Lacking any one of these (ESE) components," they assert, "the woman becomes a subsidiary partner in marriage. With all three, she is free to lead a life of fulfillment in all dimensions, without even choosing to marry." Thus an equal support role becomes "one of those historical and even evolutionary inevitabilities about which there finally can be no argument." [13] (One might argue, though, that when women can freely fulfill themselves "in all dimensions" without a husband, there finally can be little marriage either.)

In any case, it is refreshing to find our two anthropologists at last discover an "evolutionary inevitability," even if anthropology doesn't happen to be one of their strong points. Their citation of anthropological evidence and argument is everywhere shallow, distorted, and tendentious. When their notion of marriage is closely scrutinized, in the end it remains afloat only on the "expanding energy system" of their own rhetoric. Marriage itself must have stronger sources of support.

Their opening hypothesis, that the institution is essentially based on "man's innate need for structure" and desire for "one-to-one intimacy" and "companionship," is shared in essence by almost every recent book on marriage. But it is nonsense. Structure and intimacy can be and are provided in any number of other ways in societies throughout the world. These values are desirable in marriage but are not essential causes or explanations of it.

In many cultures, as the O'Neills will surely acknowledge,

the wife and husband share very few one-to-one intimacies. Ties with others of the same sex—or even the opposite sex—are often much more profound in companionate terms. The most intimate connections are between mothers and their children. Beyond those are ties between sisters, sisters-in-law, brothers and sisters. There are premarital companionship, premarital affairs, passionate or perfunctory extramarital liaisons, psychiatrist-patient affiliations, and one-sex bonds (not homosexual). In the kibbutz, where unrelated boys and girls are brought up together in large numbers and achieve a profound degree of companionate feeling, they almost never marry one another.[14] Of course, marriage may bring intimate companionship and often does. But intimate companionship is by no means indispensable to marriage as an institution. The desire for intimacy, moreover, can also often be subversive of marriage, particularly in the many cultures where marriages are arranged.

Similarly "man's innate need for structure" provides frail support indeed for an institution that encompasses most of the human race. The world is full of various structures—bureaucracies, businesses, military organizations, farms, tribes, clubs, clans, extended families, communes, conventional families, grandmother-mother-child systems, mother-child units, threesomes and couples of every description. One can conjugate many variations. The need for structure may explain all of them or none of them, but it does not tell us why, of all possible arrangements, marriage is the one most prevalent. It does not tell us why in most societies it is consecrated in a religious ceremony. It does not tell us why it exists in both orderly societies and disorderly ones.

Like the desire for intimacy, the need for structure is thus completely inadequate as a definitive motive for marriage. Based on the O'Neill principles, there is no evidence that marriages would occur much at all. One would expect a pair of anthropologists to appreciate that the superficial impressions of the participants do not suffice to explain the persistence of any social custom. Marriage as an institution is far bigger than any couple—or generation—that finds itself taking part.

Equally misconceived and anthropologically unsound is the O'Neills' insistence on a marriage pattern of rigid symmetry, reciprocity, and role reversibility between the sexes. First of all, there is the obvious practical problem that at present in our society there are not enough "meaningful jobs" for breadwinners—let alone "meaningful," "growth-inducing" jobs conveniently located for couples. The idea that at relatively high levels of remuneration (Open Marriage Country), many individuals will be able to maintain successful careers on a part-time basis is ridiculous. Only best-selling authors, professors of anthropology who do not bother to keep up with their field, and other extraordinarily situated professionals can pursue the O'Neill paradigm at all, even if they want to. It is irresponsible to urge such an unlikely agenda on all American women and say that it is indispensable to a happy and edifying life or to authentic equality with their husbands.

One realizes that in all too many cases, the O'Neill vision dooms marriage and home to just another competitive arena in American society. No matter how much the O'Neills would deny it, equality interpreted in reciprocal, symmetrical terms means defining one's success in relation to one's partner. Such insidious rivalry will usually erode the foundations of love and subvert all the other values of honesty, spontaneity, and trust that the O'Neills ascribe to their image of marriage. Moreover, all this career activity will in most cases come at the expense of motherhood. Again, this idea of the O'Neills that careers are some kind of educational lark, while everything else women do is dull as dishwater, could come only from members of the American aristocracy: the professional class.

One might dismiss such practical problems, of course, as cultural perversities of the United States and other capitalist countries. The O'Neills, however, also base their open marriage on data from a number of primitive tribes. In particular, they dwell on the anthropological evidence regarding sexual roles and differences.

Although they are ready to propound "innate needs" and "evolutionary inevitabilities" for women's liberation, the O'Neills stop short of granting any innate or inevitable differences at all between the sexes. Beyond the matter of childbirth, to which "far too much importance" is ascribed, they believe that the sexes are essentially interchangeable. This assumption, of course, is crucial to their notion that sex roles are easily reversible in a good marriage and that it does not matter who is the chief provider or child nurturer.

For anthropological support, they turn with great emphasis and ceremony to the work of Margaret Mead.[15] Dr. Mead is indeed an eminent authority, having written some ten books either fully or partly devoted to the differences between the sexes, including the book cited by the O'Neills, *Sex and Temperament in Three Primitive Societies,* published in 1935.[16] In 1949, she also wrote one of the great masterpieces in social science literature, *Male and Female,*[17] summing up all her field experience with those three societies, plus four others and the United States.

Because the issues involved are important to the whole matter of "open marriage" and because Margaret Mead is the paramount genius in her field, it is worthwhile to consider the O'Neills' misconceptions of her work. Their thesis is that the great variety of roles occupied by the different sexes in Mead's three New Guinea tribes demonstrate that sexual roles and characteristics are culturally determined and subject to social control: They can be flexibly alternated, reversed, or reformed almost at will.

These three tribes do indeed display an extraordinary sexual diversity. Among the mountain Arapesh both partners tend to be warm, nurturant, and passive. Among the Mundugumor, both partners tend to be fierce, aggressive, and relatively indifferent to children. Therefore, the O'Neills observe, as does Mead, that the Mundugumor women are far more aggressive—masculine, if you wish—than the Arapesh men. They conclude that it is not sex but Mundugumor and Arapesh culture that cultivates such aggressiveness or passivity.[18] Though the neglect of possible genetic differences between the tribes impairs this argument, it is plausible as far as it goes.

The prime O'Neill exhibit, however, are the Tchambuli. In this tribe, as the O'Neills quote Mead, the woman is the "dominant, impersonal, managing partner, the man the less responsible and the emotionally dependent person." The women fish and the husbands often go to market. The men are catty, bickering, and mercurial, walk with a "mincing step and self-conscious mien," and spend most of their time in narcissistic ornamentation, art work, and elaborate male rituals.[19]

Obviously the O'Neills could find in this pattern evidence that the conventional sex roles were so little determined by biology that they could be completely reversed. Together with the Mundugumor and Arapesh, the Tchambuli seem to give the O'Neills the go-ahead for their role reversal schemes.

But who has the open marriage? Is it the Arapesh, the Mundugumor, or the Tchambuli? The answer is none of them. In all three, the separate roles of the sexes are rigidly maintained and the activities of the male, however foolish they may seem to the O'Neills or to the rest of us, are regarded as the most important business of the society.

Nonetheless, it is worth examining these tribes further, as did Dr. Mead, though not the O'Neills. For in a way, each of these tribes may be said to exhibit some of the characteristics and the problems of the O'Neill conception. This, one could contend, is one of the reasons these groups were such pathetic failures in dealing with their environment that they were all approaching extinction when Mead studied them.

The Arapesh are the saddest because they seem the most humane. Both the males and females were deeply concerned with child-rearing. Although the chief responsibility is the woman's, the Arapesh believe that the man contributes vital nourishment to the unborn child every time he copulates with the pregnant mother. Therefore the males can claim more credit for the children than in most societies. But it is not enough, and the man not only needs an extra young wife but also spends much of his time preparing male virility rites from which the women are excluded. He is insufficiently aggressive to offer much sexual gratification, protection, or food to his family, and the tribe has been driven away from all the most productive land. He is desperately afraid of the more powerful women from neighboring areas, imagining them as witches who will come to steal his semen.

The chief positive trait of the Arapesh males seems to be their great generosity and cooperativeness, characteristic of tribes in which the males greatly value childbirth. It is in a sense an open marriage. The men are often in the home, doing work closely associated with women in most societies. The results in this case are an obsessive virility anxiety, alleviated in male rites, and "incompetence" in what Mead calls "all the assertive, creative, productive aspects of life on which the superstructure of a civilization depends." [20]

But perhaps the Mundugumor are more relevant because they do not display the Arapesh "inflation and glorification of motherhood." Like the O'Neills, the Mundugumor regard children as a great inconvenience and treat them brusquely. The lack of concern for the mother-child ties, moreover, is reflected in a general lack of cooperation or compassion in the tribe. The women are powerful, ruthless and aggressive, and gather most of the food. The men are even more vicious and strong, and spend most of their time headhunting among neighboring tribes. In a sense, the relationship partakes of open marriage principles—to the extent that there are marriages at all—because the women are extraordinarily aggressive and productive. But the males feel compelled to exceed them. The result is a society that was in dire straits because its cannibalism turned against itself, involving even small children. The group was disintegrating when Mead left it.

The Tchambuli, combining some of the female aggressiveness of the Mundugumor with the male passivity of the Arapesh, are as catastrophic a failure as either of the other tribes. The males, whom the women abuse from birth, spend their lives in a futile pursuit of their masculinity. Although they no longer have the gumption for headhunting, they purchase victims from other tribes to kill sacrificially as part of their elaborate male initiation rites. They were down to 500 people when Mead left them. Perhaps they had the most open marriage of all and the most fearful and ineffectual males, who devoted themselves obsessively to various masculine displays.

None of the conclusions that can be appropriately drawn from the experience of these three tribes is at all helpful to the open-marriage thesis. What Mead concluded from all her other studies as well, the New Guinea experience affirms: Males always require a special arena of glorified achievement from which women are excluded. Their concern with sexual differentiation is obsessive. Men can be passive without grave psychological damage only if the women are passive also. Aggressive and competitive women, unconcerned with motherhood, produce more ruthless men—and a society so competitive that it disintegrates. Men, on the other hand, when passively preoccupied with child-rearing, become incapable of effective sexual behavior and paranoid about aggressive women. A society with a great emphasis on child-rearing will, however, be exceedingly generous and cooperative. In none of the societies Mead has studied is there the slightest evidence that roles, however created, through culture or biology, can be switched back and forth. Of course, the O'Neills can dismiss all these conclusions as coming from exotic primitive tribes (the ones they chose for evidence), which had yet to be exposed to the principles of dynamic synergy through beatified couplepower.

If the O'Neill conception of what marriage is and what it can be is false, what is the alternative conception? The O'Neills cited Bronislaw Malinowski at the beginning of their book as a source for their belief that marriage is so durable and universal an institution that it can survive virtually any needed reforms.[21] Unfortunately, the reforms of open marriage vitiate the very essence of marriage as Malinowski and most anthropologists envisage it. According to him "the very essence of marriage," "the central element," the "pivotal point" is "parenthood and above all maternity."[22] The male role in marriage, as Mead has maintained, "in every known human society, is to provide for women and children."[23] In order to marry, in fact, Malinowski says that almost every human society first requires the man "to prove his capacity to maintain the woman."[24]

Marriage is not simply a ratification of an existing love. It is the conversion of that love into a biological and social continuity transcending any two individuals. The very essence of such continuity is children—now fewer than before but retained far longer within the family bounds. Regardless of whether a particular couple says it is getting married for companionship or psychoindustrial synergy or sexual massage, one must separate the professed motives of the individuals from deeper sexual and evolutionary propensities. All sorts of superficial deviations and distortions—from homosexual marriage to companionate partnership—can be elaborated on the primal foundations of human life. But the foundations remain. The natural fulfillment of love is a child, and the fantasies and projects of the childless couple may well be considered as surrogate children.

The essential pattern is clear. Women manipulate male sexual desire in order to teach them the long-term cycles of female sexuality and biology on which civilization is based. When men learn, their view of the woman as an object of their own sexuality succumbs to an image of her as the bearer of a richer and more extended eroticism and as the keeper of the portals of social immortality. She becomes a way to lend elaborate continuity and meaning to the limited erotic compulsions of the male.

This intuition of mysterious new realms of sexual and social experience, evoked by the body and spirit of woman, is the source of male love and ultimately of marriage. In evoking marriages love renders the woman transparent: The man sees through her, in a vision freighted with sexual desire, to the child they might have together. This vision imposes severe social conditions, however. For it is a child that *he* might have only if he performs a role: only if he can offer, in exchange for the intense inner sexual meanings she imparts, an external realm of meaning, sustenance, and protection in which the child could be safely born. Both partners consciously or unconsciously glimpse a future infant—precarious in the womb, vulnerable in the world, and in need of nurture and protection. In the sweat of their bodies together, in the shape and softnesses of the woman, in the protective support of the man, the couple senses the outlines of a realm that can endure and perpetuate their union.

At the deepest level, therefore, love and marriage are based on this complementary pattern. The man's most profound and indispensable psychological life must be experienced through the woman; she is the master of their sexuality. Meanwhile the woman's external existence will to some extent be sustained and protected by the man; he gives space for their worldly haven. This may be the very essence of a closed marriage but it is the essence of the institution itself.

The women's movement, and the O'Neills, will cry bondage. Yet on this foundation can be erected a huge variety of marriages. The woman may even on some occasions excel the man in the world of work without in any way seriously jeopardizing the relationship. But it is important that the woman understand her enormous innate power over the man, his psychological dependence on her, and his need to compensate with external achievement. The woman should not in general begin with the assumption that she will have an equivalent career, and she should not be made to feel unequal without it.

In the realm of sexuality she is necessarily supreme. Only she can bear the child that is the ulterior embodiment and goal of the marriage; only she can free the man of his exile from the chain of nature; only she can give meaning to the most powerful drives of his existence. If he leaves, the family may survive without him. If she leaves, it goes with her. He can have a child only if she acknowledges his paternity. Her child is inexorably hers. His position is insecure because it must be maintained by continuous performance, sexual and worldly, with the woman the judge. The woman's position on the other hand requires essentially a receptive sexuality, and it is naturally validated by the child that cannot usually be taken away. The man's role in the family is thus reversible; the woman's is unimpeachable and continues even if the man departs.

These inequalities, pertaining to the core of the marriage, can be overcome only by diminishing the woman and her maternal sexuality, reducing her to the lowest terms of male eroticism, leaving her as a man without a phallus: a veritable "female eunuch." This is the real agenda of the open marriage. It is an attempt to reduce women to the condition of men, abjectly dependent on external performance and achievement. It is an attempt to convert the rich dimensions of female eroticism into the short circuits of tension and release to which the male without marriage is assigned.

But it won't work. For in diminishing the woman, in relegating maternity to the optional fringes of her life, one attacks the "central element," the "pivotal point," "the very essence" of love and marriage itself. The O'Neills *open* marriage by emptying the womb—and thus empty marriage as well.

The remaining "innate human need for structure" and "desire for intimacy" will not sustain a marriage over the years. Deprived of his role as provider and protector, the man, like males all over the world throughout human history, will leave. As a general rule of anthropology the likelihood of his presence in the home decreases in direct proportion to the aggressiveness of the woman. Instead, he will conduct male rituals, drink, commit crimes, hunt, seek power, take drugs, pursue women on male terms. Unless he is performing a masculine service for the marriage commensurate in some way with the bearing of a child, the marriage will cramp his manhood. He will feel unworthy of the woman and thus unable to love her. The relationship will fail.

The O'Neills suavely write: "Aside from the actual bearing of the child (and even that, biologists indicate, may be carried on outside the mother's body within the next decade or so), the raising of children must be a shared responsibility" of the two sexes.[25] But the man will not be there. The woman will open her marriage only to a stiffening and probing technocracy of the child-care state.

Open marriage, therefore, fails for an obvious reason. As usual, Margaret Mead says it best: "If any human society—large or small, simple or complex, based on the most rudimentary hunting and fishing, or on the whole elaborate interchange of manufactured products—is to survive, it must have a pattern of social life that comes to terms with the differences between the sexes."[26]

The differences between the sexes are the single most important fact of human society. The drive to deny them—in the name of women's liberation, marital openness, sexual equality, erotic consumption—must be one of the most quixotic crusades in the history of the species. Yet in a way it is typical of crusades. For it is a crusade against particular incarnate humanity, in behalf of a metaphysical "humanism." It seems unlikely, however, that the particular men and women one meets in the world will ever voluntarily settle for long in an open house of barren abstractions.

Multiple Mirage

You have unmade your bed, now you must lie about it.

John Hollander on divorce

To the O'Neills and other feminists—and even to conservative publications like *U.S. News and World Report* [1]— the new, flexible forms of marriage appear the only way of saving the institution. They look at the statistics of divorce and other marital distresses; they peruse the expanding repertory of sexual consumption—the swinging singles, the switching couples, the rotatory communes; they coolly appraise the prospects of artificial wombs; and they assume that conventional marriage is obsolescent. In offering alternative forms, they envisage themselves as intelligent conservatives, providing a comfortable transition to a future that will be unrecognizable.

Alvin Toffler presents a popular version of this approach in his best-selling book *Future Shock*.[2] Toffler believes that it is the rapid pace of technological and economic progress that prevents enduring love. In a society convulsed with change and replete with individual options and possibilities, he maintains that lifetime relationships will grow increasingly unlikely. For adventurous minorities, he envisages a panoply of alternatives: childless marriages, artificial wombs, embryo supermarkets, professional parenthood, postretirement child-rearing, corporate families, communes, geriatric group marriages, homosexual family units, polygamy, and a large range of other experiments. He contends, however, that even the more conventional majority will be forced to abandon the orthodox ideal. In a technocratic, future-shocked, life-extended society, Toffler maintains, "the odds against [monogamous] success become absolutely astronomical. . . . Something has to crack." In fact, according to him, something already has: "the old insistence on permanence." [3]

The result, he says, will be whole series of marriages, corresponding to the multiple stages and careers of life in the superindustrial state. There will be probationary marriages among the young, without children or expectations of length. Then there will be marriages in which various procreative options are pondered and chosen. This parental period, however, will be steadily shortened, in Toffler's view, since women may not have to conceive, bear, or raise the children themselves.

Then the postparental stage is seen to create a new crisis, often to be resolved by a new marriage. This third coupling, without children, beginning in the late thirties, "could well turn out to be the only 'real' marriage. . . . During this time two mature people, presumably with well-matched interests and complementary psychological needs, and with a sense of being at comparable stages of personality development, will be able to look forward to a relationship with a decent statistical probability of enduring." [4]

Even this marriage, however, may not be final, for retirement from work can impose impossible stresses and impel yet another decoupling. The dynamically changing society of the future is seen as creating a similar dynamic of individual adaptation, as the family hangs on the latest word from the biology laboratories and encounter groups.

One can cavil at much of the Toffler vision on the same grounds that disqualify open marriage: the subordination of parenthood and sexuality to companionship and growth would subvert the very foundation of the institution. But even as social analysis, his disposal of conventional marriage is premature. Like most observers he overestimates the significance of the divorce rate as a radical long-term trend. While divorces are indeed increasing, so are marriages, to the point that a higher proportion of our people get married now, at least once, than ever before.[5] The highest divorce rate, moreover, comes among couples precipitately married as teenagers.[6] The current decline in early marriages thus promises eventually to diminish the divorce rate.

A further decline is predictable as the impact of the Vietnam war expires. Every war causes large numbers of opportunistic marriages, followed by a dramatic upsurge of divorces.[7] Since Vietnam enlistments and discharges have been occurring for a decade, divorce statistics have been artificially high for some time. This trend was accentuated by the prosperity of the 1960s, which brought high hopes and marriages that were later undercut by economic stagnation and unemployment.

In addition, today more than two-thirds of divorced persons soon remarry,[8] sometimes establishing more stable and loving homes for the children. This remarriage rate represents an increase of some 40 percent in the last decade.[9] Similarly, many people without children divorce several times during their lives, thus inflating the statistics. But perhaps most important is the fact that over half of all current divorces do not involve offspring.[10] Such divorces pose little threat to the family as our key social institution.

Marriages without children are fundamentally different from parental marriages in their impact on both the partners and the society. The statistics should not be combined or the categories confused. For the woman, a marriage without children may little change her life. The change for the man depends on the degree to which he assumes new responsibilities as provider and new attitudes toward his sexuality. Often the nonparental marriage will have a socializing effect on the man. He will do better as a student; [11] he will pay his bills more regularly and adopt a more conservative view of the world. He will submit his own sexual rhythms to those of the woman to some extent. But only the birth of a child can fully validate the marriage as a vehicle of social continuity. Only then does a divorce gravely tear the social fabric.

Many of our current confusions stem from the assumption that companionate marriages are analogous to parental ones. In the past, when any extended companionate union was likely to bring children, all marriages did form part of the generational fabric of the community. The community thus had a deep concern in enforcing them. But couples who do not plan children create no such public interest. Companionate marriages should not be a major concern of the law or the church, and their failure should not be considered particularly important. In fact, the current trend toward later marriages among the educated—and toward more provisional "marriage" services—signifies a recognition that the usual sanctions are wildly inappropriate to a decision to live together for a while.

Toffler's nonparental categories, therefore, are virtually meaningless as prophecy. He merely wants to codify current realities. The concern of the society is not the incidence of marriage and divorce but the creation of families with socialized males. Toffler's analysis is ominous chiefly because he assumes that parenthood will decline drastically as a familial activity. A decline of parenthood ultimately means a decline of love and sex and a further erosion of male socialization.

Also questionable is Toffler's assumption that the key reason for divorces is uneven psychological development or growth. He seems to accept the popular notion that men at work often "outgrow" their homebound spouses and turn to women more responsive to their mature needs and interests, acquired on the job. Much of the time, though, the mature needs and interests of these men turn out to be younger women, often secretaries, desired chiefly for sexual affirmation. It is difficult to see how these divorces are caused by an increasing rate of technological change and career turnover. It is also difficult to see how female careers can help overcome the middle-aged male's crisis of sexuality. It is the man's view of sex rather than his woman's failure of growth that undermines most of these marriages.

Those instances where the man truly appears to "outgrow" the woman are also often deceptive. The man has usually enjoyed some success at work and seeks to validate it sexually. He seeks to vindicate all his sacrifices—which were originally motivated by sexual ambition—by achieving the advertised ecstasies of anonymous young bodies. Again, neither technological change nor emotional and intellectual growth have much to do with it.

Nonetheless, Toffler's analysis is useful because it states explicitly what most other family reformers usually leave tacit, except in the heat of debate: a belief that conventional love and marriage are dead, victims of progress. In the future, it is implied, people will no longer identify themselves chiefly through their familial connections. Kinship will become a secondary concern. Primary will be one's "stage of personality development" and position in the marketplace. Like the O'Neills, sociologist Jessie Bernard in the *Future of Marriage* [12] as well as most of the contributors to *The Future of the Family* [13] presume that the current trend toward familial disintegration is inexorable.

The feminists offer a further argument for their somewhat avid pessimism. Conventional marriage must expire not only because it inconveniences technocracy but also because it oppresses women. It is, in fact, so much better for men than for women that it represents a trap for the wife. Jessie Bernard [14] and Caroline Bird [15] present statistics that show women are happier single than married. Bernard says every marriage is really two marriages, the man's and the woman's, and the man's is usually more satisfying. While men tend to become happier and healthier when married, women in greater numbers become sickly and neurotic. The greatest strains are caused by the birth of children. Bernard urges the usual "open marriage" reforms: a greater female role in employment, a greater male role in the home, and lesser emphasis on children.[16]

Bird and Bernard fail to explain why 69 percent of women with children believe wives have it "easier than their husbands"; or why over 10 percent more men than women endorse the women's liberation movement; or, more concretely, why married women outlive both their husbands and single women. Nor does the feminist analysis accord with Margaret Mead's anthropological finding that women are most contented not when they are granted "influence, power and wealth" but when "the female role of wife and mother" is exalted. It is when "the sensuous creative significance" of the women's role is undervalued that women become frustrated and unhappy in the home. This is probably the problem in current American society.[17]

A 15-year study by Jan Dizard of 400 middle- to upper-middle-class marriages in the Chicago area offers some confirmation for Bernard's theory and recommendations. About half the wives and a little over 40 percent of the husbands expressed dissatisfaction with the relationship in the final interviews. The most striking result was that the more successful the man in his work, the less happy was the marriage.[18] This failure of the marriages of top executives has a parallel in truly patriarchal societies. Where the men can impose their own sexual patterns, marriages are usually fragile. Thus the highest divorce rates in the world are found in Arab Moslem societies, where the men can expel their wives at will. A real balance between the man and woman produces the best marriages. In the Dizard study, the happiest unions occurred where the man had actually suffered a reduction in income during the period of the survey. Since the damaging effects of the husband's success were slightly diminished if the wife had a job or other external activity, Dizard concluded that for an ideal marriage the man should be less devoted to his work and the woman should have outside interests.

The Dizard findings offer little ultimate encouragement

to the liberationist, however. Almost all the participants were relatively successful men, functioning adequately as providers.[19] There was no evidence whatsoever that marriages would be improved if the woman undertook the kind of job commitments that brought success to the men. Women with high incomes and/or graduate degrees have the highest divorce rate —a rate far higher than successful men.[20] The real meaning of the Dizard survey was that marriages are hurt by the kind of obsessive job effort that is usually required for major financial or public success. The men stay late in the office and return preoccupied to the home. They give little attention to their wives and children. The couple drifts apart. The man then entertains a worshipful subordinate from the office, who does not make the kinds of complex demands that are associated with real sex and parenthood. It is a predictable result.

The mildly beneficial effect of some job, or other outside activity, for the woman gives equally little comfort to the liberationist position. It is obvious that, particularly during the increasing period of time after the departure of children, many women will want work outside the household. Marriages will clearly benefit from the women's fulfillment. No one should imagine that opponents of the women's movement object to vigorous career and community participation by individual women.

Career engagement by women becomes objectionable chiefly when it takes precedence over motherhood and family life and is conducted in a way that jeopardizes the male role as provider and achiever. Even this kind of female activity may be perfectly acceptable in some marriages. The damage of feminist "liberation" comes from the mobilization of a movement with a careerist ideology and a political program that are hostile to sexual differences and to family life— a movement really devoted to establishing the career woman as the American ideal, supported by federal subsidies and celebrations.

Since career success is a possibility chiefly for an educated minority—while conventional female roles are the lot of most women—the feminist cause has a clearly elitist bias. If Jessie Bernard thinks marriages make women unhappy, and Phyllis Chesler thinks they drive women crazy, these writers should consider the psychological effects of defining careers as the chief source of freedom and fulfillment. This careerist standard, in fact, would doom most American women—all except the professional minority like Chesler and Bernard—to feelings of inadequacy and failure.

There is an enormous difference between devotion to a career as a woman's chief concern and pursuit of jobs and other interests outside the home. Both the Dizard findings and common sense dictate that women participate actively in their community and society. No evidence, however, shows that women and marriages will be better in a society where the career ideal governs every woman's view of her identity— where women judge themselves chiefly as money-makers and public personalities. The evidence only suggests that marriages are often hurt by this orientation among women and men.

In any case, the findings of Bernard and Dizard about happy families with unambitious males—and unhappy ones headed by magnates—are not really very useful to the policy-maker. The families involved have already been created and supported; they are successful. When one advocates changes in the structure of marriage, one should consider their impact on the society as a whole. The ideal of secure jobs for un-competitive men is fine for those with luck or credentials. But most men have to fight hard to maintain a satisfactory place in the economy.

Families in which the men fail as providers are least likely to survive. The most fragile and unhappy marriages, after all, are found among the poor. Our social policy should focus on reinforcing the marriages of the poor by providing employment for poor males. The marital unhappiness and social disruption caused by some of our most productive men and women are the price we pay for their crucial contribution to our economy. These people indirectly create jobs for thousands and thus make possible the happiness of those less ambitious couples whom Dizard and Bernard understandably applaud.

The feminists once again offer a program oriented toward the upper-class woman. Discouraging work commitment by upper-class men in order to improve the marriages of their wives hurts the economy and worsens the problems of the poor. Encouraging upper-class women to seek employment may occasionally relieve the upper-class women. But it hurts middle-class men and women in the job force. In addition, a general bias against hard, compulsive effort deprives the ambitious poor and middle class of their greatest asset in competing with the educated upper class: their greater need and motivation. Similarly, the feminist emphasis on degrees and test scores tends to favor the dutiful accumulation of credentials over the display of leadership and initiative. Despite claims to the contrary, both the feminists and the upper classes want to emphasize reward for what one *is* rather than what one can do—being over doing.

Worst of all and destructive to all classes is the complacent expectation of familial disintegration as an inevitable result of progress. This idea, pervasive in the society, has the infectious appeal of a self-fulfilling prophecy. The feminists and futurists are wrong in treating the rising divorce rate as a portent of a new and radically different familial order; the desire for monogamous marriage remains strong. But they are right in their belief that the institution is in trouble. The culture is promoting family disintegration in a number of ways. Among the most important is the nullification of age.

The society truncates the natural evolution of life, in which three generations play active and complementary roles in families. A culture that deprives the elderly of prestigious positions—revered connections with children and grandchildren—is committing a different form of sexual suicide, short-circuiting the extended patterns of family in which our sexuality organically unfolds. Children brought up with their peers and without frequent contact with venerable elders come to regard old age as a limbo of impotence. Men surrounded everywhere with cultural advertising of sex as a province of youthful and anonymous curves have trouble adjusting to the inevitable parabolas of their own lives and sexuality. Men who lack experience with proud and fulfilled older people—with respected positions—come to fear their own aging.

One of the effects is a desperate attempt to revive one's youth by affairs with young women. This course is most inviting and practicable for successful men, because they can most easily find and afford these new relationships. But most middle-aged men in our society are tantalized by the media mirage of promiscuous sex, by the image of the unsocialized male loving and leaving one young woman after another. This vision is made nearly irresistible when the society does not affirm an alternative role of leadership and love for the old in relation to younger generations.

At the other end of the spectrum, divorces among the young are also promoted by a kind of sexual suicide. Since marriage is essentially an act of male subordination to female sexual cycles, the adoption of male cycles by the women seriously undermines the institution. Partly because the pill reduces women's consciousness of their larger sexuality—partly because of the long period of male-oriented premarital activity—all too many women today pursue sex in essentially the same way as men: as a relatively undiscriminating quest for temporary relief and gratification. Men can find partners too easily. Women become so available on male terms that men are not induced to submit to the futurity of feminine love. Wives fail to teach their husbands the cycles of femininity. Thus, even though the marriage may be happy, the man is not durably bound to the woman through her womb and the hope or presence of progeny. He does not experience the unique depth of a passion for one woman as the individual through whom he wishes to define his participation in the future of the race. At the same time, he finds other women increasingly available on the same reciprocal terms as his wife.

No matter how gratifying a reciprocal sexual relationship may be, unless the mystical drama of procreation is celebrated—at least symbolically and instinctively—most men (and women) will eventually want to move on to new conquests. Their love will not have social and psychological traction, conferred by the image of growing children. The couple is not truly married.

Of course, many such relationships may succeed. Just as there are exceptional men and women, there are exceptional marriages, and extraordinary relationships among the unmarried. There will be cases where no children are desired, and durable companionate marriages are maintained; cases where triangular groups manage to live happily together; cases where various sexual exotica are performed. Large numbers of marriages will survive adultery, and many divorces will occur despite the nominal commitment to a lifetime together.

Yet there is absolutely no reason why the failure of most people to achieve a lifetime of monogamous bliss—or the success of many with groovy new life-styles—should lead to a change in the canons of marriage. An ideal by definition cannot be achieved by everyone. The question is whether the ideal exerts a positive pressure on people's lives and whether the alternative would bring valuable benefits.

Considering the alternative of multiple marriage options, it is difficult to see a single significant gain. Couples already choose to live together for long periods under any terms they like and without any significant stigma. Why these relationships should be given legal status is difficult to understand. Similarly, adultery is often committed within marriage without terminal damage to the relationship. But to include such acts within the marital concept itself is not to condone but to invite them. Unless one regards philandering as a positive good, it is wrong to affirm it officially. The fact is that most marriages are gravely strained by outside sexual activity, and creating another impression serves no good purpose. The exceptions will know who they are.

There is no reason, however, to examine all the kinds of arrangements for which codification has been suggested. It suffices to say they are numerous enough to deprive marriage of any specific form or ideal authority. In essence, what is either implicitly or explicitly advocated is the negotiation of an individual contract for each couple. This proposal will benefit the marriages of lawyers short on work. But it will promote a view of marriage that is ultimately destructive of the institution.

Pitirim Sorokin has divided most human relationships into three categories: the ascriptive, the contractual, and the coercive.[21] The coercive occurs when the others fail. The point about contracts is that they treat the partners as functional agents, bound only by the specific terms of the agreement. You pay your money and the other provides a service. The exchange is the essence of the relationship. It is between functions rather than integral human beings.

To treat marriage as a contract is to destroy its *raison d'être*. A marriage is a commitment of two people not to exchange products or services but to escape the psychology of exchange altogether. Each partner receives the other as a whole person, for what he is rather than for what he agrees to do. Each partner serves the other not in the expectation of specific gain, but in the course of serving the larger unit they become together.

In such a relationship, an ideal image and a religious ritual are more appropriate—even more specifically useful—than any legal instrument. For the ideal and the ceremony affirm the new unity to which both partners are subjectively pledged; the law deals essentially in objects, the very imagery that the marriage obliterates and that love denies. The problem in marriage is not balancing legal obligations but in transcending them through love and family.

This ideal may be difficult. But its very existence orients the partners to seek unities rather than negotiate fair exchanges. This approach is most favorable to love. Every time one conceives of the partner in terms of what he can do for you rather than who he is, one erodes the subjective sources of love. The marriage is slowly absorbed by the marketplace, until in divorce court it is entirely subsumed by a contract of barter. But that is not how it should begin.

The advantage of complementary relationships, whether at work or in marriage, is that they avoid competition between the sexes and create emotional space for love. Sorokin believes that a major problem of modern society is the steady expansion of contractual relationships at the expense of ascriptive or complementary ones like kinships, family, and marriage.[22] This contractual expansion—this steady engorgement of subjective experience by objective formulas—this movement of the marketplace into marriage and home—constitutes a diminution of the realms of love. It also produces a degradation of sexuality. For as time passes, even the act of love becomes a reciprocation of services, and thus replaces two integral human beings with two agents exchanging pleasures. The bed itself becomes a marketplace in the Sexual Suicide Society.

A restoration of sexuality depends on a restoration of the

ideal of marriage as a unit that transcends the individual partners. All the companionship, love, and inspiration that we
now come to associate with marriage and that we seek in it
are secondary to the crucial social role that the institution
plays. Marriage attaches males to families, the source of continuity, individuality, and order in a free society. As we are
increasingly discovering in our schools, prisons, mental hospitals, and psychiatric offices, the family is the only agency
that can be depended upon to induce truly profound and
enduring changes in its members. The family is the only institution that works on the deep interior formations of human
character and commitment. Thus it is the only uncoercive
way to transform individuals, loose in social time and space—
in the O'Neill idiom, lost in "the nowness of self"—into vol-
untary participants in the nurture of society.

Through family and kinship people gain their connections with both the past and future. Although other agencies
can create objective ties, only the family can often transform
them into the ganglia of one's psychological being. The family
is effective because it is steeped in the blood, sexuality, flesh,
and flow of our unconscious lives, where true changes in
character and commitment can take root.

Of course, families can exist without marriage. Almost
always, they consist of women and children. The problem is
that they leave the men awash in the "nowness of self." Single
men all too often remain egocentric vagrants, following the
episodic currents of their sexuality. They fail to mature into
social beings, part of history and committed to the future.
Without the institution of marriage and the commitment of
women to it, the men are exiles from the natural chain of
being, their sexual experience reduced to the short circuits of
copulation. They often become enemies of society and of the
larger horizons of female sexuality: the cycles of procreation
and nurture that necessarily dictate to women a concern for
stability, community, and future.

Societies through history have recognized how difficult it
is to secure these commitments from males. The alternative
male pattern of brief sexual exploits and predatory economics
accords all too well with the many millions of years of male
evolution as a hunter.[23] Women have had to use all their in-

genuity, all their powers of sexual attraction and restraint to induce men to become providers. Society has had to invest marriage with all the ceremonial sanctity of religion and law. This did not happen as a way to promote intimacy and companionship. It happened to ensure civilized society.

Our sexual potentialities are to a great extent fixed. But what we do with them is determined by culture, which is shaped by us. The first and most important step in restoring a sense of order and purpose and community is to reestablish the social pressures and cultural biases in favor of durable monogamous love and marriage—the long-term feminine sexual patterns—that the women's movement and the *Playboy* philosophers find so "oppressive." It is women who will most benefit in the beginning, for their discomfort in the toils of male sexuality is already inducing a revulsion toward sex altogether—what Midge Decter calls the "New Chastity." [24] But ultimately the whole society gains. For as we cultivate more profound patterns of love and sexuality, we will create a deeper sense of community, a more optimistic embrace of the future, and a more tranquil, orderly, creative, and productive society.

Part Two

Work and Society

After the Hunt

A fugitive and a vagabond shalt thou be in the earth . . .

Yahweh to Cain

Anthropology is an attractive arena for the ideologue looking for a settled image of human nature. It is harder, however, for the serious anthropologist. For he knows how little he knows and how ravenous is the appetite for each glimpse of the primordial human: the *anthropos*. Every artifact discovered—each shard of a primitive hatchet (or is it a hoe?)—is used to grind someone's ax. Every theory is quickly entered in academic or political battle, to defend some vision of an Edenic or Hobbesean world: a state of nature from which *anthropos* has either lamentably fallen or precariously escaped.[1]

In general, the women's movement is Edenist. The feminists envisage a Golden Age dominated by agriculture and women. They point to the large amount of archeological evidence that early man worshipped female deities.[2] The male "conservatives" incline toward the Hobbesean vision: human life began in a state of nature where life was "solitary, poor, nasty, brutish, and short." [3] Observing the complete absence of true matriachy anywhere in the world today,[4] even among primitive tribes—and citing evidence of weapons as the first human artifacts—these anthropologists can confirm their plausible speculation that the original man was a patriarchal hunter and fighter who evolved for millions of years in a nomadic pursuit of land and game. But the debate, of course, can never be resolved. Depending on one's taste or polemical needs, one can always envisage one idyllic or predatory society preceding whatever *anthropos* is currently in fashion.

In recent years the matter has been complicated by the ethologists (students of animal behavior). Entering the fray under the leadership of Niko Tinbergen,[5] Robert Ardrey,[6] Desmond Morris,[7] Konrad Lorenz,[8] and others, these scientists bring various herds of baboons and gorillas in tow, and even, because of its pertinence for homosexual studies, a crowded school of ten-spined sticklebacks.[9] In general, the ethologists present an image of naked apes, pugnacious primates, battling baboons. But their observations have been challenged on grounds of irrelevance (we are dealing with modern man, after all) and scientific inaccuracy (an ethological Heisenberg principle: the animals are upset by the [male chauvinist] observers).[10] But the chief problem of ethology is the existence of nearly infinite varieties of animal life from which opponents could pick and choose convenient evidence.

Then a British feminist named Elaine Morgan offered the charming theory that mankind did not descend from the trees as a naked ape at all, but emerged from the waters as a wading hermaphrodite.[11] Thus at once she explained our erect posture, elevated mammaries, smooth skin, and urgent need for women's liberation. Her book was popular, and her theory represented perhaps the last word in freestyle anthropology the week it came out.

The expedient way out of this debate—beyond simply reaffirming *Genesis*—is to accept all these theories and images of man as valid under some circumstances and treat them as evidence of man's diversity and adaptability. Mankind has sometimes been brutal, sometimes pacific, conceivably matriarchal, often matrilineal (inheriting through mothers), and usually patrilineal and patriarchal. The important question is not what man most authentically is in the state of nature, but what human relationships lead to what kinds of societies; what observable problems arise in most societies; what patterns of behavior seem important to civilized human communities. If, for example, no one denies that humans are sometimes aggressive, how does one mitigate this tendency? If one acknowledges that males and females have long played different sexual roles, which differences are important to a civilized community and which are culturally dispensable?

This pragmatic approach does not fully obviate the matter of distilling an essence of pure man. One still must suggest certain limits to human adaptability. Certain adaptations, while possible in the abstract, or in the state of nature, or in the primordial tides, will not work in a complex and civilized human society like ours. One must admit that such limits are definitions, and they embody implicit histories and anthropologies. But at least the field is reduced to anthropology as it immediately pertains to current civilized society rather than to millennia past or promised.

It is obvious that depending on environment, men and women, baboons and marmosets, even ten-spined sticklebacks, can play roles of great variety. It is also obvious that the roles adopted interact with environments in important ways. Modern man, however, may be distinguished from all primitive human and primate life by the extent to which he creates both himself and his surroundings.

Man's environment—civilized society—is a prodigious and precarious achievement. If one accepts that sex is nothing less than the life force in a community, one may conclude that particular sexual arrangements contributed to the birth of this prodigy. One may suspect that its maintenance depends on an intelligent ordering of our sexual relationships. And one may speculate that our current cultural stresses, which could conceivably destroy our democratic civilization, derive from and reflect sexual disorders. Sexuality is not simply a matter of *Games People Play;* it is one of the few matters truly of life and death to society.

Apart from the diversity of mankind, this is perhaps the clearest lesson of the anthropologist. How a tribe manages its sexuality—its births, matings, kinship ties—determines the nature of the tribe and its durability. The kinds of families and customs of inheritance may have a decisive impact on whether a nation or community undergoes an industrial revolution. In modern America, the immense edifice of civilization may conceal from Ms. Ephron and other feminists, indeed from most contemporary men, the critical influence of our our sexual management on our nature as a society. But it is likely that in all its many facets our civilization also largely derives from our sexual arrangements and the energies they release or stifle.

A job, a custom, a ritual, an institution should be considered not only in terms of its ostensible function—its relation to the means of production or consumption—but also in terms of its role in the management of our sexuality, the sexual constitution of the society. We must consider the part each of our economic and social usages plays in the intricately woven armature of eros: the generator of our will, commitment, vitality, creativity. It is possible that a society is more profoundly identified by its sexual than by its industrial and political management.

One of the concerns of every society is how to respond to the essentially unprogrammed form of male sexual energy. Mead goes to the heart of the matter: "The central problem

of every society is to define appropriate roles for the men." [12]
The tie between sex and male activity is perhaps the most important variable in shaping a civilization.

Many communities have been able to solve this problem
rather easily. The men have simply performed those tasks of
hunting and defense which through the long millennia have
allowed women time and space to procreate the species or
gather and prepare food. Hunting and defense fortunately are
activities that accord with the brief but intense rhythms and
compulsions of male sexuality. A hunt proceeds to a violent
climax when the game is found and killed. A battle erupts
suddenly, requires frenzied activity, and soon ends. The men
can rise to the occasion and then subside; tension grows and
is released. Gratifications are immediate and transitory. The
men travel in gangs. They may copulate with the women but
otherwise often have little to do with them. If in the state of
nature as Hobbes described it, human existence is "solitary,
poor, nasty, brutish and short," this, excluding solitude, is the
masculine pattern.

Whether or not this hunting and gathering life is the
earliest human arrangement, it has certain attractions today.
In primitive hunting communities the males are not "sexually
insecure." In Nancy Chodorow's terms, perhaps they act with
the "full expression of their humanity." They are not threatened by female intrusion on their realms of activity. Women
often take part in the hunt in various capacities, provided the
hunting party itself is not jeopardized. Lionel Tiger, in his
controversial book, *Men in Groups,* assumes that in most instances the hunting party would be endangered by female participation, and he concludes, plausibly enough, that segregated
groups won natural selection.[13] Critics of Tiger point out that
among the Australian Bushmen, the Eskimos, and the other
few observable hunting societies, women sometimes participate
in various ways.[14] The segregation is not legal and complete.

But surely this scholarly conflict is spurious. In hunting
and gathering societies within a hostile environment, the position of males is so spontaneous, so secure, so indispensable,
that no *de jure* exclusions are needed. Male roles and male
sexuality coincide and affirm each other in an authentic unity.
In addition, because the men in hunting and fighting parties

would be most likely to succeed if they acted together, a co-operative inclination evolved. Whether or not Tiger is justified in canonizing this tendency as a universal "male bonding instinct," such a phenomenon seems evident in virtually every society and in most men. Of course, the inclination to exclude females from purposeful groups may merely reflect the intense distraction created by sexually eligible women in any gathering of men, particularly over a long period. Natural competitive instincts are exacerbated, and trust and unity may be impossible to maintain.

In any case, the role pattern of these hunting societies is clear. The men hunt and, when necessary, defend. The women gather and prepare food, as well as bear, nurture, and raise children. The family unit thus effectively consists of the mother and child, with the man an occasional visitor seeking sexual release and sometimes displaying little interest in young children. In the pure case, where there is no agricultural activity and food is scarce, the tribe is likely to be nomadic. The female cycles of procreation and nurture—the long-term chronologies of women—are found only in the female procreative activities themselves. The rest of the society marches to the beat of the hunt and the battle.

A rather vivacious debate has erupted over the primacy of the hunting pattern. Prompted in part by the women's movement, there is an attempt to revive the theory that agricultural communities, in which women provided the food, preceded the aggressive hunting units. The Edenic vision of a matriarchal Golden Age can be supported by more evidence—in religious sculpture of female deities—than can the hunting pattern. The hunters did not leave much reverential statuary.

In any case, the feminists are correct in their assumption that agricultural societies represented an important advance over the hunting pattern. For in general, civilization evolved through the subordination of male sexual patterns—the short-term cycles of tension and release—to the long-term female patterns. Anthropologists often credit women with the initiation of agriculture. Just as the movements, crises, performances, and recoveries of nomadic hunting embodied the rhythm of male sexuality, so the seasonal phases of the farm community accorded with the extended cycles of the woman's life.

But this advance for mankind nonetheless came at some psychological cost for men. The problem called by Mead the central issue of every human society arose: what to do with the males. Unlike hunting groups, static agricultural communities had to stress diligence, regularity, and control; they left little room for male initiatives and aggressions. A mistake would not merely mean the escape of a single prey; it might ruin a whole season of crops. In farming, a bold initiative offers more danger of disaster than promise of gain. Under those circumstances, male sexual insecurity arises as a social problem.

Different societies—and different kinds of men—react in different ways, but virtually every community has to respond. In some the men continue to hunt compulsively, even though game is no longer really needed. The Kalahari Bushmen devote most of their time to hunting giraffes, rather ineffectually; women provide most of the food. In other tribes, well described by Mead and by Spencer and Gillen, the men conduct elaborate initiation rites for adolescent boys that suggest a profound reverence among the males toward their women.[15]

In ceremonies shrouded in mystery, with women excluded, the men ritualistically reiterate the processes of childbirth. The boys are brought into a great womblike structure; they are sometimes maimed in the genitals, as if to provide them with symbolic vaginas; they are ministered blood, as if through an umbilicus; they are fed, as if from a mother's breast—all before being issued in a great tumult of sound and movement into the world of men. The apparent purpose of the ritual is to assert that even though the women perform the indispensable marvel of producing babies, it is the men who can create men of boys. These initiation rites, found in hundreds of cultures, are evidence that the creative ventures of man emulate the organic creativity of women.

A key point is that essentially agricultural societies— where female rhythms prevail and little of the work entails typical male skills—tend to show the strictest role segregation of the sexes.[16] Role segregation in general is not a product of

SEXUAL SUICIDE 84

real differences in efficiency or adaptability between the sexes in performing different tasks. In fact, the question of which sex or which individuals can best do a particular job has almost nothing to do with it. The women sometimes do the heaviest labor in the fields, while the men lounge in hammocks or perform relatively untaxing work. The role segregation is not a function of economic utility; it is a reflection of the sexual constitution of the community.

Because of the amorphous sexuality of males, they must be given specific and exclusive tasks, not to accomplish the business of the society but to accomplish and affirm their own identities as males. If such roles are not given them, they disrupt the community, or leave it. Or else they subside into a torpor, punctuated with rituals of sexual self-exaltation. Such patriarchies overburden the women with all the community's real work, both procreative and productive. Found among some groups in food-rich tropical areas, it is the pattern of a stagnant society (though not necessarily an unhappy one).

Under most conditions, the males insist on some conventionally masculine activity, whether hunting or tribal warfare or elaborately mysterious religious rites. As male sexual rhythms succumb to female ones, however, the hunting in many of the agricultural communities is transformed into the management of domestic animals, either for consumption or for field work. In most instances, strict role segregation is maintained, with all the large animals and all the plowing handled by men.[17] Since women can easily handle many domestic animals, once again, it seems, the segregation is established less for the benefits afforded to the animals than for the creation of a role for males.

The industrial phase in the evolution of society offers yet another answer to the problem of what to do with males. The industrial revolution was perhaps the most cataclysmic event in history, changing every aspect of human society. Until it occurred, most communities were embroiled in a vicious cycle: Gains in agricultural production caused rises in population that negated the agricultural benefits. For example, increases in availability of food or of arable soil would lead to earlier marriages and larger families, thus both counteracting the agricultural expansion and making the entire society more vulnerable to agricultural disaster or plague. The industrial revolution overcame this Malthusian dilemma in part by substituting positive incentives and stimuli for the negative agricultural cycles. Increases in population then would accelerate economic growth at some geometric rate, more rapid than the growth in human fertility.

Now industrialization has become the professed goal of almost all the world's societies, from underdeveloped nations to economically backward parts of advanced countries. Exhaustive studies have been made on its etiology: its causes and processes. As in most social studies—from anthropology to economics—no single model will suffice by itself to explain the vastly diverse and turbulent flow of such a historic phenomenon. Nonetheless, it may well be that economic growth is most essentially a problem of interrelated motivation and demography—that is, a problem of familial and sexual organization.

Once again we may find that the success and durability of a society is less dependent on how it organizes its money and resources on a grand scale, or how it produces its goods, than on how it arranges its sexual patterns: specifically how it induces men to subordinate their sexual rhythms to extended female perspectives. "Pre-industrial men," as British demographer E. A. Wrigley puts it, "lived their lives in a moving present; short-term prospects occupied much of their attention." [18]

Wrigley believes that it was the presence of relatively isolated conjugal or nuclear families that made possible the emergence of the highly motivated industrial bourgeoisie and labor force. Maintaining that "the act of marriage is necessarily one which stands centrally in the whole complex of social behavior," Wrigley points to intriguing differences between marital customs in areas that produced an early industrial revolution and those in areas that remained economically stagnant. [19]

In industrially retarded East Europe and Asia, marriages took place at an early age within the bounds of an extended family; the couple was not expected to support itself at the beginning. By contrast, in England, where the revolution began, and in precocious parts of Western Europe, a couple generally could not get married unless it was economically independent, with a separate household. Thus sexual energies were directly tied to economic growth, and since strong sanctions were imposed on premarital sex, population growth was directly connected to economic productivity. The result was that in Elizabethan England marriages tended to occur three or four years later than in England today. As Wrigley writes, "The conjugal family, consisting of father, mother, and children only, so often held to be the result of industrialization and urban living, was normal in much of Western Europe for several centuries before the industrial revolution." [20]

The virtues of this arrangement, which also prevailed in the United States, go beyond the effective harnessing of male sexual and economic energies to the creation of family units. By concentrating rewards and penalties, the conjugal household set a pattern of incentives that applied for a lifetime. Benefits of special effort or initiative were not diffused among a large number of relatives, as in the extended family; and the effects of sloth or failure would not be mitigated by the success of the larger unit. In general, the man stood alone as provider for his wife and children. He was fully responsible for the rest of his life. Such responsibility transformed large numbers of preindustrial men, living in "a moving present," into relatively long-term planners, preparing for an extended future. [21]

In another sense, men diminished their horizontal economic ties to relatives in their own and previous generations and oriented themselves toward their children and the future. Thousands risked everything and died as failures; many struggled through lives of unremitting drudgery. But largely because their motives were tied to the future that we now enjoy, the world at least partly escaped its Malthusian predicament.

In terms of male and female relations, the industrial revolution, for all its violence and technological impetus, was probably dependent upon a draconian imposition on males of the long-term rhythms and perspectives of female sexuality. The men relinquished their sexual freedom and repressed the spontaneous compulsiveness of masculinity in order to play their role as key providers for their wives and children. Their energies were released to a great extent by greatly enlarging the importance, for life and death, of their role in wedlock. They were made to feel that their identities as males were dependent not chiefly on religious rituals, or gang depredations, or hunting parties, or warfare, but on work, initiative, love, and responsibility for a wife and children.

This new structure of motivation, which arose in agrarian England and Western Europe, created the bourgeoisie and the industrial revolution. It produced the Jeffersonian yeomen, the independent farmers, and the small shopkeepers of the American revolution. And it prompted many of the ideas of individual responsibility, dignity, and equality that are now proclaimed by the women's movement.

The same essential system persists today as the sexual constitution of every modern society. The success of other institutions will in large part be determined by the extent to which they are supported by society's sexual conformation. A nation's governmental policies, for example, may be devoted to economic growth. But as many poor countries have discovered in recent years, little growth will be achieved if the society's sexual constitution—the complex of motives and attitudes in private and familial life—does not promote industriousness, initiative, and birth control.

In comparing civilized to primitive societies—and successful modern communities with disintegrating or stagnant ones—the chief difference is in the use of male energy and sexuality. The male attitude varies widely. In some societies the males hunt and fight and perform religious rituals and do not pay much attention to their ostensible wives except for sexual activity. These men seem to be governed almost entirely by a short time horizon. In other societies the men raise domestic animals or crops, and thus have their horizons extended into the seasons. In most societies the men insist on dominating the honorific and political hierarchies, and thus partake of social continuities. But the crucial difference between a civilized and uncivilized society is the attitude of the males toward their children.

In many societies the men do not so much as identify their children, and the male role in procreation—the father as genitor—is scarcely acknowledged. In matrilineal societies, for example, the brother of the mother often plays some of the roles we now associate with paternity. In fact, it may be said that while extended motherhood is a sexual fact, fatherhood is a social invention. The male sexual impulse in nature does not go beyond simple copulation, and when it does, the elaborations often take the man directly away from the family —into the battle or the hunt or the masculine rite.

In the majority of primitive societies, of course, the men join families and, in one way or another, provide for their children. In most such families, though, the connection is far less binding and exclusive than in civilized societies. The child is not really the father's. Although the father's paternity is recognized, the child belongs chiefly to the mother and to the extended family or clan. The clan will sustain it collectively. The father bears no special exclusive responsibility.

The desire of men to claim their children may be the crucial impulse of civilized life. It is chiefly in the nuclear household that the man's connection to his children becomes indispensable. He is the key provider. His fatherhood is direct and unimpeachable, and he identifies, loves, and provides for his offspring. His role as provider then becomes almost as crucial for the maintenance of the family as the mother's role. He thus can feel equal to the mother within the family and he can join it without damage to his sense of himself as a man.

This system of male socialization is the central enactment of the sexual constitution. If we wish to maintain an advanced civilization, technologically inventive, economically productive, and democratically organized, we must either support this complex of familial roles or provide fully adequate replacements.

In the matter of replacements the burden of proof must rest fully and heavily on the innovators: both on those who believe the nuclear family can survive the compromise of the male provider, and on those who say humane values of individuality and love can survive the collapse of the nuclear family. A few partial experiments under special conditions— groovy agricultural communes here, embattled kibbutzim there, utopian speculations everywhere—offer a pathetically inadequate basis for the programs of sexual revolution.

Men and Work

A man in the home is worth two in the street.

Mae West

In the United States and other modern societies the sexual constitution is now in disfavor. Even if such disciplines were needed during the industrial age, it is assumed that we are now moving "beyond scarcity" into a "postindustrial" period, in which values of "human liberation" can prevail over values of material productivity. At last we are said to have actually reached the stage to which many prestigious economists assigned us after World War II. Then it was widely maintained that the capitalist West had exhausted its room for economic growth and should embark on a massive program for redistributing its extant wealth.

The capitalist West, of course, instead embarked on a siege of material expansion about three times greater than all the economic growth previously achieved during the entire history of the human race. Scarcity, however, continues, and much of the world has still failed to break away from the toils of poverty. It is thus only a small, affluent minority, in the richest countries, that wants to stop economic and technological expansion today. Displaying all the prophetic insight and imagination of the antigrowth economists after World War II, these analysts believe that ecological pollution and population growth are the final contradictions of industrial society.[1]

The new Malthusians are no more convincing than the old. The current technology tends to be so damaging chiefly because its inventors saw the environment as a free resource. As soon as conservation and population control become part of the economic calculus, new technologies will be developed to master them. But in order to instigate and finance such innovation, further growth is indispensable. It costs money to convert to less damaging industrial methods. And growth and innovation are also imperative to overcome poverty in the United States and around the world.[2]

Such growth will depend on the same kind of disciplined and creative initiative that has impelled all human progress. It will depend on inducing males to adopt the long time horizons and responsibilities, the dedication and commitment, currently evoked by the sexual constitution. Men will be doing different things in different ways in the world of the future. But even in the United States, most will still experience scarcity and need motivation. Perhaps even less than in the past will society be able to accept the disruptive energies of unsocialized males.

Although the central concerns of the sexual constitution are marriages and families, nearly every contact among human beings contains a sexual charge. How all these charges are organized will deeply influence the productivity and order of the community. The sexual constitution will determine whether social energies are short-circuited and dissipated, or whether they are accumulated and applied to useful pursuits. It will determine whether the society is a fabric of fully integrated citizens or whether it is an atomized flux, with disconnected individuals pursuing sex and sustenance on the most limited and antisocial terms.

At every work site, in every classroom, in every store, barroom, office, and factory, this system comes into play. The ostensible functions and purposes of human activities are accompanied—and either supported or undermined—by an ulterior pattern of sexual interactions. To an outside observer, a man at work may be seen as performing an economic task, subject to legal and political regulation. But to the man himself, this formal role probably seems incidental. He may experience his job chiefly in terms of the connections it affords with his co-workers and with the existing or prospective women and children in his life. What happens in these relationships both at home and at work will more deeply affect the commitment of the man to his job than all the nominal goals of the enterprise.

A man who is oriented toward a family he loves—or wants to create—is apt to work more consistently and productively than a man oriented toward his next fix, lay, day at the races, or drinking session with the boys. A man who feels affirmed sexually by his work environment, and his relation to other men and women in it, will produce more than a man who finds his job sexually erosive and confusing. A man who is integrated into a community through a role in a family, spanning generations into the past and future, will be more consistently and durably tied to the social order than a man responding chiefly to a charismatic leader, a demagogue, or a grandiose ideology of patriotism. Sexuality is our principal way of perceiving and relating to people, and these relationships are more fundamental, psychologically, than our responses to anything else—goods, money, ideology, or law. In fact, our economic and political activities most often are motivated by sexual connections and ambitions.

The sexual constitution is most important to males. Because men lack an elaborate internal sexual constitution of their own, they require more external guidance and socialization. They require a long process of integration into a family and community. A man's emotions and drives must be durably adapted to the roles and regularities of the larger society. Otherwise he will lack a settled identity and move from job to job, woman to woman, in the typical pattern of unsocialized manhood.

A man's commitments to his job, his career, his family —his deferred gratifications and his sacrifices for the larger community—are not the product of a simple calculus of costs and benefits. Rather this behavior pattern is motivated by a system of sexual relationships and affirmations. The outer symbols and rituals of the community—the enactments of its sexual constitution—affirm an internal structure of motivation and commitment, a durable psychology of civilization. This structure emerges at the climactic moment in the flux of adolescent identity and is usually chosen, set, and hardened in the crucible of sexual love. Crucial is the desire, conscious or unconscious, for progeny with a specific woman, who subjects the male's sexual drive to long-term female patterns.

Because the father's role is a cultural invention rather than a biological imperative, however, the civilizing impulse of love is psychologically fragile. The subordination of male sexual rhythms to the long-term cycles of female sexuality is constantly subject to erosion by short term male impulses: to give up the job, the family, and pursue a life of immediate gratification. The husband's commitment thus needs external props.

The sexual constitution has long afforded three principal props. The first is the insistence of most women on some degree of monogamy. In general, a man still cannot get sex easily and dependably with women he likes unless he forgoes others, or undertakes some deceitful drama of love that is a strain on his conscience. The second support is marriage. The culture still exalts it with religious ceremony and affirms it with legal sanctions and social pressures. Third is the male role as the essential provider. This gives the man a position in wedlock to some extent commensurate with the woman's. Otherwise he is inferior. In social terms the family is formed to create a stable home for children. The woman's role is clearly indispensable while the man's is secondary. The whole sexual constitution is based on the maternal tie.

Women's liberation tries to reject this role. One of the best ways to outrage a young feminist is to accuse her of having a maternal instinct. Most of these women assert that females have no more innate disposition to nurture children than do men. The usual refrain is, "I know lots of men with far more interest in babies than I have." One's attention is directed toward all those flower-loving young men of the new college generation.

The interest in flowers does not seem to be convertible, however. Desertions are as common in the white counterculture as in the ghetto. A "prose poem" written by Margarita Donnelly and printed in one of the best feminist anthologies describes communal life for young mothers. The motif is abandonment: "Our hip brothers forgot us . . . most of the brothers skipped out . . . the men kept walking out . . . the men kept splitting . . . we kept finding ourselves alone with the children." [3] Other reports of the counterculture confirm this image. Indeed, this is the male motif for all societies everywhere that do not strongly enforce and reward male support for families. That is the way it is. The men split.

Whether "instinctive" or not, the maternal role in the sexual constitution orginates in the fact that only the woman is necesarily present at birth. Only the woman has a dependable and easily identifiable connection to the child—a tie on which society can rely. This maternal feeling is the root of human community. If it is not deeply cultivated among the women, it does not emerge among the men, and the society tends to disintegrate. The feminists' emphasis on the male role with children in no way changes the significance of their own abdication.

The effort of the women's movement to assign males an

ostensibly equal role in nurture—in bottle feeding the child
and cuddling it—might be technically workable and after a
certain point, desirable. But to maintain that such nurturant
activities by the male would suffice as his key role in the
family is nonsense. No matter how "equally" these functions
are distributed, they will not feel convincingly "equal" to the
male, in sexual and psychological terms. He will always know
that the woman's role with the children was more important,
more organically indispensable. There is no way the man can
share in the euphoria that many women feel when pregnant,
for it is a sensation of warm separateness and independent
fulfillment. There is no way that men can share in the "mothering hormone" that many authorities believe the woman secretes in childbirth.[4] There is no way the man with the bottle
will experience the sense of sexual affirmation and sensual fulfillment felt by the woman with a child at her breast. Nor is
there any way bottle feeding can reproduce the uniquely valuable combination of nourishment and prophylaxis with psychological affirmation that the infant receives from breast-feeding.
In addition, the mother can benefit psychologically, physiologically, and sensually nearly as much as the child. The man will
experience none of these physical changes or sexual gratifications and has great difficulty transmitting a sense of peace and
assurance to the child.

As a matter of fact, any sexual feelings the man has
toward his children may be disconcerting to him. He is introduced to the children by the mother. He can enjoy them
within the aura of love in the family. But paternity, as a cultural invention, will not serve to give the man a durable role
in the family; and there is virtually no society that successfully
relies on it to keep the man actively present. To keep the man
present and to preserve the nuclear family as the prevailing
institution, even love will not long suffice. He must be needed
in a practical and material way.

In American society the critical transition in a man's life
normally occurs in the late teens or early twenties, when the
question of marriage and career arises. It is then determined
whether a specific man will commit himself to the interacting
constraints of civilization. It is a period of low deference toward parents and high responsiveness toward peers. There is

an intense preoccupation with maintaining male identity. Earning capacity is at its lowest and sexual drive is at its pitch. It is thus a time when the sexual constitution plays its largest role.

A man's socialization—his productivity and his sense of community—will be shaped, perhaps for a lifetime, by the nature of his job and sexual opportunities and pressures during this stage. The outcome is set by work and women. If he finds work that affirms his manhood and a girl who demands that his sexuality be submitted to hers—submitted to love and family—he is likely to become a valuable and constructive citizen.

But, on the other hand, he may discover work and long-term relationships to be sexually subversive, if he links them with subjection to women. And he may find women either promiscuous or unavailable—at any rate uninterested in sub-duing his male sexual pattern. Under these conditions, he will not be socialized. If he loves, he may discover that he cannot marry, because he cannot maintain his role as provider. At work, he may again find that real commitment means a life of direct subjection to females. So he will maintain a short time horizon in both his work and his sexuality.

Whether the society can socialize most of its males—integrate them into both the community and the economy—will determine its tranquility and growth. It will decide whether government has to spend much of its time and energy in controlling men or whether the men will willingly contrib-ute their labor and spirit to the larger society.

A job thus is a crucial part of the sexual constitution. It affirms in a socially acceptable way the masculine identity of its holder; it submits his masculine impulsiveness to long-term feminine rhythms without compromising his male identity; it makes it possible for him to pursue women in a spirit of long-term commitment; it makes it possible for him to be married and thus integrated into a continuing community.

In these terms, the sexual role of most jobs is far more important than their economic function. In its extraordinary complexity, modern civilization is also extremely vulnerable to the outlaw—whether the alcoholic driver or the hijacker, the guerrilla or the drug addict, the mugger or the assassin.

The real contribution made by individual men in their work rarely exceeds the real damage they can do if their masculinity is not socialized or subjected to female patterns.

It takes an extraordinary worker indeed to give as much to the community as the criminal takes away, even financially for psychiatric commitment and law enforcement. When the impact of the criminal or psychopath on our social confidence, tranquility, and productivity is weighed, it becomes clear how important the sexual constitution of jobs may be. These considerations bear on all our employment and salary patterns.

Crucial to the sexual constitution of employment is that, in one way or another, it assures that over the whole society, class by class, most men will make more money than most women. Above an absolute minimum that varies from country to country, pay and poverty are relative. What matters most for men, what pay is most importantly relative to, is women. A man who does not make as much money as the relevant women in his life or class, or his place of work, will often abandon his job and will pursue his women chiefly in the predatory masculine spirit that the feminists so understandably deplore.

The feminist contention that women do not generally receive equal pay for equal work, correct in statistical terms, may in part reflect a preference for male need and aggressiveness over female credentials. But in essence, the additional pay is part of a tacit social contract by which men are induced to repress antisocial patterns. On the immediate and superficial level, justice and efficiency—so stressed by the feminists—have little to do with it.

Of course, efficiency will be considered. To make the pay differentials too great would cause serious distortions. The marketplace must ultimately prevail. But a marginal bias in favor of men in the labor force will best promote economic and social order. It can be asserted with the greatest confidence that a modern society that did not socialize its males would be neither just nor efficient, nor tolerable for women.

In economic terms the preference for men in the labor force should be considered in light of the greater "opportunity cost" of male unemployment. The unemployed male can contribute little to the society and will often disrupt it, while the unemployed woman can perform valuable work in creating and maintaining families. In fact, her unemployment may make her more inclined to do her work of subduing males. The male job preference, therefore, is based on the real costs of female careerism both for raising children and socializing men. The society will have to pay these costs one way or another.

It is crucial to understand the sexual role of money. Particularly in relatively poor communities, a woman with more money than the men around her tends to demoralize and subvert them. By undermining the role of male providers, she tends to diminish their connection with the community and to increase their reliance on antisocial modes of male identity: the priapic, hunting, and warrior patterns. She can support men only at their own psychological cost.

Her money reduces the likelihood of marriage. Not only is she less likely to want to marry, but the man realizes that if he marries her, his role in the family would be inherently precarious, for he would perform no clearly indispensable function. He feels he would have to depend chiefly on sexual performance. Enduring procreative love becomes difficult, because it places the man in an impossibly inferior position.

Ironically, the woman's money thus deters the submission of male sexuality to the long-term cycles of femininity. A society of relatively wealthy and independent women will be a society of sexually and economically predatory males, pursuing the violent and short-term patterns of male activity learned on the battlefield and in the hunt, or a society of narcotized drones, who have abandoned sexuality altogether. The sexual power of women, if combined with economic power, leaves many males with no civilized way to achieve sexual identity. If they cannot be providers, they have to resort to muscle and phallus.

A male's money, on the other hand, is socially affirmative. If the man is unmarried, a much higher proportion of his money than a woman's will be spent on the opposite sex. His money gives him the wherewithal to make long-term sexual initiatives. It gives him the courage to submit to female sexual patterns, for he knows he will retain the crucial role of familial support. His sexual impulses can assume the civilizing rather than the subversive form.

As a practical matter the differences between male and female pay scales throughout the society are approximately enough to finance male social initiatives. At present, for example, male clerks and tellers tend to make more money than their female counterparts. "Administrative assistants" tend to make more than "executive secretaries," janitors more than maids, and male office workers more than secretaries.[5] Male teachers and other professionals are more likely to be promoted to administration. Only at the lowest income levels—where intact families are most rare and precarious— are males already socially incapacitated by an inadequate financial superiority.

The women's movement sometimes reply that most women work only because they *need* money in an immediate, practical way. By and large, this is true, and these women must be able to earn money. If they support children they should receive child allowances. (They will not be helped, incidentally, by the competition of non-poor women for jobs.) But men also need the money—and need an increment above the woman's pay—for compulsively nonpractical reasons: for the "luxury" spending on women that is necessary for the male role in establishing families—the indispensable act of a civilized society —and for the superior economic role necessary to perform as provider. The more men who are induced to serve as provider, the fewer women who will be left to support children alone.

The reasons for unequal pay thus are numerous: (1) the need for male social initiative; (2) the need to give men a way to counterbalance female sexual superiority; (3) the need to give money a positive effect on family creation and maintenance; (4) the social need to induce men to follow careers and validate sexual identity in a socially affirmative way; (5) the greater propensity of males to spend their money on the opposite sex; (6) the greater social damage inflicted by unemployed males; (7) the greater psychological dependency of males on their jobs; (8) the indispensability of the alternative woman's role of socializing males and raising children.

As a general rule, relative female affluence has a negative effect in each of those areas. It retards social initiatives, enhances female dominance, deters family creation and maintenance, and subverts constructive male sexual expression. The money tends to cluster around the woman rather than support a couple. Her economic superiority undermines the sexual constitution and causes social breakdowns.

It should not be surprising therefore that men are paid more than women in virtually every economically successful society in the world. It *is* surprising that American men so thoughtlessly support the demand of the women's movement for a major governmental drive to achieve genuinely equal pay for equal or comparable work. For under current conditions of sexual disorder, this "reform" would promote most of the goals of the "extremists"—particularly the dissolution of the nuclear family.

Nothing is so important to the sexual constitution as supporting the creation and maintenance of families. Since the role of the male as principal provider is a crucial prop for the family, the society must support it in one way or another. In modern society, the burdens of childbirth no longer prevent women from performing the provider role. Particularly if day care is available, it is possible for a matrifocal social pattern to emerge. Men may escape the scheme of continuities on which modern civilization is based. But this development, though feasible, would require the simultaneous emergence of a police state to supervise the men and of a child care state to manage the children. This pattern merely means that the costs implicit in a "discriminatory" job pattern are vastly increased and transferred to the public through the tax system and through the loss of our liberties. The sexual constitution is cheaper.

Of course, the male provider role can be enforced in many other ways—through coercive measures or through religious and social pressures. It is perfectly possible to maintain male providers without taking social and opportunity costs into account in determining wages and salaries. In modern American society, however, the "social pressures" on women for marriage and family are giving way to pressures for career achievement. The society no longer recognizes, let alone communicates to women, the extraordinary social costs incurred when women neglect their role in male socialization.

At this point, therefore, a government campaign for equal pay for equal or comparable work would be most inopportune. It would endorse the false assumption of the women's movement that a greatly expanded female commitment to careers would be economical—using "human resources" that are now "wasted." The fact is that the triumph of a careerist ideology among American women would impose ultimate costs to the society far greater than the net contribution of the additional women in the work force. It is also likely that except for the exceptional minority, careerism would impose heavy psychological costs on the women themselves. There is no reason the society should encourage this wastage and abuse of women.

Even if one rejects the special need to support male providers, there are persuasive practical arguments against government efforts to abolish sex discrimination. For example, the value of an employee is far more determined by his motivation and career ambition than by his education and credentials.[6] To most men, success at work is virtually a matter of life and death, for it determines his sexual possibilities and affirms his identity as a male in a socially affirmative way. A business thus can control a man by paying him well and can almost irrevocably purchase his loyalty by paying him above the amount he can earn elsewhere. The business literally has him by the balls. For a female employee the sexual constitution of money is much less important. Her sexual prospects are little affected by how much she makes. Thus even if the woman is a very dependable employee, a payment to her does not usually purchase as great a commitment as does a payment to man.

An ostensibly simple concept like equal pay for "equal" or "comparable" skills, moreover, is in fact extremely difficult to apply anywhere in the economy, regardless of sex. A government campaign for equal pay for women would in fact imply that the only inequalities worthy of government concern were between the sexes. Yet inequalities between men with ostensibly or nominally "equal or comparable skills" are ubiquitous. Different businesses evaluate different skills in different ways. Many of the judgments are necessarily personal and subjective and require rejection of the kinds of data on credentials and experience that bureaucrats and feminists find persuasive. If such "discriminations" are systematically misconceived, the firm will suffer in the marketplace. That is usually a sufficient penalty. The marketplace, in fact, is in general the appropriate arbiter in a free economy.

The marketplace will tend to pay women less than men as long as wives give priority to their husbands' jobs. Apart from lesser aggressiveness and desire to dominate, one of the reasons women do not negotiate for higher pay as effectively as men is lesser mobility. Although the woman may have to leave her job if the man moves, the woman cannot easily move to take advantage of better opportunities. She is restricted to jobs in the area close to her husband's work. Thus businesses can pay her less and she will accept less. In the marketplace what a worker is willing to accept defines his or her economic worth. Partly because women instinctively know that economic worth is a secondary and derivative value, they are usually willing to take lower pay and do not organize effectively to have it increased. Female-dominated unions are generally willing to tolerate the system of sexism. It is now being combatted chiefly by careerist male lawyers in the federal government.

Government intervention is desirable only in case of extraordinary malfeasance, destructive to the social order, such as the racist persecution of blacks. Even in this arena the government is so incompetent that it tends to concentrate on the most marketable group in the country: the black Ph.D. Sex discrimination is an enormously more complicated condition. Whatever discrimination against women escapes the constraints of the marketplace, the offenses do not constitute a significant social problem. The problem is less serious than similar discriminations against various classes of males. But all of these offenses, with the unique exception of continuing discrimination against blacks, are best left to the marketplace.

Beyond equal pay, the women's movement aggressively demands sexual integration of all jobs and professions. If men worked chiefly for money, this proposal might also make some sense. But men hold their jobs and pursue their careers only indirectly for money. Just as the males in primitive tribes attempt to make their religious rituals mysterious to women, so men in modern societies try to maintain an aura of mystery and importance about their work. Just as women are excluded from "male" activities in those societies, so they tend to be restricted here.

As irrational as this practice may seem, it is more important than ever as a part of the sexual constitution. With the rapid social erosion of conventional male patterns—the warrior and venereal mystiques—an increasing burden for masculine fulfillment is devolving on jobs and sex. The stress on sexual performance, moreover, is already imposing dangerous strains on many males. If the job becomes an arena for competition with women, a further eruption of antisocial male impulses is inevitable. As Helmut Schelsing wrote in 1935, "The sexual neutrality of working conditions and public and cultural life . . . makes a standard of male behavior that is binding on all men and attainable by all men increasingly amorphous and uncertain. . . . Masculinity is deflected into ever more arbitrary and subjective areas of personality formation." [7]

Perhaps the most quixotic of all female demands is that men at work treat women first as "human beings." Male psychology is in large part a reaction formation, shaped in relation to women. As women invade further realms conventionally regarded as masculine—and as modern technology transforms other male roles—men will increasingly define themselves as *not*-women. Their responses will be increasingly sexual. If conventional job stresses are compounded with sexual ones, the men will desperately try to escape—either to the street or to higher levels of the bureaucracy. In the Soviet Union, for example, the move of women into medicine precipitated the departure of men, within little more than a decade, to medical administration and into specialities like surgery. Now some 90 percent of all general practitioners are women.[8] Already subjected to intense sexual strains from women, men will not easily endure professional ones. Their jobs must serve as masculine affirmations if the sexual constitution of the society is to be maintained.

On these economic questions the feminists are right in

virtually every superficial way. Men *do* get paid more than women; women *are* persistently discouraged from competing with men; when sufficiently motivated, women individually *can* perform almost every important job in the society as well as men; job assignments by sex *are* arbitrary and illogical; most women *do* work because they have to; the lack of public child-care facilities does prevent women from achieving real financial equality of opportunity.

But at a profounder level the women are tragically wrong. For they fail to understand their own sexual power; and they fail to perceive the sexual constitution of our society, or if they see it, they underestimate its importance to our civilization and to their own interest in order and stability. In general across the whole range of the society, marriage and careers—and thus social order—will be best served if most men have a position of economic superiority over the relevant women in his community and if in most jobs in which colleagues must work together, the sexes tend to be segregated either by level or function.

These practices are not oppressive; they make possible a society in which men can love and respect women and treat them humanely. They make possible a society in which women can love and respect men, and sustain durable families.

What is happening in the United States today—to explain most of our social strains and disruptions—is the steady erosion of the key conditions of male socialization. From the hospital, where the baby is abruptly taken from its mother; to early childhood, when he may be consigned to public care; to the home, where the father is frequently absent or ineffectual; to the school, where the boy is managed by female teachers and excelled by girls; possibly to college, where once again his training is scarcely differentiated by sex; to a job that, particularly at vital entry level positions, is often sexually indistinct and that may not even be better paid than comparable female employment—through all these stages of development the boy's innately amorphous and insecure sexuality may be further subverted and confused.

In the end his opportunity to qualify for a family—to validate in society his love and sex through becoming a husband and provider—may be jeopardized. The man discovers that manhood affords few distinctive roles except in the decreasingly respected military. The society prohibits, constricts, or feminizes his purely male activities. It is increasingly difficult for him to hunt or fight or otherwise assert himself in an aggressive, male way. Most jobs reward obedience, regularity, and carefulness more than physical strength or individual initiative. If he attempts to create rituals and institutions like the ones used by similarly beleaguered men in primitive societies, he finds them opened to women. If he fights, he is sent to jail. If he is aggressive at his job, he may be fired. Thus the man finds few compensatory affirmations of masculinity to make possible his expected submission to female sexual and social rhythms; and without a confident manhood he feels a compulsive need to prove it sexually.

Under these circumstances he cannot submit. He must attack, asserting his male rhythms against the pervasive female tendencies of the civilization. He cannot defer to love, or to the long-term commitments to work and community that the society depends on love to evoke. Thus the society, which refuses to make him a secure man, ironically prevents his sexual commitment to women or to the essential long-term business of the community.

The American woman, meanwhile, becomes increasingly self-sufficient. While he is almost completely dependent on women for a civilized role in the society and for biological and sexual meaning, women are capable of living successful —though often discontented—lives without men. The culture no longer much disapproves of unmarried mothers. The state gives them welfare and, increasingly, day care and maternity leave. In any case, birth control and abortion give women complete control of procreation; and sexual liberation —not to mention masturbation and lesbianism—opens sexual enjoyment to them with only the most tenuous commitment to males. Well-paid female employment further obviates dependency.

Therefore, the male is not continuously pressured by women to submit to female rhythms and to civilization. He feels decreasingly needed by women. Themselves performing as providers, women are decreasingly insistent on imposing long-term female sexual patterns. In fact, they may be disconcertingly willing to accept male terms, abdicating the female role in civilization. Although the man may find sexual partners more easily than before—though less easily than is generally believed—the meaning of his sexuality is diminished, and he can derive less assurance from it. His only sex act is devalued and the world of important sexuality—the womb and its procreative mysteries—is more remote than ever. Just proving himself a man becomes a full-time job.

As he has in every such historic extremity, he turns away from the family. He frequents all-male bars and behaves loudly and abusively enough to keep them that way. He watches televised football and other male sports for hours on end and argues about them incessantly; or he bombards himself with the music of male sexuality—the aggressive, phallic rock now dominating youth culture. Otherwise he is obsessed with women. He tries as much as possible to reduce them to their sexual parts and to reduce their sexuality to his own limited terms—to meaningless but insistent copulation. Exiled from the world of women, he tries to destroy consciousness of its superiority by reducing it to his own level. He insists—against all his unconscious and ulterior knowledge—that women are as sexually contemptible as his society tells him he is.

He turns to pornography, with fantasies of sex and violence. His magazines—*Male* and *Crime* and *Saga* and *True Detective,* even refined male publications like *Playboy* —are preoccupied with barren copulation, or with war, perversion, and crime. And usually he drinks—as recent studies show, chiefly for the illusion of a potency that the society refuses him.[9] He is an exile: an outlaw under the sexual constitution. Often he becomes a legal outlaw as well.

Such single males—and married ones whose socialization fails—constitute our major social problem. They are the murderers, the rapists, the burglars, the suicides, the assailants, the psychopaths. What they are not is powerful oppressors, with hypertrophied masculinity. They are impotent figures, and as Rollo May asserts, violence is the product of impotence grown unbearable.[10] Their problem is a society inadequately affirmative of masculinity: a society seduced by an obsessive rationalism and functionalism—a cult of efficiency and a fetish of statistical equality—to eliminate many of the male affirmations that all human societies have created throughout history to compensate for male sexual insecurity and female sexual superiority. The women's movement seems determined to create more and more such exiled "chauvinist" males, all the while citing their pathetic offenses as a rationale for feminism.

Thus the society both provides for its own disruption and leaches itself of positive male energies. For male insecurity is also the "divine unease" that in socialized males, strong enough to submit to women, has produced our greatest achievements of industry, art, and science. Women, of course, have made heavy contributions of their own in addition to their indispensable support of men; and there is every reason to expect increasing numbers of our future accomplishments to come from women, as longer life and greater affluence free more of their time and talent. But everything will depend on the maintenance of civilization itself through submitting males to female sexual patterns. If women finally reject that role, there will be no "room of their own" for any other.[11] And that role can be played only in the process of persuading men to join them in creating and maintaining families under the sexual constitution.

When sociologists discuss the functions of the family, they invariably emphasize socialization of children. The family is the most important educational institution in the society. Through it children receive their first and possibly their most enduring impressions of the world. Within the family are planted the roots of the child's sexual identity and expectations. From this crucible emerge the key formations of a child's character. And as the child connects himself to the larger community, his anticipations and reactions are usually mediated and interpreted by the family.

This socializing function of the family is obviously crucial, and sociologists are right to focus on it. They naturally emphasize the role of mother, for throughout human history this socializing role has frequently been performed by the mother alone. Although the absence of the father is acknowledged to create some difficulties—chiefly for boys—these problems are usually not crippling, particularly if there are other men around and the society is relatively tranquil and homogeneous. It is widely accepted that a matriarchal (or, more specifically, matrifocal) family can work. In itself, we are told, a matriarchy can be considered "pathological" only by a white American, blinded with ethnocentric prejudice.

Nonetheless, within the highly complex, vulnerable, and demanding arena of civilized life, gynocentric families may well be "pathological." For under modern conditions, the role of the family in the early socialization of children is no more important than its role in the later socialization of males. Responding to the question of the future of marriage, Margaret Mead summed up the problem: "Women will always want to live with the father of their child—if they can catch him." [12]

Monogamous sex and marriage are the ways that women catch their men and induce them to join and support families. But as a general rule of history and anthropology, men cannot be expected to remain as integral members of the family unit if their roles are visibly inferior to the women's and require open subordination. Under current conditions, the husband usually must at least be the principal provider. In a matriarchy, he usually will not perform this function and will leave—almost always.

The men's absence does not necessarily mean a failure of socialization if he is out working to gain the wherewithal to return to his family; or if his resolute efforts are being thwarted by a hostile environment. But all too often his departure testifies to a crucial failure: the man has not been induced to submit his volatile masculine sexuality to female futurity.

This failure is not necessarily attributable to the woman. Unlike the mother's role in socializing children, the woman's role in socializing men is deeply dependent on external conditions. In a functioning modern society, a matriarchy may as often result from a collapse of the sexual constitution, as from some gratuitous assertion of female authority or failure of female sexual roles.

Nonetheless, even if the rest of the social and economic environment is favorable, matriarchies tend to perpetuate themselves into new generations, as fatherless girls establish fatherless families of their own.[13] Thus the failures of male socialization will be unnecessarily extended. The matriarchy will also reduce the likelihood of direct entrepreneurial initiatives to change the economic conditions that fostered it. Men will not exploit existing possibilities and create small businesses and other ventures. The economy and culture will be deprived of the intense male motivation and energy normally released in the pursuit and maintenance of the nuclear family.

Two critical and interrelated props for this role—procreative sexuality and the masculine symbols of work—are today in jeopardy. As a result the internal sense of communal involvement, the psychology of civilized life, is dissolving in millions of men. We are creating millions of exiles from the larger solidarity of our society. They now threaten to return and destroy it.

Ghetto "Liberation"

"That's almost impossible to explain—how you feel
when you're a kid and the king pimps come back to the
neighborhood. They pose and twirl their watchchains and
sport their new Cadillacs and Rollses and expensive
tailored clothes. . . . It's making it. That's what it meant
where I come from—proving you're a man."
"And when you proved it, what did you want?"
"Just to play music, that's all."

Charles Mingus
Beneath the Underdog

The most severe effects of constitutional breakdown come in the ghetto. Beyond the pyrotechnic riots, nearly half of our violent crimes—murders, robberies, rapes, and other felonies—are done by and against ghetto residents.[1] In proportion to their numbers young ghetto males commit seven times more homicides and 30 percent more suicides than young white males.[2] Perhaps half of our addict population—and a similar proportion of our prisoners—comes from the ghetto.[3] Desertions by ghetto husbands produce a community of female-led families and illegitimate children in far higher proportions than are found elsewhere in the society. Although such statistics are not fully reliable, it is not prejudice or paranoia that defines the ghetto, in Moynihan's words, as a "tangle of pathology"[4] or as perhaps the epitome of all our domestic malignancies.

At the same time it is a profound mistake to treat the ghetto chiefly as a racial problem. The syndrome of the ghetto —theft, violence, addiction, demoralization, familial breakdown, and educational failure—is expanding in many parts of our society. Some indices of crime and social disintegration, in fact, are rising more rapidly in white suburbs than in the central slums. Similar patterns of malignancy can be found among poor whites in the street-slums of dropouts and runaways. The pathology of the ghetto is so conspicuous, so intensely tangled, to a great extent because poor blacks have been isolated in specific areas where the various trends of dissolution interact with one another—and where social problems gather to a critical mass. The resulting explosions should be understood as premonitory signals of the larger problems of modern society. To focus on racial characteristics or on "racism" is diversionary.

It is only somewhat more accurate to describe the crisis as a problem of economics and discrimination. Employment bias is diminishing rapidly, and in the North, educated young blacks now earn about as much as comparable young whites.[5] Most small businesses, however, still hire to a great extent through kinship ties; and even in large businesses and unions, some exclusions persist, notably in the building trades. In an economy that offers limited numbers of jobs for undereducated laborers, the apparent bias in urban unions contributes significantly to the ghetto problem.

By focusing on the problem of discrimination, however, the liberal approach may become a mere racial reshuffling of poverty. As a solution to the problem of unemployment of poor blacks, an emphasis on racial bias may lead to a program of unemployment for poor whites. Unless more jobs are made available to everyone, antidiscrimination measures will intensify racial fears and conflicts. The lack of jobs is the central problem. The unemployment of perhaps a third of young blacks is perhaps the single leading symptom of the crisis. A thriving national economy, with a magnetism of growth reaching into all parts of our society, would greatly alleviate our ghetto pathology, tangled or not with psychological and familial afflictions. But the relief of symptoms, though valuable and desirable, will not reverse the underlying degeneration.

Even the provision of adequate jobs for everyone—and the total abolition of discrimination and segregation—would not solve the deeper problems of our society as reflected in the ghetto. The chaos and frustration in our city schools will not be readily overcome either by desegregation or by economic progress. The most optimistic appraisal of the results of integrated schooling—or of more expensive teachers and facilities—shows only marginal benefits.[6] Unemployment statistics explain neither the high rate of absenteeism among many ghetto residents who do hold jobs nor the unwillingness of many young blacks to take work that is available—whether driving taxis or cleaning buildings.

For example, the automobile industry in Detroit encountered the deeper problem when it opened some 25,000 jobs to unemployed blacks after the riot of 1967. The economic director of the Detroit Urban League reported so many defections during the first few months, those 25,000 jobs were held by over 100,000 men. "They drift in and out," he said.[7] Kenneth Clark,[8] Claude Brown,[9] Malcolm X,[10] and other ghetto observers have repeatedly described the disdain for the world of work felt by thousands of ghetto residents.

A response to the ghetto crisis focusing on racial bias

will raise unrealistic expectations, promote racial tensions, and slander low- and middle-income whites, hardly a privileged class in our society. Even poverty is the essential problem only in terms so general as to be nearly useless as a guide to social policy. It goes without saying that poverty should be overcome. But as one repeatedly discovers in less developed countries, simple economic remedies will not in themselves create the durable patterns of motivation needed for long-term growth.

If we are to understand the ghetto problem and respond to it intelligently, we must deal with race and poverty chiefly as they relate to the deeper realm of individual motivation and character. Edward Banfield is correct when in *The Unheavenly City* he identifies the problem as a few hundred thousand individuals blighted with "short-time horizons." [11] But he is profoundly wrong when he seems to treat this weakness as an unmanageable character flaw, relatively immune to social policy. In fact, it is the product of grave flaws in the sexual constitution of the society and can be rectified by perfectly feasible policies to promote male confidence and family creation. The ghetto crisis is merely a particular, severe manifestation of our general sexual disorder. If we cannot rectify it, our society is doomed to years of demoralization and anarchy, possibly ending in a police state.

No American can afford a pose of sociological distance. Since the family is the central unit of our sexual constitution, many analysts, led by Moynihan, have focused on the dissolution of the black family. They have been led to search for special sources of its strength or vulnerability—making cross-cultural observations about the broken black family under slavery, or the matrifocal family in the Caribbean, or the polygamous groups in Africa.

But ultimately this approach is also unfruitful. Most American black families are together and successful. In fact, outside the rural South, intact black families under age 25 now earn approximately as much money as their white counterparts, though there is smaller participation in the work force by black women in this group. Under age 35, such intact black families earn almost as much as white families, though with a slightly greater proportionate contribution by black women.[12]

The majority of black families tend to be diligent, conventional, and sexually conservative. They are no more "polygamous" than white families of the same economic class, and they produce an insignificant amount of crime despite housing segregation that forces them to live in the teeth of the ghetto. They are the victims both of crime and of abominably stupid criticisms against the "black bourgeoisie." Their tenacity, in fact, is more impressive than the strengths of white families. There is nothing wrong with the intact black family, except that there are not enough of them. The problem is to create conditions for the establishment and maintenance of more intact black family units.

Nonetheless, the large number of broken or unconsummated families, concentrated racially and geographically, creates dire problems. For broken families are ineffective in socializing males, and even a relatively small proportion of unsocialized males can make life miserable for thousands of conventional citizens in a modern urban environment. The apparent swashbuckling hedonism of the male counterculture, moreover, exerts a strong appeal to almost every man. Thus unsocialized men can have a disruptive influence—as well as direct violent impact—far beyond their numbers.

This is the ghetto crisis: a failure of male socialization and a problem of masculinity. In the most immediate sense, it is not black women one fears as one walks the streets of the ghetto. It is not black women who perpetrate the muggings, rapes, and murders or who often perform that ultimate act of social negation: suicide. Even the ghetto killings attributed to women (one out of six) usually occur in the company of males or in retaliation against them. And there are about four suicides by young ghetto males for every one by a ghetto woman. In fact the suicide rate among ghetto women does not significantly exceed the figures among white women.[13] A chief problem of black women is the volatile and disruptive behavior of unsocialized black males. To understand the ghetto problem, one must focus on the predicament of the ghetto male.

The principal reason for the failure of male socialization in the ghetto is the breakdown of the male role as provider and the prevalence of the male as stud. In other terms, the unsocialized male does not acquire the masculine assurance necessary if he is to submit to female patterns of sexuality; as much as he can, he imposes male patterns on the women. Because of the extraordinary lack of eligible males in the ghetto—perhaps only 75 percent as many as eligible women —the men often succeed in having their way.

This situation is a typical product of male sexual insecurity, often beginning with the absence of a father in the home. The young black boy displays all the characteristics conventionally associated with fatherless children. As an analysis by Thomas Pettigrew has shown, black children of both sexes from fatherless families "experience unusual difficulty in differentiating the roles of men and women." [14] The boys are less responsible, less able to defer gratifications, less interested in achievement, more prone to crime, and even, as other studies have shown, lower in I.Q. Examination of prisoners and veterans has indicated that the pattern of sexual insecurity persists, with the fatherless men scoring higher on indices of femininity, while behaving in a compulsively aggressive way, often in all-male gangs. Girls from fatherless families, meanwhile, tend to reproduce their own childhood experience, associating more closely with their mothers than with their husbands—and giving more affection to their girls than to their boys.[15]

This pattern is reinforced in the ghetto schools, where many of the teachers are women and most of the best pupils are girls. The boys are vividly taught once again that the world of regularity, responsibility, and achievement is a realm of women. Unless the boys excel in sports, the schools typically offer almost no mode of specific male affirmation. The rewards of the classroom entail direct submission to a female teacher and dangerous competition with female students.

The result is predictable: insecure males who go beyond the school to assert their masculinity through group violence and through male patterns of sexual activity. Because the males cannot dominate the women in other ways, they resort to sex and violence. The women—often merely young teen-age girls—are induced to submit to male sexual terms. Far from socializing the males through submission to female sexuality, the adolescent girls are subjected to the shallow and compulsive sexuality of the males. Because the sexuality of the girls is inherently more secure than that of the boys, the girls themselves often are not durably injured by this reversal. But they abdicate their critical role in male socialization through sex. And bearing illegitimate children, they begin a new cycle of fatherless families.

This childhood pattern of the ghetto—the fatherless families, the female dominance at home and school—blights the early lives of ghetto males. The damage would not be so grave, however, if the young men could easily undergo the later stage of socialization: love, marriage, and procreation— the later submission to female sexual cycles. But the fatherless males, predictably enough, are very low in what Pettigrew calls "marital aptitude." Because they are unsure of their male identities, they feel constrained to continually prove them. They are unwilling or unable to love, court, and marry women.

Largely because of the perverse and destructive policies of the larger society, almost all the props of male socialization are absent in the ghetto. Since all too many women in his society make more money and have more education than he does, the ghetto male cannot play the role of initiator and supporter in courtship. He cannot compensate in the outside world, through offerings of support, knowledge, and achievement, for the male limitations in the inner world of sexuality. Because by necessity the women do combine their sexual with economic self-sufficiency, moreover, he is not indispensable as provider in marriage. He can attain equality only by eschewing the deeper forms of procreative sexuality—by reducing women to the shallow and limited terms of masculine sexual desire and by pushing them around physically.

Norman Podhoretz incurred some derision when he divulged what he called a "dirty little secret" of our time— that money is an essential force in the social relationships and motivations of the middle and upper classes.[16] People who take money for granted have trouble acknowledging its pervasive influence on their own social and sexual behavior. They often fail to recognize the extent to which their social attractiveness and importance depend on their material ability to reciprocate favors.

It should not strain the imagination, however, to perceive the more decisive influence imparted by relatively small financial differences on the lives of the poor. It is a blunt fact that below a certain income level—a level much higher than most people suppose—a man with less money than most of the women in his community is a social impotent. His financial inadequacy compounds his sexual inferiority and he has great difficulty making civilized sexual initiatives. He must try to reduce the woman to what is called a sexual object. But what he is really doing is denying the woman her distinctive sexuality and vitiating his own in meaningless copulation.

Sociologists are rather casual when they report that the earnings of black women are about 80 percent of black male income, while white women earn only about 58 percent as much as white men.[17] Yet when the impact of welfare is added —and the earnings of married black males are subtracted—it becomes clear that in the ghetto the male role as chief provider has as much as evaporated, and that the unmarried ghetto male is too poor in relation to women to be needed by them. The male may still offer significant support; he may often finance the entertainment of his women on social excursions. But he is as optional financially as he is sexually. The social relationships of the community no longer revolve around the male as provider and the female as procreator, ultimately joining in monogamous love and marriage. Rather the woman is both provider and procreator, and the man and woman join only in male-oriented copulation that leads nowhere—except on occasion to a tragically unfathered child.

This impoverishment and short-term masculinization of sex is almost inevitable when the women have the money. Lacking a manifestly indispensable role in the scheme of female sexuality, the man must reject procreative responsibilities; he often does not marry, and if he does marry, he frequently deserts. By creating an economy where women can more easily get welfare than men, where women are paid as much, and where employment does not afford clear male advantages, we promote a society of violent, misogynistic, and masculine sexual patterns: a society of broken families, ravaged by crime; a society where courtship does not bring a gradual unfolding of male socialization; a society where all too often the relationships between men and women alternate between robbery and rape.

The only surprising fact about our ghetto tragedy is the way we doggedly refuse to understand it—and the way we endlessly perpetuate it. It should be clear to any sentient observer with a smattering of anthropological and psychological insight that the worst parts of the ghetto present a rather typical pattern of female dominance, with women in charge of the family, and male gangs away on the hunt. Workable in a few primitive societies with garden and game, this system brings unremitting tragedy in the tenements, and on the streets, of our modern cities.

In the absence of agricultural support, the women and children become dependent on government. The welfare bureaucracy supplants the matriarchal garden and displaces the husband's game. Expelled from the family, he becomes an outlaw under the sexual constitution and a threat to his women. And with most of the available jobs dominated by females or by white unions, he has trouble finding any legitimate manhood in the community at large.

Inevitably he turns to—or creates—a world of men: sports or music, if possible; crime, drugs, and revolution, more probably—but predictably and necessarily a realm where males command, where he can find external symbols of the internal necessities of his sex. In the absence of socialization by women—the civilizing familial processes of love and procreative sexuality—he follows the usual impulsive circuits of male sexuality. It is a familiar drama, fraught with violence, anger, and yearning, enacted on the black stage and on the blacker street, sung in a thousand blue voices, celebrated in a thousand "soul" rituals, proclaimed and transcended in the art of jazz.

But the essential pattern should not be seen as a special propensity of blacks. It is sometimes imagined that the gynocentrism of many poor black families is a strength—the secret of black survival through the harrowing centuries of slavery and racism. In a sense, of course, this is true. In any disintegrating society, the family is reduced to the lowest terms of

(mother and child. The black family has long rested on the)
(broad shouldered heart of the black woman.)

Yet this secret of black survival is also a secret of ghetto
stagnation. It is quite simply impossible to sustain a civilized
society if the men are constantly disrupting it. Whether among
blacks or whites, male socialization through love, family, and
work is indispensable to transcending the short circuits of
male sexuality and aggression.

The drama of the unsocialized black has become the
commanding motif of American culture. Driven to the wall,
threatened with emasculation, surrounded everywhere by formidable women, the black male has summoned from his own
body and spirit the masculine testament on which much of
American manhood now subsists. Black jazz is the most important serious American music, acknowledged around the
world if not in our own universities. Our rock culture finds
its musical and rhythmic inspiration and its erotic energy and
idiom in the jazz, gospel, dance, and soul performances of
blacks. The black stage provides dramatic imagery and acting
charisma for both our theaters and our films. Black vernacular
pervades our speech. The black athlete increasingly dominates
our sports, not only in his performance but in his expressive
styles, as even a Joe Namath and other white stars adopt black
idioms of talk, handshakes, dress, and manner. From the
home-plate celebration to the touchdown romp, American
athletes are now dancing to soul music. Black men increasingly star in the American dream.

This achievement is an art of the battlefield—exhibiting
all that grace under pressure that is the glory of the cornered
male. Ordinarily we could marvel and celebrate without any
deeper pang of fear. But as the most vital expression of the
culture—increasingly embraced by a whole generation of
American youth—this black testament should be taken as a
warning. For much of it lacks the signs of that submission
to feminity that is the theme of enduring social order. It suggests a bitter failure of male socialization. By its very strength,
it bespeaks a broader vulnerability and sexual imbalance. Thus
it points to the ghetto as the exemplary crisis of our society.

Women vs. Blacks

The women's liberation movement is remarkable in its ability to face all the implacable facts of ghetto life without so much as an inkling of the source of the problem. Its adherents can listen to all the soul songs, read all the statistics of crime, observe the persistent refusal of the financially inferior male to stay with his family—and still they cling to their old prejudices, making proposals that would *increase* the female advantage and render still more desperate the male plight, still more untenable the nuclear family.

It is not as if the ghetto problem is obscure. For observers who cannot follow the signals of black culture, this drama has had brilliant sociological prophets. From E. Franklin Frazier [1] and Kenneth Clark [2] we have received clear documentation of the distorted sexual constitution of the ghetto. In 1966, Moynihan, then an assistant labor secretary in the Johnson Administration, put it all together in a report so glaringly true that it all but blinded most feminists and blacks who read it.[3] Moynihan's thesis was quite elegantly simple: The black ghetto family was disintegrating because of a vicious cycle in which weak or absent fathers reproduced themselves in new generations, and women were given a dual role that only a few could adequately manage. Men were reduced to economic and social impotence in a society in which success is all too often a female attainment, achieved in bureaucracies filled with women.

Under these circumstances, it is inevitable that males reach for the great male equalizer: violence. In fact, the extraordinary level of violence among men and women in the ghetto is the best evidence that women do not finally benefit from financial dominance. Faced with the imperious combination of female sexual and financial power, the men all too often storm in with guns, knives, and phalluses high.

Pointing to this tragic mode of equalization, there are those who say Moynihan is wrong about black matriarchy. The black male maintains the power, it is suggested, through brute physical and sexual bargaining—that is, by forcing his women to submit to male sexual cycles. The ultimate triumph and disaster of this mode is the pimp and his Cadillac.

But women's lib finds all this tragedy—safely confined to another culture—rather groovy. The curious interest in prostitution shown by Kate Millett,[4] Susan Brownmiller,[5] Germaine

Greer,[6] Gail Sheehy,[7] and other feminists—together with their prurient obsession with rape—indicates the real contours of "liberated" society. Unable to love the effeminate males of their program, they fantasize, and Germaine Greer even prescribes, brief, violent, sexual tussles with exiled males.[8] This vision, of course, depicts the condition of women in a society in which males do not succumb to civilized female patterns.

The ghetto pattern is also inviting to the feminists because some of them are virulently anti-American, and the unsocialized male is prone to join revolutionary gangs. These feminists get vicarious kicks out of the macho violence—the sexy terminal swaggers and the gun fetishism—of the black guerrilla. They oppose all specifically male-oriented welfare reform and job programs that would redeem the black male from his exile.[9]

The women's movement—particularly in its moderate manifestation—is the most important remaining organized enemy of black progress in America. It influentially opposes programs that are crucial to reestablishing the black male as the chief provider and supporter of the ghetto family—programs that might help black women in their beleaguered efforts to socialize the ghetto male.

The chief requirement for giving upward mobility to any poor community is maintenance of a family and employment structure that affirms the male in his role as provider. If the male is the external prop of the family, he can venture into it without risk to his masculine confidence. One of the few successful movements for the socialization of truly indigent males in the black community—the Black Muslims—has learned this lesson—that the first step in restoring a poor community is to rectify the sexual imbalance bred by poverty. Because the males are clearly dominant in Muslim society, they can afford to submit to long-term patterns of female sexuality. They identify with their children and hence with the community and its future.

The result is that the Muslims have created an extraordinary network of small businesses, comparable on a lesser scale to the entrepreneurial accomplishment of Jews and Chinese (both of whom also employ a patriarchal religion to affirm their males). Also like the Jews, Chinese, and Catholics, the

Muslims—almost uniquely among blacks—have succeeded in establishing a school system that actually teaches poor black children to read and write at the white grade level.[10] In addition, like the patriarchal fundamentalist religions now conspicuous among whites in street society,[11] the Muslims have managed to overcome addiction and make ex-convicts into law-abiding citizens. It is unfortunate that it is a movement of racial fanaticism that hit on this clear imperative of social regeneration. But as long as the rest of the society fails to recognize the need to reestablish the male, the government will continue to reinforce the matriarchy—thus ensuring continued anarchy and crime in the ghetto.

Andrew Billingsley has offered another example, seemingly remote but nonetheless striking, of the effectiveness of special programs for males.[12] In a study of "the sources of achievement" of leading black male professionals, Dr. Horace Mann Bond found that the crucial factors were (1) "a history of family literacy," (2) "a father with a determination of iron, an ambition for his children that is illimitable, and a disciplined mind that will exemplify and induce and foster good habits in children," (3) "a mother who shares these qualities with her husband," and (4) "a good school." [13] Exploring the backgrounds of some 500 leading black Ph.D.s and M.D.s, he was surprised to find that a disproportionate number came from Perry County, Alabama, and that all of these—including Billingsley himself—had a father or grandfather who attended the Lincoln Memorial School, an institution started in 1868 in Marion, the county seat. Although neither Billingsley nor Bond emphasizes the fact, this school was free to all the many black boys in the county and gave the sons an educational advantage over the daughters.

James Baldwin has written that the "overriding horror of the present system is that it is teaching millions of Negro children to disrespect their parents and despise them." [14] Jessie Bernard, a prestigious and knowledgeable feminist of the older generation who has a respect for facts, was led to assert, "The upgrading of the Negro father might constitute a major contribution to the welfare of the nation." [15] The chief of police in Detroit has said that the problem he faces is caused by "young boys who never in their lives have seen an honest, dependable, and successful male." The women's liberationists have no valid answer to this problem of how to induce males to pursue families and careers.

The usual response, of course, is more money for everyone, better jobs, more time with the children—a cornucopia of benefits. Close examination, however, indicates that the chief beneficiaries of the women's program will be upper-class white women, and the chief victims will be upwardly mobile lower-class men, black and white. Among the psychological victims will be most men of insecure sexual identity and thus the American family.

As painful as it is to say it, only a small proportion of Americans can hold interesting and remunerative jobs. Most jobs are boring, performed by men in order to maintain their role as provider. If large numbers of women move into the job force in important professional capacities, large numbers of men will be frustrated in their careers. Increasing numbers of men will find themselves subordinate to women at work and faced with wives who are earning substantial salaries. Under such unbearable pressures on their sexual identities, many of these men will leave their jobs or families. A significant proportion of them will be blacks, since blacks are just now moving into the official, managerial, and professional roles that the highly educated women are now seeking on the basis of their superior education and "credentials."

The impact on black males will be exacerbated by the feminists' increasing usurpation of the antidiscriminatory machinery of the federal and state governments and of many private corporations. These agencies were established and financed in response to the blood and sweat of the civil rights movement. The legal basis of antidiscriminatory litigation was fought out for a century by heroically tenacious civil rights lawyers and private citizens willing to risk jail to test and extend the rights of their people. Many of the new laws involved constitutionally questionable extensions of governmental power. They were enacted against powerful conservative opposition only because of the extraordinary history of blacks in this country and the continuing atrocities committed against them.

Now the women's movement cruises in with claims of

comparable grievance, which are positively obscene from the perspective of slavery and segregation. The feminists add injury to insult, moreover, for the effect of their demands is to divert the attention of government from the discrimination against black males, which had been the *raison d'être* of the civil rights agencies. Cumulatively, the effort of government was paying off in higher salaries and better opportunities for millions of black men. But since the chief remaining institutions showing widespread bias—construction trades unions and some Southern businesses—are politically powerful, government was glad to be distracted, particularly by pretty and articulate upper-class women asking action against liberal universities, law firms, and publishing companies. Because discrimination against women is absolutely ubiquitous by quantitative standards, the young agency lawyers can generate a lot of purposeful activity, please their wives, and win a lot of ostensibly significant victories without offending anyone high in the government or jeopardizing their careers. The only losers are the millions of black men struggling to achieve an economic position from which they can acquire and support a wife and family.

The damage to the black male, however, does not derive only from lesser attention to discrimination against him, or from the promotion of upper-class white women into positions he might otherwise have won. The black male suffers chiefly because, once again, the federal government is induced to give black women a special advantage over him. Black women benefit from both thrusts of antidiscriminatory activity. Companies that previously would respond to claims of discrimination by hiring black men will now hire black women and dispose of two aggrieved categories at once.

This tendency not only hurts black men. It makes a mockery of the assumption that special measures against discrimination should help the disadvantaged and strengthen the society. This aid for black women, who despite their grueling lives already have the advantage over most of the men in their community in financial support, is a tragic misuse of government investigatory and enforcement powers that strengthens matriarchy and undermines the society.

The only greater absurdity of antidiscrimination activity

is the government efforts to force the most prestigious universities in the country—with jobs sought and coveted by almost every leading graduate student in the land—to take "affirmative action" to find women, *who do not even care enough to apply.* It is hard to believe, but that is the bathos to which J. Stanley Pottinger and his "don't call them quotas" gang at the Department of Health, Education and Welfare (HEW) have reduced the exalted cause of civil rights.[16] Who would have anticipated that it would be liberal Republicans in the Nixon Administration who would fulfill the cynical dream of Judge Smith when he added the words "or sex" to the bitterly won civil rights laws of the sixties. Smith thought that the thicket of sex discrimination would ultimately confound and discredit all the antidiscrimination efforts of government—in fact all the highest egalitarian impulses of liberalism. And he may have been right.

Women's liberation also attacks a further imperative of male socialization in the ghetto—in fact everywhere in the society: the creation of a world of work that is attractively masculine. One of the principal problems of every male without full professional credentials is that when he reaches the age of socialization, his sex drive is most intense, his male restiveness greatest, and his marketability lowest. The only way he can be disciplined is by integrating his sex drive with his career. The sexual constitution must favor and connect work, male sexuality, and marriage. At present the ghetto male enters a society where most of the accessible institutions are heavily female. The schools, bureaucracies, businesses, and even, increasingly, the politics of the ghetto are ruled by women, particularly at the entry levels where he must begin. The sexual constitution of a job under or with women tends to erode a man's motivation and will, particularly if the work is not palpably masculine. He can endure it only if his masculinity is extraordinarily secure. Unfortunately, this is not the case in the ghetto.

When the women's liberation movement forces conspicuous entry by women into one field after another in the established society, conventional work becomes decreasingly attractive, and men resort increasingly to athletics and outlawry. A political system led by Shirley Chisholm symbolizes a society dominated by women. Her election reinforces the inclination of black males to drop out or to turn to revolutionary pursuits. The increasing number of black women elected to office reflects this process. A substantial majority of the ghetto vote is now female.

It should be understood that any one of the activities of women's liberation may not be deeply damaging. The sexual division of labor is constantly changing, and if female entry into a particular profession is sufficiently massive, its sexual constitution will change and men will do something more affirmative or remunerative. Just as medicine became a female profession in the U.S.S.R., so political conventions may become increasingly a female arena in the United States, as major politicians defer to worthy women. The problem arises when all the available entries into the established order are feminine, and when, as Elliot Liebow's study indicates, legality, marriage, and work are themselves identified as female.[17] This is the problem in the ghetto, and woman's liberation only exacerbates it.

Unfortunately, the movement women bitterly oppose the kinds of male-oriented programs that are needed to alleviate this crisis. Ghetto boys need preferential treatment; they need special training—special male affirmations—designed to overcome their relative disadvantages in relation to ghetto women. A job program that provides genuinely equal opportunities for ghetto boys and girls will only reinforce the matriarchy. The girls, in general, will be better able to exploit the program and will thus increase their advantage. Social dissolution will be promoted. Thus women's liberation, by insisting on equal treatment in governmental programs, prevents redress of grave psychological inequalities between ghetto men and women.

This is not a mere theoretical quibble. The whole multifarious apparatus of federal job programs is rendered worthless or even destructive by its tendency to give job opportunities on an equal basis to men and women. Women's liberation prohibits any legal recognition that men need jobs, both for psychological affirmation and for socialization, far more than do women.

A particular absurdity is the use of large amounts of the taxpayer's money on job training for welfare mothers with small children. Having deprived the black family of fathers, the society is now moving to take away the mothers as well. One might think we had vast quantities of social funds we do not know what to do with—or that it is all some inexplicable bureaucratic blunder. But no, this program of inducing indigent mothers to leave their children and accept menial jobs or undertake employment training—all at a total cost, in day care and other expenses, much higher than welfare—this is a top priority program of women's liberationists and American politicians, liberals and conservatives alike. That it is an indefensible waste of money, with destructive social consequences, can be seen only by people who are willing to recognize that men and women are different in their need for work, that our ghetto unemployment problem is not welfare mothers but their men, and that every cent of our employment money should be spent on males.

The disastrous impact of women's liberation on black progress goes beyond our current policies. The feminists also have day care, child development programs, and welfare proposals worse than our existing system. But perhaps most destructive is the general effect of the movement on that complex of problems and political reactions often called the "social issue," but better termed the crisis of our sexual constitution.

Once male has left home what is a mother of small children to do? How will she feed her babies. How do you make a man stay when he doesn't want to? What is this training is her ticket out of the ghetto? To a better life for her and the children. Dealing with male in the ghetto is the most importance. Again, does white America really care.

The Sexual Sources of Demagoguery

Every politician knows that there are some issues on which private prejudices—no matter how apparently irrational—cannot be safely affronted. Views disdained as superstitions by most sophisticated Americans, casually rejected by most young people, nonetheless sometimes hold firm as democratic verities.

In November 1972, for example, 62 percent of the voters of Michigan and about 80 percent of the voters of North Dakota—including heavy majorities of both sexes and all races—voted against liberalized abortion laws,[1] thus making them an electoral proposition even less popular than George McGovern. The opposition of the blacks and poor—the supposed beneficiaries—was greater than the opposition of the rest of the electorate.[2]

Yet the women's demand for "control of our own bodies" seems eminently justifiable. The tragedy of an unwanted baby is easily comprehensible. The dangers of abortion mills are well known. Polls indicate, moreover, that this is an issue on which people have relatively strong and considered beliefs; they are not, as is sometimes said, "innocent victims of priestcraft." [3] In other words this is not an issue—like the antiballistic missile, for instance—that is too complex for most people to understand. We must assume that this large majority of the electorate acted with relatively knowledgeable deliberation. They thus consciously asserted the uncomfortable principle that at some point a woman should *not* "have control over her own body."

Another apparent mystery of public sentiment is gun control. Everyone knows that an important cause of the American carnage by firearms is the proliferation of handguns. Yet the Senate—a relatively liberal body dominated by Democrats and passionately exhorted by Edward Kennedy—has adamantly refused to enact so much as a meaningful registration requirement.

There are other such issues on which relevant public sentiment is directly hostile to the consensus of informed Americans. Although the voters in California in 1972 turned down an antiobscenity proposition (it was so extreme that even John Wayne opposed it), the public in general supports antipornography laws.[4] They also oppose liberalized divorce [5] and granting birth control pills to teenaged girls.[6] One could extend the list to busing, welfare, and marijuana—three other matters on which respectable opinion radically differs from public opinion.[7]

This divergence is even more significant than the immediate statistics would indicate, because public opinion is largely shaped by the kind of small minority that holds the sophisticated view. The articulate, knowledgeable elite has influence far beyond its numbers. Thus the tenacity of public opposition on this group of issues suggests a resistance sufficiently profound to demand explanation.

What is it about liberalized abortion, for example, that leads a 62 percent majority of Michigan's voters to violate the considered views of perhaps 90 percent of the American intelligentsia? And what is it about the other so-called social issues—embracing such varied matters as desegregation and guns—that makes them analogous to abortion on reasonable demand?

The answer is that all these measures directly impinge on that sensitive psychological terrain, involving sexuality, children, and the family, which underlies the sexual constitution of the society. Unlike many intellectuals whose lives are devoted to legal and scientific abstraction, most of the people still instinctively recognize that preservation of the sexual constitution may be even more important to the social order than preservation of the legal constitution. They recognize that no laws can prevail against the dissolution of the social connections and personal motivations that sustain a civilized polity. They acknowledge, with Carl Jung, that though the society can resist epidemics of physical disease, it is defenseless against diseases of the mind. Against "psychic epidemics," our laws and medicines are virtually helpless.[8]

Now it may well be that in most of these programmatic instances the intelligentsia is right and the public wrong; that the threat of easy abortions, for example, is less grave than the threat of unwanted and unaccommodated children. But the people perceive these proposals as a symbol of a more profound menace to our community. Before we can casually dismiss their prejudices, the progressive positions regarding abortion, gun control, marijuana, pornography, welfare, and busing should be examined for their impact on the sexual constitution. For if the public is right—if these measures do gravely threaten the sexual infrastructure of our society—then the changes probably should not be enacted regardless of how practical and realistic they seem.

One might even argue that the very belief, held widely, that certain measures jeopardize our sexual fabric is in itself a sufficient case against them. Government should tread lightly indeed when entering the murky arena of sexuality, where we may find at once the most critical and least negotiable, the most sensitive and least understood of the terms of our social contract: the source of motivation, commitment, and solidarity. Changes that affront the sexual prejudices of the people may cause a demoralization more serious than the nominal or real limits on freedom—and the protective surfaces of hypocrisy—entailed by the status quo.

The relationship of each of these issues to the sexual constitution, though perhaps not immediately clear, is psychologically profound. Guns are a good example. The United States is a nation of households, each containing a man who deeply feels his responsibility for defending his family—and who fears that his ability to do it is diminishing in modern society. The ultimate nightmare of almost every male is to witness helplessly the rape of his wife. Only somewhat less threatening to the very core of male consciousness is the possibility of the violation of his home.

The role of protector of wife and children is as old as the family nexus itself, as old and deeply ingrained as the role of provider. A move by the state finally to incapacitate the man in this responsibility—and usurp him—undermines the validity of the family itself and the man's part in it. In this role, the gun is not a mere symbol. It does objectively increase the man's capacity to defend his household.

In addition, a gun is an emblem of the male as hunter. This, according to many anthropologists, was the primordial role of the evolving male *homo sapiens*. Many of the male's distinguishing physical characteristics—his greater throwing ability and running speed, his more volatile hormonal pattern, and his greater muscular energy and aggressiveness—all were said to have begun in the anthropoid hunting party.[9] Lionel Tiger even contends that the male propensity to work in all-male groups originated in these early expeditions.

Today men across the land continue to hunt compulsively, despite a possibly declining need or appetite for the available game. They early give their male children guns and ceremoniously teach them the rules of their use. As anyone who has undergone this paternal instruction knows and remembers, it is a portentous event, conducted in the atmosphere of an initiation rite.

The obstinate refusal of many males to support gun control is not chiefly a product of conditioning by the weapons industry. It is not simply a fear of disarmament at a time of rising crime. Nor is it a paranoid response to black revolutionary rhetoric and violence. Rather, millions of men fear gun control because they are losing life-control; they are losing the sense of a defined male identity and role in the family. They cling to these weapons and persist in their hunts as totems of masculinity, as rites and symbols of their continuing role as protector and provider in the family. In this sense, the guns have a virtually religious import, and gun restrictions pose a serious psychological threat.

This is not to say that gun control is unimportant, particularly in congested urban society. But the crisis of crime and violence itself is to a great extent a product of familial disintegration and male incapacitation. Unless this erosion of the sexual constitution is recognized as a major social problem—for which realistic solutions rather than utopian incantations must be provided—gun control will remain politically difficult and practically unenforceable outside a police state. In addition, the controls may exacerbate the syndrome of male insecurity, violence, and frustration that they are designed to restrict.

The sexual dimensions of the abortion issue may be more obvious, but they are little better understood. The usual assumption is that opposition to abortion on demand stems from a puritanical aversion to premarital sex, combined with a religious superstition that feticide is murder. The real reasons, however, may be significantly different. Beyond the import of the Michigan vote as a repudiation of the women's movement—and of sexual liberation in general—it may be seen as a symbol of resistance to the erosion of male sexuality.

When the women demanded "control over our own bodies," they believed they were couching the issue in the least objectionable way. But as only Norman Mailer fully understood, they were in fact invoking one of the most extreme claims of the movement and striking at one of the most profound male vulnerabilities.[10] For, in fact, few males have come to psychological terms with the existing birth-control technology; few recognize the extent to which it shifts the balance of sexual power in favor of women. A man quite simply cannot now father a baby unless his wife is fully and deliberately agreeable. There are few social or cultural pressures on her to conceive. Male procreativity is now dependent, to a degree unprecedented in history, on the active pleasure of women.

The psychological consequences of this change are greater than they might at first appear. Throughout the centuries, men could imagine their sexual organs as profoundly powerful instruments. If they performed a normal amount of sexual activity—"spread their wild oats"—they could assume that they would cause a number of women to bear their children. Male potency was not simply a matter of erectile reliability; it was a fell weapon of procreation. Women viewed male potency with some awe, and males were affirmed by this response.

This masculine attribute is now almost completely lost. The male penis is no longer a decisive organ in itself. It has become an optional accessory of the woman's will and body, and an instrument of sexual pleasure somewhat inferior to the clitoris and a Coke bottle. In a profound sense, the male has now lost control of it—of his own principal masculine endowment.

Thus the feminist demand that women have control over their own bodies accentuated an unconscious recognition that males have almost completely lost control of procreative activity. Women are only marginally dependent on men—women can conceive a baby artificially or in one passing encounter. But a man cannot validate his procreative powers, his role in the chain of nature, without the active, deliberate, and now revocable cooperation of a woman. A man's penis becomes an empty plaything unless a woman deliberately decides to admit a man's paternity. This change in the sexual balance between men and women is still being absorbed by the society. Legal abortion on demand is resisted as a symbol of this radical change in the sexual constitution.

The campaign for abortion on demand is not simply a drive for better government, with laws more congruent to real social need and practice. It is part of a movement that is changing the sexual dimensions of every human relationship and every exchange of love. Recognizing this, Norman Mailer argues that abortion is actually preferable to prophylactic methods of birth control. He believes that the sure knowledge of sterility, conferred by the pill, itself aborts the deepest resonances of every sexual experience. Abortion after conception, on the other hand, or perhaps a "morning-after" pill, may not so directly intrude on the act of love itself.

He may be right, and his position should not be considered a quirk. If intercourse indeed can fathom the reaches of our unconscious and shape the innermost flows of personality—if it is our paramount ritual of biological community—then we must be extraordinarily careful how we choose to reform it. In choosing among the various birth-control possibilities, it may be that some advanced form of abortion is least disruptive of the sexual constitution—least damaging to the sources of male identity and least impoverishing of human sexuality. But the issue is formidably complicated. The reluctance of the people to authorize abortion on demand stems from a profound sense of justifiable conservatism in interfering with our deepest human experiences.

Busing further symbolizes the diminishing control of a family over its own children, the *raison d'être* of families. If the state can take children and use them for dubious social experiments, actively opposed by the parents themselves, parental protection of, and authority over, offspring are gravely reduced. Yet protection and socialization of children are perhaps the definitive functions of the family. To displace them is to subvert filial ties and undermine this crucial institution of civilized society.

Busing violates the implicit contract by which parents relinquished their children to the state to be educated. The assumption is that the children are being taught more effectively than they could be at home. They are relinquished for this educational purpose, not for the engineering of a more just and integrated society as debatably envisaged by judges.

The forcible creation of a broadly integrated urban school system, at a time of ghetto disorder, is an enterprise radically different from the consolidation of dual school systems in relatively small and tranquil communities. The current busing effort does not reduce total educational costs in most instances or demonstrably improve the education of the participating students. It is undertaken to promote broader and more abstract objectives—often at a cost in time and convenience or even at the peril of the students involved. The response—"not with my kid, you don't"—is not chiefly racist. It is a reaction to what is felt as a further encroachment on the rights of the family, a further encroachment on the sexual constitution. If one understands the critical role of the family in the society— a role that no other institutions have shown any significant ability to perform—one understands the positive character of attempts to defend it from the state.

Again, the racial crisis is perhaps our most grievous social problem, testing the viability of our democracy and its ideals of equality and fraternity under the law. An ultimate failure to overcome racial conflict would represent something of a final moral tragedy for our nation. But this crisis, too, is to a great extent a crisis of the sexual constitution—of a breakdown and incapacitation of the family, particularly in its role of socializing ghetto males. Until the problem is addressed in these specific terms—how do you give men a sense of civilized participation in the community and restore the family to its appropriate role?—busing will just spread demoralization.

Marijuana is similarly perceived as a threat to familial authority and thus to the *raison d'être* of the family. Although legalization would be universal, it is feared by the older generation as an assertion by the state that children under 18, who are among the principal users, should have the right to autonomy at a period in their lives when the family is still trying to instill values of industry, thrift, and continence, values that pot tends to subvert. The state would be implicitly legalizing a life style profoundly hostile to the values of the elders. As with guns and abortion, people are being treated not principally as members of families and subject to familial disciplines, but as individuals primarily subject to the state and its social and legal priorities.

The role of the family is thus constricted and the sexual constitution infringed, even while plausible legal rights and social ideals are being promoted. When determining policy, it will be wise to consider not only the abstract principles being applied and the specific grievances alleviated, but also the impact on our most intimate institutions. For it will be hard indeed to maintain a just or orderly or idealistic society without the crucial socializing work of families.

Public opposition to marijuana would not be so intense if it were not a symbol of social disintegration. Liberals cannot seem to offer any effective programs of communal affirmation and male socialization that would actually reduce crime, violence, and narcotic escapism, divorce, abandonment, and sexual disorder. So they advocate programs of adaptation, often individually desirable, which collectively exacerbate the crisis of the sexual constitution. The public reacts with a general revulsion toward social liberalism. To overcome the revulsion—with all the injustices it entails—one must resolve the ulterior crisis of motivation, masculinity, and the family.

Until a serious effort is made in this direction, one can plausibly maintain that the blighted lives of millions of our urban citizens constitute an injustice far more grave than the occasional incarceration of a user of marijuana. One can admit that it is not logical or inspiring to think in terms of such morbid trade-offs. But millions of Americans are losing patience with the social engineers who demand ever greater payments for a used war on poverty that looms increasingly like a war on middle-class males. Unless some of our liberal programs start to work—and unless our conservatives start to provide plausible alternatives—the people are likely to seek immediate symptomatic relief: repression.

Welfare is one of the programs that not only does not work but also attacks the sexual constitution. The people resist it not out of some vulgar misanthropy or stinginess, but from an instinctive knowledge, probably more sound than most sophisticated analyses of the subject, that free money has a corrosive impact on the motivation of its recipients. Doubly corrosive is money that goes to women under conditions that deter marriage. Our welfare program—particularly Aid to Families with Dependent Children (AFDC)—is not a tragedy, therefore, because it gives inadequate aid. It is tragic because, as currently designed, it promotes social disintegration.

It is often maintained that nearly all welfare recipients have no other way of supporting themselves; the chiselers and frauds are said to be a figment of demagogic speechwriters. The leading recipients—the blind, the disabled, and the deserted mothers with small children—are unimpeachably qualified for public assistance.

No one begrudges money for the blind and disabled, and the sight of a deserted mother and child strikes a deep emotional chord in everyone. Yet it is this welfare effort—AFDC—that chiefly qualms and frightens every lower-class male. He is not resentful toward the subsidized women and children themselves. It is the notion of the male deserter, lovin' and leavin'—in the glamorous pattern of every male fantasy hero—that makes the lifelong husband and worker, with wages little greater than welfare, feel like a cuckold. He remembers all the sexual opportunities forgone, all the payments dutifully made, all the disciplines arduously observed, and the image of the fugitive fathers tears at the very ligaments of his identity. He feels that the social contract by which he has ordered his life has been broken. The society that entwined his sexuality in social cords—reaching from the depths of his psyche into the womb of a woman, and thence into the future of mankind—has betrayed him. It has failed to maintain the civilization he arduously sustained. It has used his money to subsidize the primal mode of male behavior that he painfully relinquished.

It is difficult for the financially comfortable to appreciate the psychological impact of money on the poor. The liberal looks at welfare payments and sees them as pitifully low. He cannot imagine how this amount of money appears to a man required to submit to forty or even fifty or more hours of drudgery a week to earn only slightly more after taxes. Unlike

AFDC payments, moreover, his earnings must sustain not only his wife and children but also himself, and his few stinted indulgences. If his wife is restive, he sees welfare as a positive invitation from the state for her to dissolve the marriage. If he is restive, he finds welfare—and the example of other unchastened deserters—an implicit moral exemption. In addition, he sees welfare as an imposition on his familial authority, forcing him to give his wife almost all his money. This pressure, in effect, undermines the poor man's role as provider by depriving it of its moral quality as a deliberate act. He has little choice; thus he loses the psychological affirmation for which, in many cases, he holds a job and supports his family.

In any event, the welfare payment, from the point of view of the poor, is anything but negligibly small. It is the chief single source of funds in the community; it is free and can be augmented by unreported part-time or criminal income, more difficult to come by if one is working full time. It is, in fact, the dominant economic influence in the lives of the indigent, and it exerts a continuous and morally corrosive pressure on the lower middle class. Because their socialization, despite the stringent discipline required, is so little rewarded in material terms, it is not surprising that so many millions of lower-middle-class Americans, black and white, look with the greatest cynicism on welfare dispensations.

This complex of problems—often termed "the social issue"—is at once the chief vulnerability of American liberalism and the greatest opportunity for American conservatives. Contrary to a popular impression, the deep resentments aroused have little to do with bigotry or avarice. They are the natural reaction of honest Americans who are trying to defend their families against the poisonous emissions of a decaying sexual constitution. Neither the liberals nor the conservatives have any answer. The liberals would make the problem a lot worse by enlarging welfare, day care, and other government programs that promote matriarchy. But the conservatives are little better. Not only do they lack the guts to rebuff the upper-class feminist ladies, but they lack a fundamental interest in the problems of the poor and the lower middle class. They fail to show the resolution and decisiveness needed to develop a complex of new and expensive social policies designed to strengthen families and socialize males. Thus the problems keep getting worse, and the people, demoralized and confused, show a rising and justifiable contempt for the world of politics.

A key reason for our current failure is the tendency of bureaucrats and social theorists to look upon the society chiefly as an aggregation of individual units, scarcely differentiated except in income and employment. This bias is understandable. It derives from a seductive misconception of democracy and of the great moral mandates of our founding fathers. The assumption that "all men [meaning men and women] are created equal . . . endowed . . . with certain unalienable Rights" has been interpreted to mean that the laws of the land must be sex-blind: that men and women are essentially the same and wherever possible should play similar roles in statistically similar patterns throughout the economy (and where impossible, we should feel guilty about it). As government attempts to foster equal opportunity for liberty and the pursuit of happiness, it is urged to apply the same standards to all citizens, as individuals, whether they are married or single, young or middle-aged, male or female. Similarly, when the feminists speak of the need to consider us all "human beings" and "people," what they mean is autonomous rational individuals: men and women without powerful sexual drives reaching into all their relationships and without kinship ties binding them to their very identities. But such "human beings" exist only in actuarial tables and in the minds of fastidious economists and sociologists.

When such thinkers address the problems of equal opportunity, moreover, they seem to think exclusively in terms of individual financial prospects. The pursuit of happiness and the promotion of the general welfare are to be measured in the comparative income, housing, and employment of independent citizens. The sexual constitution is to be ignored. A conspicuous instance of this mode of thought is, of course, the Equal Rights Amendment, which declares it unconstitutional to differentiate between men and women in most public policy.

Yet for most people, the pursuit of happiness is inextricably tied to sexual relationships. The general welfare is best served when most men and women are socialized through love, marriage, and family. At the very core of these relationships and institutions, moreover, are differences—sexual, financial, and motivational. A policy that ignores or counteracts these differences in the name of statistical or numerical equality will tend to retard familial creation and male affirmation, and subvert the general welfare and the pursuit of happiness. The numerical symmetries will come at the expense of possibilities for real equality in human fulfillment.

In designing a social policy, we should consider the society not as an aggregation of undifferentiated individuals but as an organism consisting of interdependent men and women, largely defined in terms of their different relationships to families. Each adult can be seen as occupying a different position on the continuum that begins with psychological and economic preparation for marriage, is punctuated by marriage itself, and proceeds to parental and postparental stages.

During this process, of course, people will often see themselves in different ways, unrelated to family. Many individuals will make large contributions to the society in spite of, or perhaps in some cases even because of, their failure or refusal to follow the usual cycles. But we should not be unduly concerned with the exceptional individuals or the geniuses who can find inspiration and commitment outside the usual pattern of biological fulfillment. Their artistic or professional creativity often comes in a drive to compensate for their failure to marry, whether deliberate or not. In addition, their early work and education—their discipline and resolve—may have been motivated, consciously or unconsciously, by sexual ambition. Even their unmarried identities may be defined in terms of a rebellion against marriage and thus in a negative way are dependent on the institution. In any event, most of the unmarried, no matter how stalwartly self-reliant, were originally products of marriage and beneficiaries of the sexual constitution.

The women's movement would have us focus attention on the unmarried—particularly on talented unmarried females —and devote our social policy to removing any pressures that encumber their success or impel them toward marriage. The fact is, however, that most unmarried men and women either aspire to or once aspired to marry and would find life most rewarding if marriage were made less onerous. They may reject marriage largely because the society did not provide them with a stable family example in the beginning and made marriage financially or sexually uninviting.

Women may not face the same problem as men. Most women are capable of quietly enduring civilized society without marriage. According to a survey by sociologist Jessie Bernard, single women seem to suffer fewer psychological strains than do wives.[11] But almost every woman wants to marry at some point in her life if the conditions are right; and virtually everyone in the society, male or female, would benefit from better socialization of currently disruptive or predatory single males.

Although the best process of socialization seems to be love and family, even men who never marry will be favorably influenced by an environment in which most men are committed to the long-term patterns of family life. The values promoted by families will create a social order within which the unmarried will be most likely to contribute.

It is objectively sound, therefore, to define the society as chiefly an assemblage of families, family aspirants, and unmarried units within the familial order. Unless we take this reality into account, our politics will fail to achieve its goals —will fail to foster the happiness and fulfillment of our citizens. A sound social policy will devote itself to promoting the creation and maintenance of family connections.

Such a policy will have to acknowledge and accommodate sexual differences. It will have to come to terms with the special frustrations of older women during the increasingly extended period after their children grow up, and with the loneliness of women isolated with their children. Under the pressures of population and the need for increasingly inventive and sophisticated manpower, sound social policy will have to encourage an emphasis on the quality rather than quantity of child-rearing.[12] At some point, it may also have to face problems of motivation and identity leading to inadequate procreation. It will have to meet the increasingly dire

threat of the new biochemical technology of artificial reproduction. And, perhaps most important of all, it must respond
to the interlocking crises of masculinity and family breakdown.

All these responses will require sexual discrimination of
various kinds. By insisting on a view of society as an aggregate
of individual units—however well they may fit the computers
in the labor department or the ideologies of liberation—we
will prevent ourselves from responding to the real and different, though interrelated, problems of men and women.
And we may not be able to preserve the family as an obstacle
to the dehumanizing threat of the new technology of reproduction.

If, on the other hand, a family policy is established and
the sexual constitution renewed, we can probably overcome
most of our current domestic distresses, which feed on and
derive from our sexual disorders. We can restore our confidence as a people and prevent the rise of demagogic movements exploiting the resentments of the social issue.

But first we have to resist the alternative "family policy"
of women's liberation—an antifamily program advocated
even by the "moderates" in the movement.

The Moderate Extremists

The changes necessary to bring about equality were,
and still are, very revolutionary indeed. They
involve a sex-role revolution for men and women which will
restructure all our institutions: child rearing,
education, marriage, the family, medicine, work, politics,
the economy, religion, psychological theory, human sexuality,
morality and the very evolution of the race.

Betty Friedan
New York Times Magazine, *March 4, 1973*

The moderate feminists do not admit any basic hostility to the family. They say they want to change it only to make it stronger. But the same "moderate" leaders who in one breath piously aver their support for marriage, in the next testify before Congress in favor of "more equitable" tax treatment for single people. If one observes politely that tax treatment for singles is more favorable in the United States than in any other industrial nation, one is met with incredulity. If one points out that, in general, better terms for singles mean higher burdens for families, the feminists just raise the pitch of their voices and proceed with further poignant description of the plight of the unmarried. In fact, the intensity of their concern for this economically favored group is one of the most revealing aspects of their program. Only the willfully single, moreover, will appreciate their concern. Other beneficiaries either aspire to marriage or recognize its primacy among our social relations.

On this issue, the moderate feminist position thus represents a rather extreme minority view. At a time when the real need of tax policy is to strengthen family finances, these women would weaken them. But such perversity should not surprise us. It is characteristic of the entire moderate agenda and is well exemplified in the "Bill of Rights" promulgated by the National Organization for Women (NOW).[1]

This "historic document of feminism" [2] consists of proposals, including abortion, equal pay, and daycare, that are accepted by virtually the entire movement and in several instances have been enacted by Congress and endorsed by both political parties.[3] Because the positions are so likely to become law, they represent the real cutting edge of the movement. Far more than appeals for revolution or lesbianism, these proposals will shape our national future. Yet there is scarcely a single one that is sound or desirable. Nearly all would subvert our most essential institutions and relationships.

Even the Bill of Rights' demand for unrestricted abortion is couched in language so garbled, pretentious, and absolute that it is hard to accept. NOW asserts the "right of women to control their own reproductive lives by removing from penal codes laws limiting access to contraceptive information and devices and laws governing abortion." All right, it can be figured out and affirmed in essence. But wouldn't one like to know just how late in pregnancy an abortion might be legally secured; and just what "the right of women to control their own reproductive lives" means in connection with the responsibility of the husbands in this realm? In view of movement praise for those "brave women" who raise children on their own, this question is not academic.[4]

At any rate, the other demands are all at least as problematical. There is a demand that pregnancy be considered a "temporary disability" and that women be paid maternity leave under social security. For the most part unexceptionable, this proposal is a sleeper, because it would give official sanction to the feminist view of childbirth as a mere inconvenience, like appendicitis, in the lives of women.

In another major demand, NOW "insists" that the Equal Employment Opportunities Commission (EEOC) devote itself to fulfilling the noble legacy of Judge Smith: the EEOC is to enforce laws against sex discrimination "with the same vigor as it enforces prohibitions against racial discrimination." Once again the women are trying to ride on the shoulders of aggrieved blacks. Once again they try to foist on us the notion that the differences between men and women are of no more practical significance than the differences between whites and blacks. Apart from being stupid, this effort is most inopportune. Racial discrimination remains a significant, though politically sensitive, problem in many parts of the country.

Beyond these peccadilloes, the group's demands display typical feminist irresponsibility. They fail to acknowledge any conflicting concerns of government, such as progressive distribution of wealth, maintenance of democratic politics, or preservation of the Constitution. A good example of their attitude was their campaign for the Equal Rights Amendment (ERA).

Most unfortunately—in view of its revolutionary implications—the ERA is superfluous. By artful association with the civil rights movement and laws—and with the guileful cooperation of Southern reactionaries—the feminists have hectored all three branches of the federal government into accepting almost all the principles the Amendment embodies. At the insidious behest of Judge Smith, the 1964 Civil Rights

Act was amended in Title 7 to prohibit discrimination by sex in private employment. The courts have frequently upheld the applicability to sex discrimination of the Fifth and Fourtenth Amendments.[5] The Equal Employment Opportunity Commission (EEOC) is active in the cause and has even outlawed the listing of jobs by sex in newspapers as "psychologically" damaging.[6] The antidiscriminatory agencies of the huge federal cabinet departments, particularly the Department of Labor's Office of Federal Contract Compliance (OFCC), are all too readily betraying their real civil rights mandate in order to aid women (black and white). Beginning under J. Stanley Pottinger's fatuously aggressive leadership in enforcing Executive Order 11375 of President Johnson, the Department of Health, Education, and Welfare requires colleges to institute "affirmative action" programs to find women who have not shown sufficient interest to apply for available jobs or pursue them aggressively.[7] The ERA would add virtually nothing to these already exorbitant activities under way in every part of the federal system.

Of course, the courts have not been as absolutely and immediately compliant as the movement would wish. Women are still not drafted, for example; nor are the elaborate virility rites of the military and naval academies yet open to females. Other separate educational facilities for boys and girls persist here and there against NOW's wishes.[8] Although juries are all legally open to women, women with children still can be more easily exempted, on the grounds that their domestic role is more indispensable than the male's role at work. A few other shreds of protective legislation persist and the Supreme Court has upheld—though in remarkably narrow terms —the concept of a "bona fide occupational qualification" by sex (i.e., *Playboy* Bunnies). In family law, some states still require the man to support his family but impose no similar requirement on women. In general, however, the purposes of the ERA have been all too fully recognized in the law.

None the less, the women's movement urgently demanded that we trivialize the Constitution with this obviously unnecessary amendment. With the moderates in the lead, the feminists assumed an absolutist stance, as completely indifferent to the sanctity of the Constitution as were their spiritual forebears years before in instituting the Prohibition Amendment.

Apparently by oversight, NOW's Bill of Rights failed to mention one of the most notable concerns of the moderate wing of women's liberation: equal representation in politics. Displaying a spectacular indifference to American democratic principles, the movement managed to get both political parties to accept the idea that a truly representative national convention would be half female. Although the women were willing in practice to accept somewhat smaller proportions, every state was expected to make a good faith effort to achieve a delegation composed 50 percent of women. A state whose delegation was not over 30 percent female would bear a heavy burden of proof in showing that it had obeyed the rules.

Although the Republican convention was less submissive to the women than was the Democratic assemblage, both parties accepted the crucial and inadmissible principle that democratic representation could be promoted by quota and that a fully open and authentically representative convention would be 51 percent female (and by extension, 12 percent black, 10 percent young, and so on through the fashionable categories of the year). Of course, the women denied that their approach in fact involved quotas. The targeted figures, toward which the state parties were to aim, were said to be mere evidentiary devices, useful in assigning the burden of proof but inconclusive in themselves.

But even as tests or targets, quotas bear the implication, radically inimical to any democratic process, that the electorate consists of separate, homogeneous, and identifiable groups, each best represented by one of its own kind. Such conception of American voters is, of course, profoundly wrong. Women vote for men most of the time; young people vote for their elders; blacks vote for whites and whites for blacks. Plausible categories can be endlessly multiplied, through ethnic, professional, economic, cultural, and intellectual indices. But it is all a frivolous undertaking because people are usually best represented by politicians whose effectiveness in serving their constituencies is registered through their election. In accord with this test, the women's movement ranks high among the groups from whom women seem least likely to choose their representatives.

A good illustration of the quota problem can be found in the Chicago challenge of the 1972 Democratic convention. Using categorical quotas as an evidentiary test, the Democratic credentials committee found deeply suspicious the small number of women (9 percent) [9] on the regular Chicago delegation. The regulars had been overwhelmingly elected in the primaries, but the democratic test of election was of little avail against the evidentiary test of quotas. So after citing some trivial infractions of the rules, which could have had no significant effect on the result (for nobody denied that Mayor Daley was the choice of the people), the Democratic convention seated an alternate Chicago group. Consisting of men and women defeated by the regulars or unwilling to challenge them at the polls, it was an impressive reform assemblage of variegated sex and color. Its failure to include significant representation from the white ethnic groups that dominate Chicago demography was compensated by a high sense of moral and financial worth.

This is a familiar story, but a key facet of it was little remarked. The women chosen were almost totally unrepresentative of the city's females. Helen Lopata, in her book *Occupation Housewife*, summarizes her in-depth interviews with a demographic sampling of some 600 Chicago women.[10] She found that, in general, they lived more challenging and varied lives than their husbands. However, they left politics to their men. In a city where most males do work of uncommon drudgery, this system may have been a significant part of the sexual constitution.

What the movement demanded was not representation of Chicago women, for they demonstrably wanted to be represented by men. The liberationists wanted a cultural revolution in the city and a significant change in its sexual constitution. Whatever one thinks of these goals, they have nothing to do with democratic processes.

The fact is that for almost every state, in both conventions, a truly open selection process would have produced far fewer female delegates than actually appeared in Miami. The large number of Democratic women was chiefly attributable to the manipulations of the liberal Democratic reformers, who displaced elected officials with women and young people. The similarly large number of Republican women was also a product of bossism, as people like Nelson Rockefeller deferred chivalrously to them.

The heavy representation of youth, moreover, signified a further attack on the sexual constitution, which in societies all over the world has usually treated political power as a perquisite of maturity, earned by service to the community. The accession of youth, hailed with high sanctimony, was actually a demagogic response to the rise of the 18-year-old vote.

If there is morality in politics, it does not consist in displacing men who have devoted long years to politics with youths who have their whole lives before them. There is something to be said for respect for the aged, just as there is something to be said for allowing men and women to keep politics as essentially a middle-aged male preserve if that is what they want, evidentiary tests and quotas notwithstanding. The alternative of categorical quotas is a system that would find its *reductio ad absurdum* in a President who is an exact ethnic and sexual composite of the American demography—some kind of multiracial hermaphrodite from Kansas City.

The final irony is that quotas are inimical to the development of real political power by women. If women could be induced to vote only for their own sex, they could control not just 51 percent, but all our political offices. The best approach for the women's movement in pursuing political influence is not to agitate for proportionate representation at the top but to organize for political control in the field. If they succeeded, the results might not please them (polls indicate that Pat Nixon is the favorite of America's women).[11] But the women who won elections would not have to fear the disdain of male politicians on reaching the convention, for such women will have shown they can deliver votes as well as speeches.

The women's movement has still shown little sign of choosing this arduous course. It prefers a politics of style and cosmetics, superimposed on democratic political processes.

Pretending to be an excluded minority like the blacks, the women have adopted the same theatrical and gestural repertory: threats, demands, proclamations. It is no credit to our political process that—unable to distinguish between sound policy and political noise—politicians are capitulating at every turn. They accept quotas and spurious analogies to racism at one moment, and then support gratuitous constitutional impositions at the next. The "moderate" demands, as destructive as they are, seem mild beside the lesbian posturing of the extremists. The politicians, mostly men, are afraid to affront any group that even seems to speak for so many women.

Nonetheless, the extremists objectively pose much less a threat than do the moderates. Obviously eccentric, the fringe women can ultimately be accommodated by a system that tolerates eccentricity. The moderates, on the other hand, want legislation and power that will apply to everyone and change the very nature of our society. They want to establish the professional woman with secondary family affiliation—themselves, that is—as the American norm. This is their ultimate vision, and it is more important than any of the others.

In pursuing this goal, moreover, they are proposing several other changes of equally far-reaching impact. Several are included in the NOW Bill of Rights, and they are central issues in our politics today. They deserve full appraisal. These proposals relate to welfare, day care, and job discrimination, and it is in these areas that the women most gravely impair the sexual constitution. It is here that they attack the male role, subvert poor families, incapacitate federal job and educational programs, and generally prohibit any serious attempt to break the vicious cycles of poverty.

Finally, it is in these areas that the persistent upper-class bias of the movement becomes apparent. Unconsciously promoting the needs of the affluent, the women would create an ever more rigidly stratified society and engender a social crisis of unprecedented severity in American life. The "progressive" programs of the feminists, in fact, simultaneously invite revolution and reaction, while undermining the most important source of stability in civilized society—the female role in the family.

The Child Care State

The care of children would be paid
employment; the primary relation of adults to children
would be the cash nexus.

Walter Karp

The central demand of women's liberation—universal day care for children—is a program that exacerbates most of the mistakes of our previous social policy. Indeed, the potential costs and effects of this new proposal are so catastrophic that blocking it should be a major endeavor of American liberals and conservatives alike. Instead, one discovers that under the guise of "child development," day care has become a virtual crusade of American liberalism and an attractive approach for many conservatives as well. It joins Democrats and Republicans alike, while inducing the few conservative opponents to grope desperately for "private alternatives," often virtually as bad. It even unites the entire women's liberation movement—a feat that could otherwise be achieved only by a campaign to put Norman Mailer in stocks.

The political and ideological stakes are high. Senator Walter Mondale of Minnesota is basing his future presidential prospects partly on his ability to get a child care program through the Senate. Nixon vetoed the Senator's 1972 effort and charged that it favors "communal modes of child-rearing as against the family-centered approach." But Mondale is irretrievably committed. He called the President's veto message "cruel, irresponsible, hysterical, and false."[1] (Did he think Nixon had said "Communist"?)

Mondale is not exceptional in the intensity of his feelings. Senator Gaylord Nelson of Wisconsin described the President's mild strictures as "the most irresponsible statement I have heard in all my time in public life"[2]—a strong assertion, since the Wisconsin Senator goes back to the Joe McCarthy period. Ogden Reid of New York explained his switch from the Republican to Democratic parties partly in terms of the President's veto. In fact, there is not one Democratic liberal and all too few Republicans who recognize nationally subsidized day care as the monstrosity it is.

Upper-class Republican women tend to be sympathetic. Several, like Martha (Mrs. Kevin) Phillips of the Republican Congressional Policy Committee and Jill (Mrs. William) Ruckelshaus of the Women's Political Caucus, are influential with key Republican conservatives. In view of the growing impetus of the women's movement and its disproportionate impact on both political parties, it seems unlikely that this gargantuan waste of money and bitter betrayal of the poor can be stopped. Nonetheless it may be possible to keep appropriations down from year to year when the real nature of the proposal becomes evident.

The various federal day-care programs differ superficially. One of the most inexcusable, enacted in 1971, came directly from the NOW Bill of Rights, courtesy of Senator Russell Long of Louisiana. Senator Long, chairman of the Senate Finance Committee, had run into a "servant problem"; the NOW ladies would understand. His amendment to the tax bill was designed to liberate more women from their own homes to serve in other, richer ones. He proposed a system of tax exemptions for day care and home care costs. Available for families with incomes up to $18,000 annually and for offspring up to 16 years old, the exemptions covered expenses of $2,400 for one child, $3,600 for two children, and $4,800 for three or more.[3] Of course, this program may not help much with the servant problem. Like most tax exemptions, it is chiefly useful to upper-income families and would not give enough help to the poor to release them from their homes.

There also exist a number of federal day-care accommodations for low-income families, at a total cost of some $700 million in 1972 (some 800,000 spaces at a cost of $900 each per year).[4] Largely associated with various job-training programs for AFDC mothers, these provisions are useful chiefly as part of welfare "crackdowns." The most notable feature of such "get tough" campaigns is their fiscal softmindedness. The jobs, in the 20 percent of cases where they actually materialize,[5] almost never pay as much as the costs of the training and day care—which in turn are higher than the welfare payments. The mothers do drudgery; their children get institutional care, otherwise unnecessary; the politicians are acclaimed for "toughness"; and the taxpayer foots the bill.

The chief remaining federal child-care programs are Head Start and Title 4 of social security. Designed for abandoned and neglected children, Title 4 day care has been expanding rapidly in recent years.[6] It is unfortunately necessary. Head Start, on the other hand, suffered a devastating blow when a Westinghouse survey, conducted by perplexed liberals sympathetic to the program, discovered that it did not seem to do any measurable good, at least in educational terms.[7] Any initial gains evaporated quickly in the public schools. The result was consistent with other recent findings indicating the ineffectiveness or even damaging impact of much preschool education outside the home.[8] Of course, these findings do not mean that all preschool programs are useless—just that it is hard and expensive to design good ones, particularly for more than a few hours a day.

Such research does not daunt the proponents of child development legislation, however. Nor do existing day care and tax shelters satisfy them. Some advocates of child development maintain that Head Start does not get the children early enough (a few experiments indicate that with elaborate and continuous ministrations from infancy, I.Q.s can be significantly improved).[9] In any case, the advocates say, it is urgent to remove small children from the clutches of ghetto mothers. In addition to citing the estimated 12,000 "latchkey kids" left to make their way on the streets every day while their mothers work,[10] poverty officials tell horrible stories about battered and abused infants, and mothers who sit for apparent weeks and months in front of television sets.[11] One top former OEO official declares, "It would be worth anything to wake up these women and get them out of the house. Any job would be good for them and would help with their children." [12] But this view is disputed by child psychologists like Arnold Gesell, who points to the maternal capabilities of black women, and John Bowlby, who maintains that "children thrive better in bad homes than in good institutions" (see note 9 for further discussion).

In any case, if one decides that ghetto families can be reached only through day care, an immense sum of money is needed. Since these problem cases, as well as ordinary welfare mothers, are widely dispersed across the country, only a universal program can efficiently encompass them all. It would, of course, be possible to reach large numbers of them through a program focused on indigent communities. But day care advocates wax suspiciously indignant at such an idea, calling it "ghettoization of poor children." [13] Since

for convenience to home and work many facilities will have
to be dominated by one or another race or class, this argument is obviously spurious. Or does Senator Mondale envisage a day care busing program? In any case, a group of
liberationists who started a private center on the edge of Harlem, and opened it to the poor, were surprised to discover
that black mothers would have nothing to do with their liberal
child-raising methods. "They're just a bunch of hippies," one
said. "It's a mess," said another.[14]

Nonetheless, day care advocates want a universal program or nothing. NOW and most of the other women's groups
demand a comprehensive, free, public effort "on the order of
the public schools." [15] Senators Mondale, Jacob Javits, and
the other key day-care advocates, sensitive to political and
economic realities, propose to begin with more limited efforts
that accept the idea of universality only in principle.[16]

The practical problems and expenses of setting up a national system are enormous. Child development experts are
unanimous in insisting that only trained personnel be used.
Yet at present there is a lack of trained people for existing
day-care centers. As to costs, day care authorities maintain
that anything much less than $2,500 per space will produce
an inadequate, merely custodial program, damaging to children.[17] The current legislation envisages "child development,"
with animated educational environments, full of mobiles and
bright colors. The facilities are to be open around the year
and around the clock to accommodate the hours of the working poor; they are to be staffed at "teacher-pupil" ratios much
higher than are presently found in the schools.[18]

But regardless of the problems, there is little question
that if we make day care a top national priority, we can overcome all obstacles. A universal national system will cost approximately $20 billion annually [19] (compared to about $12
billion annually for the first six grades of school).[20] Less ambitious programs, with higher payments by users, will cost
substantially less. The Long-NOW tax exemptions, however,
mean that if significant charges are imposed on affluent parents, the public system will have difficulty competing with
private centers. Since day care advocates strongly oppose any

program that would segregate poor children, only nominal charges are envisaged. Virtually no one urges that nonpoor families pay anything near the actual costs of the service.

The $20 billion estimate therefore seems realistic as an ultimate annual cost for programs currently being considered. Of course, lesser programs serving chiefly the poor, or chiefly the middle class—or merely providing "child garages"—are feasible. But even these alternatives will not be cheap. Even if the child development people have enormously overestimated the demand for their service, none of the projected programs could cost less than the present $5 billion spent on AFDC.[21] If we embark on a major day-care effort, it will clearly become our chief new social initiative of the 1970s. And despite all the usual and understandable cries of "get it from the Pentagon," the money will have to come out of existing and prospective social spending.[22]

It should give our liberal senators pause, therefore, to learn the likely effects of the program. Universal day care would hurt the poor and the family, while giving a multi-billion dollar impetus to upper-class "women's liberation." These ladies obviously should support it. They and a relatively small number of middle-class mothers will be the chief beneficiaries. But it is outrageous that so many moderate and liberal leaders are jumping on the bandwagon.

The damage to the poor comes in several forms. The jobs available to poor mothers are poor jobs, many of them not even covered by the $3,960 minimum wage. In pure financial terms, the women lose. They give up welfare, which pays as much or more if they have a large family, and they incur the expenses of their job in transportation and other costs. They also submit their children to institutional care—though most of the mothers can do better [23]—and submit themselves to low-wage drudgery. Their benefits are hard to see.

An even larger loser may be the taxpayer. He pays some $2,500 per space for day care, plus training and accessory costs, to achieve no discernible social gain whatsoever—except in that small number of instances where the day care helps abused or undernourished children. These cases, however, could be reached far more cheaply and effectively by other programs specifically aimed to treat them.

The chief financial beneficiaries are the low-wage employers. The massive day-care effort among the poor will release large numbers of workers who would not otherwise be available. It thus constitutes a subsidy for the businesses that employ them. These businesses should obviously pay day care costs themselves.

Beyond the aid to businesses, the benefits of day care in poor communities become more abstract. Local and federal officials can claim to be "removing people from the welfare rolls and putting them on the payrolls" as the President demands. Although this shift represents a real social gain chiefly in the case of men rather than mothers, such pertinent distinctions are no longer in fashion. So Senator Mondale's program may make the ill-conceived Nixon "workfare" effort look better.

There is a more menacing implication, however, in day care for the poor. If facilities are indeed established widely, the program can enable government for the first time not merely to encourage but to force welfare mothers to work. A program seen by its proponents as a source of options for liberated women may thus mean compulsory labor for indigent mothers. These mothers in many cases find as much joy and fulfillment in raising their children as the upper-class women find in leaving theirs. Poor women should perhaps be allowed the options of motherhood.

The danger of draft labor is not mere speculation. The federal government's WIN program, ostensibly a job training and day care effort, is already being used to force welfare mothers to work.[24] In addition, all across the country state legislatures are "cracking down" on welfare recipients.[25] The conservatives who want to force them to work, however, are usually unwilling to finance adequate day-care facilities for their children. Ironically enough, therefore, it is the women's movement and its liberal allies who may open the way for a truly repressive new assault on the options of poor women.

Nonetheless, the financial and ideological gains for upper-class feminists are more than sufficient to blind them to the effect on the poor. For the professional woman, day care subsidies are pure gravy. In many instances, she would just pay for the service out of her salary if the government did not provide it. For women in lower salary brackets, free day care may make the difference between keeping a job (and an upper-class standard of living) or staying home and depending on a husband's middle-class pay. For a certain number of unmarried or widowed mothers, day care will mean the difference between going on welfare or not.

No doubt many other specific families will benefit from the program, including many lower-middle-class couples who avoid poverty by having two breadwinners. Particularly poignant among the possible beneficiaries are the couples who work around the clock, alternating eight-hour shifts in order to assure the presence of someone in the house. Day care would give them a fuller married life by allowing them to take simultaneous jobs and thus see—and sleep with—each other more often.[26] The possible uses of a universal day-care program are indeed multifarious, impinging on almost every family. Usage, moreover, might be greater even than current demand, since the free public facilities will relieve couples of the need to find the informal and private accommodations that comprise the chief day-care program today.

But, in general, the chief gainers will be educated, young, middle- and upper-class couples with two breadwinners and a liberationist philosophy, for the women who are pursuing the most potentially remunerative careers tend to be married to similarly qualified men. The day care program allows them to inflict much of the cost of their liberation on less affluent families who do not agree with them on the relative priorities of motherhood and career. These taxpaying couples with one income and no use for public day care will have to contribute to the day care costs of families with two incomes.

This ideological insult is compounded by a more damaging financial and psychological injury. The upwardly mobile breadwinner will face a labor market contracted by the entry of large numbers of educated women. Benefiting from good connections and qualifications and relieved by liberation and day care of the usual career inhibitions, these women will become deadly serious competitors with him for the relatively few top-level jobs open in every field. The presence of female rivals, moreover, will undermine the sexual constitution of lower-level work that otherwise might offer a perfectly acceptable livelihood. These jobs will now become sexually erosive, although in the past they would have affirmed him in a realm of men. Because at long last the seventies are bringing large numbers of young blacks into the career contest, the federally aided presence of upper-class white women becomes racially as well as sexually invidious.

Irving Kristol has written that "the unintended effects of social policy are usually both more important and less agreeable than the intended effects." [27] Many of the advocates of day care imagine that they are merely providing "options" for beleaguered mothers and preschool training for disadvantaged children. Their intentions are generally good. Yet our current problems can virtually be defined as the gap between the purposes and the effects of our previous policies. The people whose good intentions produced AFDC, public housing, rent control, the interstate highway system, and the minimum wage did not expect to pave an asphalt jungle. They did not anticipate, as the fruit of their efforts, the Detroit riots, or the crime-ridden Pruitt Igo Housing Development in St. Louis, or a 50 percent youth unemployment rate in Harlem. The men who formulated counterinsurgency warfare as an inviting course for American policy—and romanticized the Green Berets as its protagonists—did not foresee B-52s raining bombs on North Vietnamese hospitals, or expect to estrange a whole generation of young people from their nation's politics. The intentions and emotions and high expectations of the day care movement are typical of all efforts for social betterment. They have very little to do with the real nature of the program or its probable impact on the society.

The proposal for universal day care is more portentous than any of our previous social initiatives and more likely to produce acute and unexpected consequences. This is because its impact will be ubiquitous rather than restricted to one class or group in the society, and because the cost will be immense and entails forgoing other more suitable programs. In addition, the proposed system would be an important instrument of a powerful, crude, and naïve ideology of social transformation. It will deeply and directly attack the sexual constitution in the time of its most acute vulnerability. Yet the program has not been examined at all in these terms. In all the thousands of pages of congressional testimony, there is not a single coherent analysis of the broad social impact of the proposal.

The system is to be essentially free to all. In a society largely governed by economic motives, such a program acquires an enormous public authority. Just as a college education becomes increasingly indispensable as the government makes it more cheaply available, so public day care will become a crucial part of our lives. In fact, to a family with two children, free day care will be worth over $5,000 a year, approximately as much as an unsubsidized year at college for two students. Just as qualified students find it increasingly difficult to renounce a subsidized college education, so women will find it hard to reject "child development." The mother who does will be subject to the same kind of moral pressure that is exerted on graduating high school students. It will seem somehow culpable to reject a service so immensely valuable.

Of course, many mothers will reject it anyway. But throughout the society this program will impose a serious pressure on every woman who is disinclined to continue at work after the birth of her offspring. Until recently most social and economic pressures have favored motherhood as a rewarding profession in itself. The day care program, however, swinging the heavy club of free money, will tell every young mother that the government wants her to remain on the job. In addition, many husbands will find it difficult to maintain their chivalric convictions in the face of so strong a financial dictate. For there is an enormous difference between day care as an option, which one can purchase if one can or will, and day care removed from the calculus of scarce resources within which most of our choices are made.

Subsidized day care is not a neutral program, even-handedly extending options of motherhood and job. Rather it is a massive $20 billion federal endorsement of one option: the uninterrupted career. Such a program will inevitably have vast consequences over time. It is not comparable to a temporary wartime effort, like the U.S. Lanham Act required by the absence of men; or Soviet child-care systems, which were necessitated by the loss of some 20 million young males before and during World War II.[28] Both Soviet and Eastern European programs are under attack and retrenchment today and Communist day-care experts are mystified by what seems to them a regression by the United States.[29] The system in Sweden is as yet neither universal nor comprehensive, and is subject to significant fees.[30]

In any case, the universal day-care scheme reaches the United States not at a time of labor shortage but of potential surplus. It is accompanied not by rhetoric of patriotic expediency, but by a revolutionary ideology, designed to reorder the foundations of our sexuality. It brings to programmatic climax all the trends in American life destructive to the family. By further subverting the male role as provider—depriving it of its special or sexually distinctive character—the program attacks one of the foundations of familial unity. It thus promotes a further male flight from marriage, and into the short circuits of untempered male sexuality.

Beyond the impact on the male, however, is the effect on the woman. One sees emerging, for the first time in human history, a matriarchy without mothers. At a time when there is an acute need for qualitative child-rearing—with an active father—the government seems to encourage the bearing of children without full responsibility by either parent. Officials claim that "child development" centers are better than the home.[31] Not only is the father made economically superfluous, the mother is made optional. Her own sexual constitution is significantly attacked.

The AFDC welfare program, which dictated that a man could best support his children by leaving them, is therefore followed with a national day-care system, which says the same to a mother. She can best serve her children by depositing them in public care under a nonsexual "child development act."

This prospect is no triumph for women, for it releases males from the civilizing constraints of female sexuality. But it is a victory for the feminists, particularly the upper-class women pursuing careers. For them it means government ratification of their liberated life styles. They can imagine that their "interesting," "meaningful" careers are not what they are—special advantages of wealth and position—but "options" available to women throughout the society. While enjoying the privileges of affluence, the feminists can even fantasize they are leading an egalitarian social revolution.

They need not recognize that poor women are being manumitted not to plush offices but to mops and switchboards; or that the program imposes severe strains on millions of men and women inclined to follow the traditional pattern; or that the feminist emancipation entails the sexual impoverishment of the entire society. Instead they can hold firm their dissident and revolutionary credentials.

In effect, universal day care seems to remove from the feminists the moral burden of privilege. It exempts them from the need to see their profound dependence on capitalist prosperity. While they enjoy a uniquely advantageous position in the world economy and society, they can proclaim their identity with the oppressed.

The final irony is that they may be right, for in a sense, they *are* oppressed. But they are oppressed chiefly by the very decline of familial sexuality that the feminists wish to hasten. Without knowing it, these women are discovering a paramount fact of modernity: The material and sensual rewards of modern society are meager compensation indeed when one loses the ability for profound fulfillment of biological sexuality.

Supporting Families

Writing in the 1930s, Edwin Wight Bakke described the sexual constitution of welfare and its impact on white families. "Consider that the check normally goes to the woman and is often accompanied by female social workers. The man, already suffering from his failure as provider, is further demoralized by becoming dependent on two women, one of them a stranger. He is reduced to an errand boy to and from the welfare office." [1]

Nothing in this picture had changed very much forty years later, except that the man was less often found in the home. Welfare still erodes the sexual constitution of society. Yet those few feminists who concern themselves seriously with the plight of the poor demand a steady expansion of welfare payments, to the point that every citizen would receive an adequate income regardless of familial role or employment. George McGovern's famous elastic $1,000 bill exemplified their approach, as do the various guaranteed annual income plans that have been adduced from time to time by Robert Theobold and others.[2] Even liberals who recognize the budgetary and political realities believe in the desirability of ever larger grants. Few perceive that every increase in payments under current and proposed formulas may relieve immediate distress only at the cost of intensifying future poverty. A durable escape from need will almost always require a reorientation of psychology: the submission of males to female sexual patterns. Crucial to this process is the very commitment to long-term work that welfare destroys.

The feminist failure to understand the role of work is easy to explain. The women refuse to acknowledge that work plays a different and more important role in male than in female psychology. They cannot recognize that while women may work because they have to—or because the job is "interesting" and "meaningful"—men usually work to validate their very identities as males.

Poor women without jobs can find sexual affirmation in the bearing and raising of their children. Welfare affronts them chiefly because of its inadequacy. But it is the relative *adequacy* of welfare that affronts poor males. Even if the amounts are relatively meager, they suffice to displace the man as provider and profoundly damage his sense of manhood. He leaves and pursues it elsewhere, in the usual ways.

The sexual constitution of welfare is particularly disastrous for young men. It tells them money is a bequest for women rather than the earnings of men. It indirectly deprives them of the example of a male provider in the home. In conjunction with the absence of jobs and apprenticeships for youth, it discourages the early acquisition of work habits and employment records. Worst of all, the welfare system gives the impression that work is optional for men, to be pursued only for brief periods, when sufficiently remunerative or interesting. This pattern may be acceptable for women. But without long-term work commitments—whether interesting or not—men are doomed to lives of poverty and crime, and to exile from the sexual constitution. Anyone, or any program, that gives a different impression is profoundly destructive to both men and society—and thus to women as well.

Welfare is, of course, necessary. But there is absolutely no way for the society to escape the mandate of providing jobs, apprenticeships, and training for all poor males and promoting the formation and maintenance of families. Enlargement of government payments has the opposite effect. As one young black told Governor Romney, "Welfare is just the way the honky keeps the black man down." [3] He was perfectly right, except he might have added that it keeps plenty of white men down as well, while relieving the consciences of those unwilling to face the real needs of the society.

Thus even the one ostensible virtue of welfare programs—that they progressively distribute money from the wealthy to the poor—is deceptive. For while poverty is real, escape from it is largely a state of mind. Upward mobility usually comes from regular work, integrated in male psychology as part of one's sexual identity. By preventing this state of mind and creating an easy-money psychology, welfare actually retards a long-term redistribution of income in our society. It means that young poor males are likely to remain poor all their lives.

Again, welfare does not have the same impact on women. They suffer in another way, through subjection to the male sexual patterns. Otherwise feminine sexuality is naturally ori-

ented toward the commitments and regularities required in
most modern employment. Most women can receive welfare
without serious damage either to their sexuality or to their
job potential. Any program seriously designed to alleviate
poverty must take these differences into account.

One of the peculiarities of American social policy—remarked by Daniel Patrick Moynihan some years ago—is its
failure to use the most popular device of all: child or family
allowances. This system, consisting of a monthly payment
given to every family for each of its children, exists in various
forms in more than one hundred of the world's countries, including Canada, Britain, France, and Sweden [4] (though Canada is permitting other social programs to supplant it). Most
affluent countries spend a far higher proportion of national
income on family assistance than does the United States. Indeed, every other industrial country maintains a variety of
supports designed to promote marriage and family. France
even has a "single income" allowance available chiefly if the
mother does not work.[5]

The attractions of family allowances are great. In an
administratively simple and automatic way that does not reduce work incentives, they complement other income, reduce
poverty, support families, and promote distributive justice.
They are not now advocated by the women's movement, but
they accord with its professed concern for families.

Many of the virtues of the allowance derive from the
lack of other income sources that increase payments in proportion to family size. Wages, salaries, interest payments,
profits, unemployment benefits, and social security all tend to
be governed by broad economic concerns. They fail to respond
to the acute increase in need entailed by family additions. Not
only do children impose direct new costs for food, clothes,
and housing, but they also may force the mother to leave work
or purchase expensive day care.

As a result, in countries without special family support,
most large families tend to be poor. Children now comprise
about half of all Americans living in poverty and nearly three-
quarters of the indigent in working families. Child allowances,
therefore, tend to complement other income and to reduce
poverty more efficiently than one might expect in so compre-

hensive a program. Simple themselves, they also improve the simplicity of other income systems by relieving them of the need to consider family size.

But perhaps their greatest appeal in the current American predicament—when various means-tested programs interact almost as a conspiracy to dissuade men from work—is that family allowances scarcely affect incentives at all. You get them, in general, no matter how much you earn. Thus family allowances help the man function as provider rather than threaten to usurp him. As much as any welfare program can, they tend to confirm the sexual constitution.

The weaknesses of the program are the converse of its strengths. Administrative simplicity reduces overhead costs, but also diminishes responsiveness to the varied problems of poverty. Support for children is an investment in the future, but it is also regarded—quite erroneously according to the evidence—as a stimulus for population growth.[6] Universality means ease of distribution and obviates the work incentive problem. But it also means that rich people benefit and raise the total cost in a politically embarrassing way. For example, a usual proposal for the United States, $40 a month per child, would cost some $34 billion, four-fifths of which would go to the technically non-poor; and unless adjusted, about 20 percent would go to the relatively wealthy.

Many people are thus attracted to programs like the negative income tax, which more efficiently and exclusively helps the poor. If a device to cover family size is included— perhaps some kind of reverse child exemption—such a program could be made to correspond almost exactly with the incidence of poverty (give or take criminal earnings, domestic labor, unreported capital gains, and other anomalies). The Internal Revenue Service (IRS) would simply set a minimum income level and impose a tax on every family above it while giving a payment, a "negative tax," to every family below it, with an adjustment according to the number of children. It should be noted that the payments for children represent a significant move away from the kind of pure system originally advocated by Milton Friedman and toward a family allowance concept. But a negative income tax minus a child adjustment factor could not in fact eliminate poverty in large families without necessitating payments so large that the attractions of efficiency and responsiveness would be lost.

For the last several years American social thinkers, often led by Moynihan, have been vacillating between these two approaches and seeking a synthesis between them. Various teams of administrators in the Department of Health, Education, and Welfare—and legislative technicians on the Hill— have worked out a number of detailed schemes. Motivated to a great extent by a concern for the 50 percent of the poor with full-time jobs who were ineligible for public assistance, Moynihan began by strongly and cogently advocating a program of family allowances. But upon discovering the extent of political resistance, he too joined the search for a compromise. By the time of his appointment to the Nixon Administration, he was urging adoption of a program of income supports strongly suggestive of a modified negative income tax. HEW officials were arriving at a similar position. The growing public umbrage toward AFDC—its rolls rising at a time of prosperity— created the political opportunity for welfare reform. The Nixon Administration moved in with the Family Assistance Plan (FAP or "workfare").

Great emphasis was placed on the potential effectiveness of the program in giving the poor incentives to work and the working poor incentives to keep working. The final version in 1972 gave an outright grant of $2,400 in regular payments to a family of four with earnings totaling less than $720. Two-thirds of any earnings above that amount would be applied against the $2,400 grant, reducing it by two dollars for every three dollars earned. This two-thirds (66⅔ percent) figure is called the marginal tax rate. In other proposals, the marginal tax rate was set at 50 percent, meaning the recipient could keep one half of what he earned. This plan brought the total cost of the program to $7 billion. Also involved in the HEW computations were various proposals for "forgiveness" of social security taxes and for total exemption from marginal taxes of the first $1,000 of earnings. Such benefits, needless to say, increased the costs and raised the cut-off point. But all such changes occurred later, after the bill was before the Congress.

As we know, FAP foundered. Although Ways and Means

Committee Chairman Wilbur Mills ushered it briskly through the House of Representatives—as if it were a guest from the White House too important to stay for interviews—the program stalled in the Senate. HEW Secretary Robert Finch got a going-over from the Senate Finance Committee; and by the time his successor Elliot Richardson appeared with a new endorsement from the President and spruced up statistics, the program was in trouble from all sides.

Liberals wanted more work incentives, conservatives more coercion, and welfare mothers more money. Some experts, like Frances Fox Piven, looked at the rising AFDC payments and the diminishing FAP prospects and concluded that the existing system was not so bad after all. Or it was so bad that it was good. She hoped the recipients, suing for their "rights," would keep getting more money until the system collapsed and we could start over.[7] Perhaps the key man in the entire debate, however—at least according to popular analysis—was the President. He kept averring his support and then letting some Administration conservative deny it.

It would seem, however, that we must ultimately conclude the real fault was in the program itself. Although it was far better than AFDC or the McGovern $1,000 bill, FAP had a fatal flaw, and wily Russell Long found it. The problem was not the President, or Finch, or Richardson; the problem was work incentives. A program introduced as "work-fare"—a welfare reform designed to get people "off the welfare rolls and onto the payrolls"—should at least have better work incentives than does AFDC. But as Russell Long charged, and as Jodie Allen of the Urban Institute demonstrated,[8] FAP did not. Although AFDC had a nominally high marginal tax rate of 60 percent, in practice this figure was drastically reduced by a $1,000 earnings exemption, a social security tax forgiveness, and a host of interpretive loopholes, applied loosely by social workers under the pressures of Welfare Rights activists. Without work incentives better than AFDC, workfare began to look very much like just another, more expensive, version of welfare, extending its tentacles over an even larger number of recipients and imposing new job disincentives on the working poor. If it passed, so it appeared, poor people now with permanent jobs could do better by leaving them, perhaps picking up unreported earnings on the side.

Somehow HEW officials were taken by surprise. Although they were well aware of the problems, they seemed to hope that no one else would understand them. Pressured on the work incentives issue, they began to talk about the huge number of people the program would lift from poverty. Moynihan also seemed to shift ground. Rather than emphasizing work incentives—"We all would like higher ones"—he stressed the high degree of correspondence between FAP's coverage and the real incidence of poverty. "Hundreds of thousands of Indians, migrant workers and Southern sharecroppers will have their incomes doubled and tripled over night." [9] He also maintained, plausibly, that the benefits to the working poor would help keep families together by supporting the man's performance as provider.

But by this time Russell Long had won. Although FAP was such an improvement over AFDC that it should have passed, one can argue that its defeat was no great loss. The years of attempted compromise between the negative income tax and family allowance concepts had failed to produce a single really satisfactory synthesis. One doubts, moreover, that a satisfactory compromise is possible within the context of our current social policy.

All the debate about work incentives, all the statistical manipulation of marginal tax rates, appears rather frivolous beside the overwhelming disincentives actually faced by the poor. Welfare does not operate alone. It works in conjunction with a group of other social programs based on means tests that impose their own marginal taxes on the earnings of the poor. Medicaid, for example, is worth an average of almost $1,000 to impoverished families. [10] But if their incomes should inch above the poverty level, it vanishes. Similarly, public housing, for those who can get it, is worth at least as much. But if one's income rises too high, one's rent goes up or one is evicted from the project. Food stamps also are based on need, and the program has been greatly expanded by Congress. Graduated housing allowances are now being contemplated as an answer to our housing imbroglio. [11] They will add still more to the disincentives. Moynihan correctly observes that few poor families can parlay all these benefits—"It's like going to the race track and winning all the races; it just doesn't happen very often." [12] Nonetheless, Medicaid and food stamps are a daily double in the lives of millions, and public housing expands annually in various forms. Against this array of rewards to the nonworking poor, the "marginal" work incentives in a program like FAP become nearly irrelevant.

In designing new social approaches, first of all we must decide exactly what we want them to do. What we should want them to do is in essence what Daniel Moynihan had in mind in 1964 when he wrote the Moynihan report and began considering the issue of child allowances. We should want to restore work and family as instruments of male socialization among the poor. We should try to establish the conditions in which large numbers of families can stay together and cultivate the motivations and disciplines of upward mobility. This is already happening—despite all the obstacles—among millions of poor people today, black and white. It is even happening among those most disadvantaged of blacks who turn to the Black Muslims. [13] It is happening among the hundreds of thousands of young black couples from indigent backgrounds who are now earning as much or more than their white counterparts. [14] It is happening among hundreds of thousands of Chinese and Italians and Puerto Ricans, from equally poor families, who manage to resist the myth of easy money, the government blandishments of matriarchy, and the short-circuit economics of the unsocialized male. But these processes of social progress are leaving millions behind in the familial ruts of stagnation. To overcome the antifamily pressures, we must deliberately work to restore the sexual constitution.

Viewed from this perspective, the dilemma of FAP and child allowances becomes clearer. We must abandon the idea of completely eliminating poverty by distributing money to the poor, in accordance with formulas artfully designed to repress costs and enhance work incentives. There is no way it can be done. Welfare reform cannot eliminate poverty because as it approaches an "adequate" level, it necessarily subverts the male role as provider and promotes family disintegration. Family breakdown in turn prohibits emergence from dependency. With the male gone, the woman gets the money, begets the children, and becomes a financially unmarriageable burden on the state. If welfare is high enough, she may be technically unpoor. But her family is an instrument for the perpetuation of poverty, and she no longer seriously attempts the socialization of males. She can not afford to.

The negative income tax idea and most of its derivatives are falsely conceived. They are based on a static and statistical conception of poverty, as a problem of individuals lacking money rather than families lacking providers and men lacking both families and jobs. There is no alternative to integrating the poor into the larger society. One part of such an effort should be the family allowance, as universally available as possible. As Moynihan put it, such a program can be a "unity" that brings the society, and the liberal coalition, together.

Large middle-class families experience intense strain raising their children to meet community standards. Every father who sees a colleague thrive on a smaller paycheck because he has fewer children—or no family at all—must feel a pang of resentment. Every mother who finds that because of her husband's inadequacy as a provider, she must stint on the children she loves is to some extent embittered. And these qualms and frustrations can cumulatively poison the sexual constitution of a whole society—can make motherhood seem a "baby trap" and fatherhood a treadmill. For poverty is to a great extent relative—relative to others in one's community, to others of one's sex and of the opposite sex. Family allowances will help all families. It will reduce what a poor mother loses by marrying and it will reduce male jealousies toward the men who maintain their own masculine circuitry.

At this point it will be anticlimactic to observe that family allowances themselves will be too expensive unless they are phased out at high incomes. Here enters another "marginal tax rate" problem (although at a financial level that will affect only people who have already "made it"). In addition those who have endured the endless statistical juggling of FAP will be wearied to learn that a family allowance program will admit of enormous variations; there are more than 100 in existence already in various countries. But when we overcome the siren lure of the statistical poverty gap, we can face the real problems. We must get over the idea that with just $16 billion artfully distributed in a negative income tax, poverty could be abolished. Then we can devise more promising approaches, without too much concern that some people will not be directly covered by each plan. Then we can realistically devise a family allowance that performs the functions a family allowance can, but no more. Then we can try to create an environment in which families can durably escape from poverty.

Among the devices useful in reducing the cost of allowances is to make them taxable and substitute them for the current child exemptions. Or it may be easiest just to cut them off flatly at $18,000 or some such figure. In any case, they will be expensive, as expensive as day care, for example. But if we want to spend $20 billion, we might as well make sure it does good. The financial possibilities, as well as various schemes for cheaper programs, are well described in Harvey Braser's contribution to *Children's Allowances and the Economic Welfare of Children*.[15] This book also contains valuable analyses of programs in other countries. Although some of the statistics are dated, it is the best currently available study of the problem, and it presents powerful evidence that the allowances do not affect the birthrate (even when adopted for the purpose).[16]

Family allowances are an extraordinarily flexible instrument. In New Zealand, at the appropriate time a family can acquire in a lump sum—for the purchase or renovation of housing—the total allowance due to a child from that date to the age of 16. More fundamentally, in intact families the allowance can be assigned to the man (to encourage his paternal role), or to the woman (to help ensure that the money goes to the children). It can be used to defray some child care expenses. It can be adjusted to raise benefits if the male is present. It can be reduced, as in the French "single income" device, if both partners work. It can be diminished for later children, on the grounds that the marginal cost goes down. Or it can be increased for the first two, because it is then that the mother has to leave work.

All these adjustments, and many more, are used in various countries. It is probably best, in our current predicament, to use such devices as much as possible to keep the man in the home. But they will have this effect to some extent under all existing schemes. As important, the allowances can help keep mothers in the home, rather than out pursuing boring work that hardly pays for day care. And although no program alone can abolish poverty, this one can greatly alleviate it in the places where money itself can do the most good, particularly in those vulnerable families headed by a male who works full time but still cannot lift his children from privation.

Regardless of child allowances, however, restoration of the sexual constitution will depend on the creation of jobs, particularly for young men. Liberated life-styles, leisure, creativity, fashionable rebellion, transcendence of competition —all the displays of "consciousness III"—are upper-class indulgences, which will succeed in greening only the eyes of the poor. Only a small number of Americans can escape scarcity and competition. No publicly guaranteed income that will be fiscally possible for decades to come can satisfy the rest. They can only be demoralized, and demoralization of potential competitors almost seems the purpose of much upper-class ideology. As the new generation of ambitious middle-class youths approaches the citadels of affluence, the new Brahmins turn up the music and cry, "Let them smoke pot."

The Liberated Job Disaster

All their interest in job opportunities for
highly qualified women is basically counterproductive.
What will happen is that providing jobs for these women will
create a squeeze at the bottom. Those who suffer
most will be the working men, who, under the present system,
have enormous family responsibilities and who will
be pushed out of work. That, unfortunately, will be the
result of abolishing discrimination against females.

Germaine Greer

. . . The basic theme of the initiatory cult . . . is that women, by virtue of their ability to make children, hold the secrets of life. Men's role is uncertain, undefined, and perhaps unnecessary. By a great effort man has hit upon a method of compensating himself for his basic inferiority. Equipped with various mysterious noise-making instruments, whose potency rests upon their actual form's being unknown to those who hear the sounds—that is, the women and children must never know that they are really bamboo flutes, or hollow logs, or bits of elliptoid wood whirled on strings—they can get the male children away from the women, brand them as incomplete, and themselves turn boys into men. Women, it is true, make human beings, but only men can make men. Sometimes more overtly, sometimes less, these imitations of birth go on, as the initiates are swallowed by the crocodile that represents the men's group and come out new-born at the other end; as they are housed in wombs, or fed on blood, fattened, hand-fed, and tended by male "mothers." Behind the cult lies the myth that in some way all of this was stolen from the women; sometimes women were killed to get it. Men owe their manhood to a theft and a theatrical mime, which would fall to the ground in a moment as mere dust and ashes if its true constituents were known. A shaky structure, protected by endless taboos and precautions, . . . it survives only as long as every one keeps the rules. Iatmul men who see their whole social order threatened by the coming of the European threaten in tearful rage to complete the ruin by showing the flutes to the women, and the missionary who shows the flutes to the women has broken the culture successfully . . . To the Occidental, bred in a society that has exalted the achievements of men and depreciated the role of women, all this seems far-fetched, perhaps the more far-fetched when he realizes that the men who depend for their sense of manhood on a phantasy structure of bamboo flutes, played within leaf hedges imitating man-made wombs, are not peaceful shepherds, but bold and fierce head-hunters, men often six feet tall, well set-up, and capable of magnificent anger . . .[1]

MARGARET MEAD

It is in writing about jobs that the liberationists become most fanciful. It seems that college girls now attach to careers the same romantic reveries previously attached to beloved young men. "How meaningful," "how socially conscious," "how revolutionary," "how importantly mysterious," "how gratifying" seems the world of work when encountered in the essays of the younger feminists.

Of course, men have long encouraged these illusions. The young college males with whom these women consort all expect to perform great deeds in the world of careers; and the men of the older generation—the girls' fathers and uncles—seem to work nearly as hard in mystifying and consecrating their jobs as they do in performing them. It is almost the same pattern that Margaret Mead found in her four New Guinea tribes: the men all performed secret initiation rites, conducted with rather modest and mundane devices—bamboo pipes, drums, knives, and masks—and consisting of various bloody acts of sexual mortification, symbolic procreation, hierarchical devotion, and sham contest. All the activities gained their magical authority chiefly from the exclusion of women. In fact, these rites usually represented a rather absurd effort by the males to simulate the awesome female achievement of childbearing and to compensate for their own organic feckless-ness. When missionaries moved in with the attitudes of modernity and displayed the pipes and other devices to the women, the whole system would collapse. Some of the men would wander off to be eaten by a neighboring tribe. Others would sulk. But the rituals would end.[2]

In civilized, utilitarian societies—where an animist view of the world gives way to science and function—the men try to give their ceremonies a useful purpose, often with great success. But in essence they are the same old rites, similarly devoted to incorporating young males and compensating for male sexual limitations, and similarly vulnerable to exorcism by females: "Would you believe, at their Monday conference, they just collect bets on the football games?" "Look at the whiskey flask in the Senator's closet." "You know, corporate law is kind of simple, after all." "Look at the pornography in the dean's desk." "That secretary near the door is really much smarter than the editor." But the men do their best to preserve the pretenses of their work, and sometimes they can for a while—from their sons and daughters. And though their wives and secretaries usually catch on pretty soon, it is best they do not rub it in.

Now, the daughters have grown up. Having gone to school with males from kindergarten through graduate study— and having often outperformed them—they naturally want to move on with them into the professional world. Having enjoyed considerable sexual activity they know their attraction to men. And aware that they probably can have children when they want—or forgo them when they wish—they enter the offices of the land without the male need to enact a sexual identity. They don't realize, therefore, that for men the only immutable fact is the burden to perform, and that their offices, and their jobs, are a prime arena of sexual validation.

They come as young men and are tested for competence and loyalty in the enactment of the rites; they compete with their fellows in elaborately sublimated struggles; and they are finally admitted to the portentous banalities of power. The job is "meaningful" to them if it is sexually affirmative, and if it is sufficiently remunerative to finance a provider's role. The ceremonial trappings, the ritualized competitions, are more important to the men than are the corporate or bureaucratic purposes. Few things are as frightening as having the ceremonies suspended. For then, the men would have to compete in a raw and open struggle for which civilized society little prepares them.

The college girls arrive on the scene, full of high purpose, and for a while they enjoy the accessory role they are given. But as time passes, so do the gratifications of proximity. Accustomed to full participation, they not only want to listen to the bamboo pipes; they want to see and play them. They not only wish to attend the conference; they want to be heard respectfully when they speak. They wonder why they are resented.

It is at this point they discover that the office is not really so devoted to high purpose as it pretends to be. Their male colleagues seem distressingly obsessive and competitive, oddly concerned with trivial symbols of rank. Some of the bosses, from whom these women with all their refinement and degrees, are expected to take orders, are the kind of men they have been taught to disdain. What these men seem to have is a fanatical commitment to their own advancement, all very gauche, and they compound their insults with sexual innuendo.

Why, the women ask, can't we be sensible and work together cooperatively as "human beings," and just get the job done? Why all this worry about hierarchical symbols, about money and status and competition? The reason is that the job is often as dull as dishwater and diapers—and the struggle as ugly as a cockfight—if the ceremonial disguises are not maintained. Most of the men are not only working to perform a task; they are fighting for their lives and the competition is deadly real. If they have to choose between their own sexual identities and the ostensible purposes of the work, the contest is not even close. The whole complex of rites and symbols in the working world is designed to avoid the conflict, to allow men to affirm their manhood in the course of productive labor. When the rites and symbols are exorcised, the masculine affirmations removed, and only the work and struggle remains—in all its pedestrian relentlessness—the men are reduced to functionaries in front of their women. They must find their masculinity elsewhere. In modern society there are few places to go.

If this scheme seems hopelessly melodramatic and unreal to many, it is because the pattern has been elaborately camouflaged. At the highest levels the rituals have reached a degree of refinement and elegance that all but conceal their nature even from the votaries themselves. Many men, unconsciously believing the pretensions of male superiority and the importance of the charade, fail to recognize the male predicament at all. Others have so easily attained their manhood—feel so invulnerable to female competition—that they cannot appreciate the struggle going on below them. Thus a radical sociologist like Frank Reissman—from three different prestigious professional offices—can happily acclaim the virtues of cooperation.[3] Thus the editor in chief at Simon and Schuster can write a book in favor of women's liberation and the radical reordering of office relationships.[4] Thus John Kenneth Galbraith—from his eminence of 6 feet 8 inches and his similarly elevated prestige—finds all the male exclusiveness in the business and professions just too silly for words.[5] He makes similarly silly proposals for change. But the realities are not thereby abolished.

Consider that in the United States today, conservatively estimated, there are about 11 million unemployed males who would work if suitable opportunities were presented them.[6] Only 3 million are acknowledged by the Labor Department but the rest are easily found if one scrutinizes the statistics. Some 3 million are cited but excluded from the totals because they have given up looking for work. An additional 1.5 million men in their prime, between the ages of 25 and 54, have dropped out so completely they aren't even accounted for. But it is reasonable to speculate that .5 million of these would work if they could. Some 1.5 million more males under 64 were also unlisted, but a good many of them were forced into early retirement; perhaps 1 million would work if possible. Some 1.5 million students, at the very least, would take jobs if suitable ones were available. At least 3 million others are in dead-end training programs, or on ghetto streets, or listed as unemployable to qualify for welfare, or in seasonal labor or on strike, or so underemployed that their inclusion in the rolls is a cosmetic deceit.

The figure of 11 million, as may be deduced from several scrupulous accounts, is modest indeed.[7] Total unemployment, including women who would like jobs and teenagers who desperately need them, is estimated at 25 million. This figure, it should be stressed, does not represent the full mobilizable manpower of the country. If everyone worked, including some people over 65 and some of the disabled, the figure could be higher still. But 11 million males is a reasonable estimate of the number now unhappily out of work. There are an additional 3 or 4 million deliberately or irretrievably out of the work force.[8]

Many readers will be acutely conscious that unemployment reaches into the ranks of the educated. Doctoral degrees in history, sociology, modern languages, economics, even education, provide no assurance at all of academic jobs. Over 5 percent of young scientists and engineers are unemployed and their average desuetude lasts seven months. The market for elementary and secondary school teachers is glutted. Incredibly, there may even be an excess of physicians toward the end of the decade.[9]

The problem will not be readily overcome. Though demand for educated manpower is likely to remain relatively even for the rest of the 1970s, the supply will soar. According to figures assembled by labor economist Eli Ginzberg, the labor force as a whole will increase by 20 percent between 1968 and 1980. But the number of college graduates will rise by 50 percent, the number of master's degrees will double, and the number of doctorates will more than double. The proportion of educated persons seeking jobs, moreover, will be higher than ever before. Peter Drucker has estimated that every new job created entails some $15,000 in new capital investment, and jobs for the educated cost more. He calculates that even at present ratios of male and female employment, the economy will have to produce 40 percent more jobs every year than it has during the last decade.[10]

If there are relatively few available jobs of any description, the number of good or "meaningful" jobs is still fewer. Only a small minority of the people can hold them. But they have psychological importance to millions more. They serve as goals, if not for this generation, for their children. To millions of people, they mean access to a comfortable life—of the sort taken for granted by almost all U.S. students at prestigious colleges, including the countercultural dilettantes, and by almost all middle-class women when they consider a family. Such jobs mean a house, car, some travel, some cultural activities, music and movies, diversions and edifications for the children. They are the sort of work that college graduates expect to acquire relatively soon after graduation and less fortunate Americans expect to earn over the years. The competition is very difficult for all who cannot transcend it and there are lots of losers, but most men with education and resolve ultimately succeed.

It is inalterably a competition in scarcity, however, and in proportion to the numbers of contestants and the material expectations of most of them, the scarcity will be growing more, not less, acute for at least the next decade. Even if economic growth soars, moreover, the kinds of lives that virtually all Americans anticipate—and come to demand when forced to maintain a family—require diligent competitive effort over a lifetime. Few dropouts or dilettantes need apply, although they will, soon enough, as they grow older.

Unless we pursue policies of stunning improvidence, it appears likely that the worst of the crisis will be overcome by the 1980s.[11] Until then, large numbers of educated males will be festering in jobs they regard as below their contempt or will drop out of the labor force altogether. Unemployed males at any level pose a grievous social problem. Unable to find their manhood in the usual role as provider—their marital and procreative possibilities curbed—they will try to fulfill themselves in other ways. The United States, like underdeveloped countries today, will find itself with a surplus of dissident intellectuals, seeking alliances with other aggrieved groups for acts of self-destructive male validation.

Though radicals might find this prospect exhilarating, in fact it consists of millions of blighted lives. Not only will the intellectuals suffer, but by taking thousands of jobs that would ordinarily be available to less qualified men, they extend the tragedy throughout the work force—to men with large families, to blacks just overcoming the barriers of discrimination, to veterans recovering from an excruciating war, to ex-convicts precariously clinging to legitimacy, to teen-agers yet to develop the work habits they will need for a lifetime.

The prospects are grim in mere statistical terms. But they are made incalculably dangerous by the disintegration of the sexual constitution. At other times the persistence of the family and the ties of kinship and marriage—and the affirmations of religion—have provided a safety net below the struggles of the marketplace. Now the relationship is reversed. Today millions of young Americans of both sexes are trying to use the marketplace—the world of enterprises and professions—as a net below the struggles of hedonistic sexuality. No longer committed to the search for familial stability, many use sex as an arena of transitory pleasures, and embark on an effort to find meaning in careers. But if the young feminists are now disillusioned with men and love, they have some bitter lessons to learn about jobs. One expects them to learn soon enough, and attempt a qualified return to deeper feminine fulfillments. In the meantime, however, they can wreak terrible damage in our current crises of employment and masculinity.

There are some 30 million women of working age not now holding regular jobs. There are millions more women who work but do not envisage themselves as full contestants with men in the career marketplace. Although there are relatively few jobs for middle-class women in which they can compete with men, work force participation rapidly increases with educational attainment. If millions more educated women enter the work force—and most important, if they get over their emphasis on "credentials" and begin fighting for advancement like men—they will acquire many of the jobs most affirmative of masculinity. Moreover, they will come to be seen as part of the competition for the higher jobs in every area. The entire arena of careers loses its quality of maleness and the struggle will assume the edge of sexual bitterness that already anguishes so many professional women when they find it at work. Many more men will drop out, as they have been in recent years, virtually in proportion to the entry of women seriously into the work force. While female participation has risen to nearly 40 percent, the real male participation rate has sunk from almost 90 to just above 70 percent.[12]

No more than a tiny proportion of these males are upper-class experimenters with gratifying new life styles, or are men happily supported by their wives. Most are males permanently prevented from socialization, pursuing opportunistic and escapist lives. They can be found in the crime rate, among the addicts, in institutions, and on the street.

Their number will inevitably swell as more women enter the career market in male fields. If radical women currently feel compassion for lower-class men in their dreary toil, they should understand that this work will become insufferable if it is done in competition with, or under the direction of, women. If their wives or eligible girls are also approaching the male income levels, the challenge will be extended to home or social relationships. Love and marriage will gravely suffer.

This is a situation never before undergone by males anywhere in the world, except perhaps in a few decaying tribes and in the ghetto. Here we do not have a relatively few exceptional women assuming roles reserved for them; or women temporarily assuming positions where they are needed; or women performing important professional roles in separate areas; or gifted individuals earning their isolated triumphs. Rather we have the prospect of the collective and systematic entrance of millions of women—including many of the most qualified and best-connected in the society— professing a determination to compete in remorseless equality, and calling on the intervention of government to assure their "rights." We have women who decline to withdraw from the work force even for children and who demand heavy day-care subsidies to prevent the usual interruptions. We thus have an all-out attack on the male role as provider and on the masculine rituals of work. We have a prescription for social paralysis and a concerted lapse of male socialization unprecedented in a civilized society.

This trend will be accompanied by increasing class bitterness. As usual the upper classes will be able to adjust to a great extent. They will be able to benefit from double incomes and part-time work, expanded leisure and cultural activity. Many of the males will find new modes of masculine validation in music, athletics, aviation, appropriate physical recreation, sex. These diversions will be insufficient in many cases, and tensions between the sexes will rise in every level of the society. But money can offer many compensations.

These new life styles, however, are almost completely foreclosed to the lower and middle classes. For them any relaxation in their commitment to work, any resort to part-time enterprise, will be disastrous to their careers and to their immediate standards of living. They know that they must work not less, but more, if they are going to succeed. For them the pastoral vision of a couple holding two part-time jobs—chiefly a reverie of academics anyway—is preposterous. Part-time work prohibits reward for the greatest assets of the middle class in competition with the upper class: desire and diligence. As for their wives, the job possibilities are less good than for the upper class, and the man's job has to take precedence.

Middle- and lower-middle-class men value their families deeply, moreover. If asked why they work, they will show you a picture of the wife and kids. For these men, work is "meaningful" almost exclusively because it sustains their role as provider and affords an arena of masculine associations. The higher purposes are of little importance. If the world of work becomes a realm of women, many of these men will leave it and their families as well. The society's underclass of males will steadily expand, and policing it will become the chief concern of the state. The upper class of educated, sexually competitive men and women, meanwhile, will seem more happily situated. But their money will be tall cotton for the psychiatrists. For competition is deadly to love.

In his book, *The Mountain People*, Colin Turnbull has written poignantly about the moral destruction of an African tribe—the Ik—when the processes of male socialization broke down.[13] It had been a hunting and gathering tribe and the men had held a fully affirmative role. They were generous and cooperative with each other, affectionate toward their women, and solicitous toward children. Kinship ties and responsibilities were elaborately maintained.

Then the Uganda government banished them from their hunting area and turned it into a game preserve. The sudden change to a largely agricultural mode of life left the men with no crucial role and the tribe with little food. The result, described in excruciating detail by Turnbull, was a sexual suicide society: the destruction of all family ties, the expiration of compassion and cooperation, and the emergence of a completely predatory and opportunist mode of existence, which was dominated by hatred and contempt for human life and which did not change even when food became plentiful.

Turnbull writes about our society:

"Family, economy, government and religion, the basic categories of social activity and behavior, despite our tinkering, are no longer structured in a way that makes them compatible with each other or with us. . . . At the best they are structured so as to enable the individual to survive as an individual, with as little demand as possible that any vestigial remains of mutual responsibility should be expressed in mutuality of action. It is the world of the individual, as is the world of the Ik.

"The Ik teach us that our much-vaunted human values are not inherent in humanity at all, but are associated only with a particular form of survival called society, and that all, even society itself, are luxuries that can be dispensed with. That does not make them any the less wonderful or desirable, and if man has any greatness it is surely in his ability to maintain these values. . . . But that too involves choice and the Ik teach us that man can lose the will to make it. . . . We pursue those trivial, idiotic technological encumbrances and imagine *them* to be the luxuries that make life worth living, and all the time we are losing our potential for social rather than individual survival, for hating as well as loving, losing perhaps our last chance to enjoy life with all the passion that is our nature and being." [14]

Now, one can easily reject such facile analogies. We are an affluent civilization, the Ik a disintegrating tribe. We, a thriving democracy, can reject any human connection with this twisted and malignant form of human decline. Nonetheless, a mere decade ago the Ik were also thriving, their sexual constitution secure. Even if we assume, as we must, that our degradation would assume a radically different form; even if we maintain that our humanity, intelligence, and social controls would prevent such a moral catabolism; no matter how we define our exemption, such a sudden collapse of human relations should serve as a warning, as we ourselves disrupt the foundations of our sexuality, the source of all our social connections.

Part Three

The Sexes at Bay

The Male Imperative

A man whose cock is soft is not useless,
but he *thinks* he is. . . .
A stiff cock is not all that necessary.

Germaine Greer

The revolutionary members of the women's movement have a more valid position than the moderates. The revolutionaries say that our sexual relationships are fundamental to all our other institutions and activities. If one could profoundly change the relations between the sexes, they contend, one could radically and unrecognizably transform the society.

But because they announce their destination, the radical feminists cannot get anywhere—except to television talk shows and best-seller lists. The moderates, on the other hand, merely profess a desire to improve the relations between the sexes. They want to maintain our society in essentially its present order—with the usual liberal reforms. But the result of their program, if fully adopted, would be revolutionary.

The conservative position—that is to say, the view taken by most liberal males when detached from their moderately feminist women—corresponds with the nonrevolutionary view. These men say, in essence: Let them have their political demands; nothing fundamental will change because men will remain men, and women women. Even if they pursue careers in far greater numbers, the women will want to be sexually submissive, have babies, and be loved by men; and despite a newly titillating aggressiveness on the part of their women, most men will retain their current dominance as initiator, provider, and protector. The changes will all be perfectly manageable.

In the view of many young males, much of the feminist program is reducible to domestic logistics. The man will more often hold the baby (and, on occasion, heroically change its diapers) or baby-sit while the woman attends a political meeting or a consciousness-raising session. The man will more often take out the garbage, wash the dishes, and do other chores around the house.

These young men do not feel threatened at work. Their jobs are fairly secure, and it is exciting to have that pretty blond lawyer on the staff. (Who is she sleeping with now, anyway?) Although they endorse equal pay for women, they almost always make more than their own wives, or are engaged in training or business that promises a superior career. Mention procreation, and they talk about the population explosion. They believe it is just as well that many women indicate uninterest in having children. And they profess delight (somewhat uneasily) with the new female sexual freedom.

The personal experience and expectations of these men are real. But they are living in a dream world. As long as everything goes reasonably right in their lives, the sexual revolution will affect them little. But for most men today, things go wrong. They lose their jobs or their wives (often both together) and find themselves suddenly in an insecure and hostile situation. Then their sexual security vanishes. The aggressiveness of a girl in bed becomes menacing. The competition of women for high-level employment is alarming. For a man in this situation, it becomes impossible to find reassurance from the women he meets on the mediocre job he finally accepts. It turns out that these women are dead serious about their work and know too much about his. If his finances are low, it becomes impossible to take new women out; and somehow when he accepts, more than once or twice, the old friend's offer to pay, her attitude changes.

At this point, his own view of women has undergone a shift. He wants to use them for sexual validation. Intercourse, the only male sex act, looms greater among his priorities. Long-term relationships, though desirable, diminish in attraction. He doesn't pay bills. He drinks a great deal with the boys, watches football on T.V., and enjoys crude jokes about females. When someone challenges him, he wants to fight. He finds himself gravitating toward women he wouldn't have considered before—submissive and intellectually inferior. He turns to his parents for support and is grateful if it is there.

When an upper-middle-class world collapses, it can often be restored. In most cases, a good job will do the trick. When disaster strikes precariously risen middle-class men, however, the damage is more difficult to repair. Many men find themselves outside the social order altogether, following the impulsive and predatory patterns of fallen masculinity. When too many men are subverted, the society itself is jeopardized. The real menace in the mild proposals of the women's movement is that they threaten to expand vastly the numbers of fallen males, while removing the modes of recovery: the supports and consolations of women who clearly need men.

The reason the revolutionaries are right and the moderates revolutionary is that the movement is striking at the Achilles' heel of civilized society: the role of the male. They are correct that it is a cultural contrivance and that it can be destroyed. But they are wrong to suppose that men, shorn of their current schemes of socialization, would mildly accept the new roles provided by the movement. New roles can work only if they come to terms with the sexual inferiority and compensatory aggressiveness of the male, only if they afford a distinctive male identity that accords with the special predicament of male sexuality in civilized society.

Neither the moderates nor the revolutionaries—nor current American institutions, for that matter—provide male roles sufficiently distinctive and affirmative. The feminists of both schools imagine that they can adequately enfranchise men by giving up current female power in sex and family. Although they are unclear on the ways, one can deduce them easily enough. First, women will have fewer children and give men greater responsibilities in nurturing them. Secondly, women will submit to male sexual patterns by making sex more available and less bound to long-term commitments. Thirdly, women will withdraw their claims on male earnings.

Each of these sacrifices, however, has a severe limitation. The new male nurturant role neither really reduces the woman's control of the child nor affirms the man as a male. As desirable as it may be for the man to participate more, the role itself is inexorably female, evinced in every line and softness of her body, face, and voice, and accentuated by her breasts, with all their portent for men. There is no way that early nurture of children will be sexually affirmative for males.

The further female accommodation—the woman's new sexual compliancy and aggressiveness—is initially exciting. But soon it becomes upsetting, and the man is undermined by it. The woman's attitude, which devalues the procreative symbolism of intercourse, encourages the man to abandon the long-term sexual commitments that are the basis of his marriage and his role in civilized society. For if sex is not profoundly important—if the woman treats it as a perfunctory pleasure, a matter of tension and release like unsocialized male eroticism—then the structure of male socialization itself is imperiled. The man is subtly pushed toward the uncivilized patterns that come so naturally to him and that are insistently propagandized in the society.

The third prospective sacrifice by women—abdicating their claim on male earnings—is similarly upsetting. For it reduces the importance of the man's role as provider without replacing it with anything else. Thus the man is again deprived of props for his long-term civilized commitments. The three female offerings may grant the man new powers. But it is not new powers he needs to affirm him in his uncertain role in civilization. What he requires are signs and assurances that women really need his own submission to them, that they are as dependent on his masculinity as he is on their femininity. Women's liberation has an opposite, uncivilizing impact. And the ostensible compensations fail to affirm him as a male, deny the deepest fulfillment of his sexuality, and finally deny him his distinctive role in the family as an economic institution.

If the feminists fail to offer an appropriate male role, however, the emerging American technocracy does hardly better. It provides neither enough jobs and opportunities, nor the right kinds. Even without women moving in and destroying the male mystique of work, the world of employment affords paltry male affirmation as it is. In fact, one of the reasons the female entry poses such a threat is that many jobs as now constituted offer only two masculine uses: association with other men and endowment as provider. The exercise of power, the sense of productivity, the expression of personality are all so restricted in many jobs that men are little affirmed by them.

Even the rituals of hierarchy and promotion—the new office, the name on the desk, greater access to secretaries, or nominal control over a group of men on a work site—no longer have the heft and spirit of similar symbols in smaller institutions. For the bureaucracy looms so far above and reaches so wide that a promotion does not significantly change the psychology of the work experience. There are still men above and below; the secretaries are part of a pool and change confusingly; the assignment is marginally more challenging but in essence the same, structured by impersonal authority above. In general the man must gain his affirmation less from the job than from the provider role it endows.

We are all familiar with the critique of modern organization: the gray-flannel mind, the status seeker, the outer-directed automaton—impersonality, inhuman scale, monotony, alienation. A few men wield huge power, take risks, act decisively, see consequences. For them, work is a supremely masculine exercise.[1] But for many of the others, work is a matter of impotent dependency.

We are also familiar with the litany of alternatives, which is often summed up as nostalgia for the irretrievable, a past of intimate and personal productivity that will never return. Nonetheless, the list of prescriptions is worthy of interest: decentralization of power; revival of small business; new male groups; expansion of ownership; rise in personal craftsmanship; smaller ventures in education; proliferation of personal services; reorganization of industrial work; a multiplication of cultural and informational outlets; expanded political participation; a renewal of religious activity; an increase in specialized entrepreneurship; new modes of young male apprenticeship; new opportunities for the creative use of leisure time; increased spectator and participant athletics.

Although most of these possibilities affect both men and women, all afford special benefits to males in their crisis of sexual identity. They permit men to exercise in civilized society the kind of personal creative power they are organically denied. They give to men an opportunity to conduct activity that is as individual and expressive as management of a home and nurture of children; they make it possible—within the constraints of a utilitarian marketplace—to elaborate the kind of performance found in the initiation rights of primitive tribes: a drama of male creativity.

Our nostalgic list, moreover, is surprisingly open to realization. For the critique of large bureaucracy and organization is in many ways accurate. Although bigness often affords huge efficiencies of scale, valuable accommodations for technology, and flexible resources for financing, it also cultivates a kind of sclerosis. It magnifies wealth but not wit. It requires the emergence of its own antidote: a rise of personality—what William Irwin Thompson calls "the individual as institution." [2] But the man can rarely produce positive individualism without women's help. At present, too few of the male energies are finding such socially beneficial purposes. Rather we find an efflorescence of virtually primitive rites, in which unsocialized males gang together in activity devoid of feminine sexual transcendence.

When masculinity is repressed in schools, assembly lines, and offices, it flares out kaleidoscopically on the streets and in the parks. Sometimes it is violent, but as in much tribal conflict, only the most stylized violence is sought by many of the males. The tens of thousands of male gangs in the cities (there are 300 male groups for every female one) are usually willing to have their "rumbles" broken up by higher authorities before blood is shed. In fact, youth workers often find themselves tacitly colluding with gang leaders in the production and abortion of violent dramaturgy.

Similarly the mock wars of youthful protesters seek the semblance of danger, but not the reality of violence. Tear gas is perfect, because it allows the youth to experience acute physical distress—as if the war is real—only to recover completely 15 minutes later for more telegenic heroics. One can feel as immortal as Steve McQueen. Anyone who saw the guerrilla parties attacking the FBI building during the 1970 March on Washington—the manic gleam in their eyes, the bellicose cries—became aware that for all the high seriousness of the antiwar purpose, the male protests assumed their own momentum as rites of masculinity. The boys were conscious of some connection missing in their passage to manhood.

In this sense, the activities are tragically misunderstood when the police or National Guard takes them as serious combat and fires real guns—or when radical women, in a fury of effort to be accepted in the male groups, start producing and planting real bombs. The activity of these desperadoes closely resembles the pathetic belligerence of marginal males, always ready to fight as a display of manhood.

The virility games assume a more socially positive character in the outburst of pseudocultural expression. Every small town—and urban block—seems to have not one but several rock groups, usually all male, cooperating intimately in the production of music that often shows all the subtlety of a bayonet charge. In its early stages, this music usually seems a raw macho assertion. It finds its perfect complement in the groupies, those pathetic girls who completely abdicate feminine sexuality and glorify the phallus, even to the extent of making plaster replicas.

Music, in fact, offers a rich field of metaphor for our sexual condition. Morbid extremes of macho consciousness can also be found in the music of some female rock stars. Janis Joplin, in all her tragic genius, seemed to proclaim the despair of a woman who has short-circuited her womb. Her deadly adoption of what one might call male sexual rhythms was evident in all her later music. "Get it while you can, there is no tomorrow, it's all one fuckin' day, man," she implores with an urgent whiskey breath of faith.

Soul music tends to be more mature than macho white rock. Here the male expresses an awareness of his exile and declares a profound knowledge of the power of women and the existence of a world where feminine rhythms prevail. Otis Redding, Ray Charles, James Brown, and Wilson Pickett as well as all the great kings of the blues are forever singing of the exile of men from the deepest and most durable levels of sexual experience. "Let Me In," "Open the Door," "Let a Man Come In," "It's a man's world, but it ain't nothin', nothin' without a woman and a girl," "World," "Try a Little Tenderness," "Sitting on the Dock of the Bay," almost all of the great soul classics bespeak a realm in which men and women merge in profound complementary sexuality.

Similarly the great black women from whom Janis learned her music—Bessie Smith, Billie Holiday, and later the Franklin sisters—all expressed what seems a deep feminine consciousness. They were engaged in an effort, however forlorn, to bring men into the world of feminine horizons. Whether defiantly hurling Otis's appeal back to him, "All I Want Is a Little Respect," or singing of departed lovers, all the best female soul-singers, with their full gospel resonances, sang of the complex and poignant realm where men and women join their crucial differences and attain a greater sexuality.

Of course, not all these singers write their own songs, nor does all their music partake of this spirit, even as metaphor. But the deviations have a deviant sound. After all his explorations of real sexual pain, Otis Redding sounds ludicrous trying to render the anthem of the masturbators, "I Can't Get No

Satisfaction" (by the Rolling Stones). And when the soul-singers do sing a pure macho chant, they usually do it with an ironic chuckle; they are being bad boys, while the Doors and the Stones much of the time seem to think that macho violence is the only sexuality there is. In general, the message of soul music is epitomized by Dyke and the Blazers in the fine hit that begins by reciting the crises of the day and goes on to offer the answer in a refrain: "Let a Woman Be a Woman, and Let a Man Be a Man."

The mysterious creativity of male groups reaches its pinnacle in Black American jazz. Although there is the usual canonization of individual leaders—and the immensity of genius —the music is essentially a group phenomenon, in which the competitive solidarity of men is beatified. Here, perhaps, the musical form shows a comprehension of intricate female commitments and suspensions transcending the insistent beat of male desire. As do all great artists, Charles Mingus knows there is a tomorrow, an extended cycle of life, and a possibility of more complex and remote resolutions beyond the next bar. As his book *Beneath the Underdog* clearly suggests, this music, like all great art, exemplifies the necessary convergence of the two sexual principles: male anxiety and energy, and female time and space and transcendence.[3] It is the process that is embodied in the great classical works, as well as in great literature and films; and indispensable to it is the knowledge of extended time—innate in the body of women—that is not "all the same day, man."

Although one can carry such schemes of sexual duality too far, the lesson is that male groups, in fact all men, can attain civilization only by submitting, in one way or another, to female sexuality. A further lesson is that males in groups can find the masculine assurance that allows them to submit: to swim deeply in female time and space before surfacing in the now, redeemed. It is a sexual baptism that does not necessarily come with intercourse. Even homosexuals can achieve it. But it is indispensable to art.

What is necessary for art is also required for all other male enterprises. Only socialized males can usually contribute either to the great corporations and bureaucracies or to the alternative modes of activity arising in modern societies. And only through the maintenance of affirmative male roles can the society assure the long-term sexual patterns on which civilization depends. Thus it is urgently important that this crisis in the nature of work be seriously addressed.

As Sennett and Cobb show in their study of American workers, *The Hidden Wounds of Class*,[4] and as Patricia Cayo Sexton documents in her book on boys,[5] what males most want from their jobs is a sense of active mastery and control. This feeling does not necessarily have to come from organized power over others; in fact, Sennett and Cobb point out that the men particularly admired people, such as doctors, lawyers, and professors, who were seen as performing necessary services for their clients. What the men most abhorred was the sense that their work was controlled from above in ways that made it impossible for them to be themselves and to produce results that they identified as their own. Those findings to some extent confirm the Marxist theory of the alienation of industrial workers, as well as Margaret Mead's thesis that male activity was often devoted to an attempt to duplicate the irreversible personal creativity of women in childbirth.

Neither the assembly line nor the bureaucracy fulfills either of these criteria. Nor do they often afford the further gratification of male camaraderie. What they do achieve for males in many cases is the production of wealth and the extension of leisure. These compensations may be sufficient, if they are granted with some regularity and dependability. But they do not create a society in which the largest human possibilities are often fulfilled for the majority of the people. And they tend to make males so defensive, so unsure of themselves, that long-term submission to women is difficult and detraction of women is pervasive. In producing males who do not respect themselves, such jobs also fail to foster respect for women.

Although corporate and bureaucratic size remains indispensable to modern society—to the creation of the wealth necessary for the solution of most of our problems—we must at the same time afford more men the kind of mastery and autonomy that makes them confident males. This is the core of our sexual crisis. It means as an absolute imperative that jobs be made available to every male who wants one, from the age of 15 on. For younger workers it means an expansion of training programs and apprenticeships. For every man with a productive idea, it means the opening of a reasonable opportunity for financing and managerial advice. And it means, in particular, a special concern at every level of government for the promotion of small business.

Such recommendations have worn very thin over the years. But they have rarely been seriously tried. As Geoffrey Faux and others have shown,[6] the black capitalism program, presented with such fanfare in 1968, has been a sad charade. The Emergency Employment Act has been stymied by civil service and unions in most cities.[7] The minimum wage is raised annually, with little concern for its catastrophic effect on youth employment, particularly in small businesses. (A further benefit of a system of child allowances, incidentally, is that it can remove one of the pressures that leads to continuous and uneconomic increases in the minimum wage.)

The transformation of the United States to a dominantly service economy will present a valuable opportunity to create jobs that are gratifying to men. Many services are highly labor intensive, open to relatively small enterprises, and responsive to new organization. Small businesses, moreover, hire many more people per dollar of investment than do large ones.[8] Government should be alert during this period to foster new entrepreneurs and restrict labor and professional practices that inhibit the responsiveness of new services. The delivery of medical aid, for example, can be facilitated by promoting the use of paramedical personnel. New postal systems can supplement the Post Office Department, if the government is not restrictive. New newspapers and magazines are emerging in almost every major city across the country. They should not be burdened with impossible mail rates and other governmental harassment.[9] The enormous ferment of energy among youth must not be repressed and aborted by the too tenacious and inflexible maintenance of old economic structures.

One area of particularly great importance to the sexual constitution is ownership. In the past, acquisition of house and land has been a prerequisite of marriage and family. The drive to own has thus been directly connected to the sexual drive. John McClaughry, in his fine study, *Expanded Owner-*

ship,[10] has presented a large body of evidence showing the salutary psychological effects of ownership—of homes, land, and business—on a variety of Americans. The benefits are particularly striking in poor communities, where groups of houses purchased by the residents are far better maintained than rented structures. Home ownership, in fact, confers a strong socializing impact on males.

Sennett and Cobb indicate, in addition, that ownership of a small business is still the highest ambition of most workers.[11] Despite the great decrease in small business possibilities in recent years, the notion of owning a store, a service station, even a truck, exerts a powerful attraction that an intelligent capitalist system should not fail to use. Although less successful to date, stock ownership programs may also give workers in otherwise unrewarding jobs a sense of participation in a larger undertaking.

The U.S. economy is at a crucial juncture. It can allow the increasing size of business to crowd out smaller ventures. In league with large governmental bureaucracies and labor establishments, it can create a society in which the natural drives of its males—even their capitalist instincts—are all but stifled. This trend would produce a society consisting of large horizontal classes, identified by qualifications and status— professionals, workers, corporate executives, government bureaucrats—all defending their realms of activity from others, but little interested in the purpose of the enterprise. Or, on the other hand, we can assert as a fundamental goal of our system the opening of vertical opportunities for ownership— of houses, businesses, and other property—thus endowing men with a new sense of masculine identity and reaffirming the sexual constitution.

A more entrepreneurial system, moreover, could help overcome the growing tyranny of credentials. People could be tested by what they can do rather than by how they can fit a prefabricated image of suitability. Blacks could more easily exploit their knowledge of their community to serve it profitably. Thus they could escape to some extent what many regard as the onerous need to adapt to stylistic standards of white society. Small businesses and politics were the chief channels to success for other ethnic minorities that arrived in American cities without the usual credentials. It would be more than unfortunate if as blacks take control over American cities, they find all former patronage jobs protected by civil service and unions, and find small business equally foreclosed. In addition, countercultural ventures could more easily join the establishment if the economy were open to the special talents of the unorthodox. And the economy in general would benefit from the abilities and resources of ever larger proportions of our people.

Finally, of great importance would be the opportunity for women to succeed in ways that create new jobs for others. Talented women find themselves oriented too much toward jobs in services and professions that offer little but money and status. This work is most likely to be surrounded by sexual mystiques and restrictions. But the realm of business offers opportunities for undeniable contributions that little disrupt the sexual constitution. Clothing and artifacts of various kinds can be made in the home and sold from a single room, at times and on schedules set by the woman herself. Success can lead to an expanded effort, creating employment for significant numbers of people, male and female. Small publications and other ventures can also begin on a relatively small scale in many areas. Again, few sexual complications will arise.

McClaughry's study presents an elaborate catalogue of legislative proposals designed to expand ownership possibilities of every kind.[12] Such efforts are vital to the restoration of our sexual constitution and the creation of a society in which men and women can live more happily and productively together.

If masculinity is reaffirmed, many of the resentments that women now bear toward it will be dissipated. Women now associate maleness with their own oppression. In fact, it is the restriction of masculine fulfillment in modern society that leads men to seek sexual validation by oppressing women. If men grow sexually stronger, women will become more powerful as well, because men will be able to submit to them more happily. Sexuality is not a zero sum game.

In examining the power of men and women, one has to decide whether one is interested in absolute or relative authority. Men in the Arab world and in parts of Latin America tend to be the most powerful in relation to their women, both within the home and in the marketplace. In Lebanon in 1970 they were still debating whether to retain on the books a law allowing men to kill their wives for various trivial infractions.[13] Moslem women often cannot appear in public without a veil, and polygamy is widely practiced. Divorce, available at the whim of the man, is even more frequent than in the West.[14] But a patriarchy so complete tends to produce stagnation, as the women fail to commit their men to long-term economic activity. The total power of all men and women, therefore, tends to be limited by lack of money and opportunity.

If bound by familial ties, patriarchic tendencies may represent a stimulating change in such stagnant matriarchies as parts of the American ghetto. But in general the triumph of males is a Pyrrhic victory. Much of the underdeveloped world is in the grip of stagnant patriarchy, and neither men nor women have real control over their futures. The problem is similar in matrifocal tribes. In a society where childbirth is paramount to everyone, the women will have an exalted position. But major economic growth does not occur. It may be a very happy society, but it will be shaped by the pattern of subsistence.[15]

The kind of freedom and autonomy of which the liberationists speak occurs chiefly in societies where the women are strong enough to socialize the males but not so "powerful" that the men have no constructive role. The creation and maintenance of a modern industrial society thus largely depends on a complementary balance between the sexes in the nuclear family. This is the fundamental male imperative.

The current power of both sexes is based on the wealth and freedom found in modern industrial democracies, the scene of Western civilization. No program of liberation that undermines civilization will end up making either sex more free or powerful. In fact, the more primitive the society, the greater the emphasis on force, and the more ostensibly "powerful" tend to be the men. The great irony of the women's movement is that it may effect a relative increase in the power of men and an absolute decrease in the freedom and happiness of both sexes.

15

Six Inches for the Holy Ghost

Until recent years most American parochial schools have maintained strict sexual segregation. The boys and girls joined chiefly on ceremonial occasions—assemblies and graduations. Even the playground was divided into male and female territories. The restrictions were lifted only during carefully supervised dances, when young couples made their way chastely around the floor of the gym under the watchful eyes of nuns. Any unseemly body contact brought a swift reprimand: "Leave six inches for the Holy Ghost." [1]

There is no room for the Holy Ghost any longer at most of our schools. The bodies and minds rub together from kindergarten to graduate study. The result is perfectly predictable. Sexual activity occurs at an increasingly younger age. In communities where the family cannot impose discipline, illegitimate children are common. Classrooms become an intensely sexual arena, where girls and boys perform for the attention of the other sex and where unintellectual males quickly come to view schoolbooks as a menace to manhood.[2]

This happens, moreover, at a time when education is becoming increasingly important, and the distractions of early sex are increasingly subversive to one's future. Our society enforces an ever longer period of objective latency, before full participation is allowed, and at the same time refuses to grant its children the "latency period" of sexual separation provided in societies where marriage comes at age fourteen.[3] Boys and girls, often forced to write before their hands can manage a pencil,[4] are later thrust into sexual contact before their minds and bodies can deal with sexual emotion. This enforced precocity does not even improve later sexual adjustment. The anthropological evidence suggests that societies like Samoa that separate the sexes in youth enjoy the most generous sexual relationships in maturity.[5]

But there is "no turning back the clock," as they say. The few remaining sex-segregated schools dwindle in an ideological void—as a species that survives the death of its philosophy and rationale. The issue today is not the desirability of coeducation. Coeducation is about as universal in American schools as dissatisfaction with their performance. The issue is whether the remaining male or female schools should rapidly open their doors to both sexes and whether any future institutions should experiment with sexual segregation.

The abandonment of separate education, peculiarly enough, has occurred without any visible national debate. Prestigious prep schools like Exeter and Andover, eminent women's colleges like Sarah Lawrence, and male institutions like Yale and Princeton have all quietly adopted coeducation as if it were inevitable. New elementary schools are universally co-ed. The reasons for the trend seem to be as much financial as academic. No one seems to have been able to offer cogent answers to the question "Why not?" The Holy Ghost, needless to say, is no longer much consulted.

The assumptions seem to be that segregated education is "unnatural," that males and females are best educated as similarly as possible, and that the change is of no profound significance. Exeter or Yale with women students are assumed to be not essentially different from those same institutions without them; coeducation at Exeter is regarded as essentially the same as coeducation at Yale or Sarah Lawrence—or, for that matter, at a kindergarten, grade school, or junior high.

Yet, regardless of whether one considers the trend as ultimately desirable, most of the assumptions that accompany its adoption are demonstrably fallacious. A shift to coeducation is in fact "unnatural" by most anthropological criteria. It represents a radical change in the learning environment for both boys and girls, who mature in very different ways and phases.[6] Its effects in grade school are drastically different from its effects in college. And whatever the benefits, many of the problems of America's schools—and disorders of the society—are attributable to the presumption, rare in all other human societies, that boys and girls should be thrown together whenever possible.

Let us begin with a few simple, crucial, and apparently unmentionable facts about a typical high school classroom. First and most important, most of the boys and a good number of the girls are thinking about the opposite sex most of the time. If you do not believe this, you are a dreamer. The only thing about a classroom more important to adolescent boys than whether girls are present is whether or not it is on fire.

Advocates of coeducation will tell you that the boys are

learning to regard the girls as "human beings" rather than
as sexual objects. These are the kinds of people who imagine
that most males anywhere, under any circumstances—short
of affliction by senility, homosexuality, or Bella Abzug—ever
refrain from regarding females as sexual objects. These are
the "imaginative" types of people who run our schools. They
tend to think that their sexual interest in budding adolescent
girls is their own secret perversion. It happens to be shared
by the boys in the school (as well as by all the other male
teachers).

If the educator is particularly creative and imaginative,
he will suppose that these young "human beings" are learning
a lot about life in their work together. What in fact the boys
are learning is that unless they are exceptionally "bright"
and obedient, they will be exceeded in their studies by most
of the girls.[7] Unless you are imaginative, you will see that this
is a further drag on their already faltering attention to Long-
fellow's *Evangeline*. Clearly in a losing game in masculine
terms, the boys react in two ways: They put on a show for
the girls and dominate the class anyway, or they drop out.
Enough of them eventually drop out, in fact, to disguise the
otherwise decided statistical superiority of female performance
in school.[8] But they do not drop out soon enough to suit
educators for whom aggressive boys are the leading problem
in every high school.

Adolescent boys are radically different from adolescent
girls. The boys, for example, are at the pinnacle of sexual
desire and aggressiveness. In school, what they chiefly need is
male discipline and challenge, ideally without girls present to
distract them. Girls, on the other hand, are less aggressive and
sexually compulsive at this stage and are more willing to
study without rigid policing and supervision. Thus a classroom that contains both boys and girls will hurt both. The
boys will be excelled and demoralized by the girls; the girls
will be distracted and demoralized by the boys. Both sexes
will be damaged by the continuous disciplining that the rebellious and unsuccessful boys require.

There are benefits to coeducation, however. It allows
our educational system to avoid "sexism," reduce costs, and
get rid of rambunctious lower-class males. It conditions a

good many boys to compete with women on female terms. The classroom successes of these "grinds" and "apple-polishers" are somewhat tarnished after school or in the men's room, when they are brutally harassed by gangs of unsuccessful male students. But what happens after school—or in the men's room, God forbid—is of little concern to the school management. The only after-school that interests them is college admissions.

Coeducation also allows the educators to avoid the problem of finding new ways to meet the sexual identity crises of most schoolboys. As Patricia Cayo Sexton has elaborately documented, it is the most "feminine" boys, by every index, who tend to excel in school. Obedient and submissive in the classroom, their aggressions emerge fitfully in other arenas. They raise hell on college campuses, for example. Otherwise they masturbate incessantly, worry about it even more than about their grades, and generally turn their energies inward where they can cause serious distortions of character. Homosexuality and violence are frequent outlets, drugs a frequent palliative. But they *do* do well in school.

Surprisingly, to imaginative educators, these types have less trouble in all-male institutions. Contrary to the widespread notion, homosexuality is evident neither at prep schools nor at parochial schools. Boys with masculinity problems are reinforced by an all-male environment, while less competent though virile students are not so estranged from education by their failures. Competition with females is destructive to males in any arena, but nowhere is it so damaging as among impressionable adolescents preoccupied with their intense but inchoate sexuality.

Nonetheless, enough boys are surviving school with their masculinity intact to deeply distress women's liberation. It has become clear that in order to extirpate "sexism," it is necessary to attack it at the root—to give boys a "head start" in emasculation. Thus the movement is striking at the early stages: nursery school, kindergarten, and the lower grades. Exploiting their great strength in the teaching profession, particularly at the elementary level, the feminists want to remove every vestige of sexual differentiation from textbooks and class activities. They are succeeding widely and no one seems willing firmly to resist. Even *Sesame Street* has succumbed.

The National Education Association has adopted a militantly feminist position,[9] and many teachers across the country are turning elementary school into an even more destructive experience for little boys than it long has been. These boys will still ultimately have to face the problem of becoming men, of dealing with the imperious claims of their adolescent bodies. The only difference will be their lack of a developed psychological framework for masculine expression. The confusions of the more vulnerable ones will blight their lives. The liberationists seem to imagine that the sexuality of small children is some kind of ideological playground. They should recognize that these are not fetuses whose lives they are aborting.

Ideally, the best compromise probably would be to let the movement change the teaching of little girls if it can. Girls may be less vulnerable sexually. But the attacks on little boys should be terminated by establishing separate facilities for them. Since this solution will not be adopted by many schools, it seems necessary to fight the movement on every point, while moving men into elementary school teaching as rapidly as possible. This means paying elementary school teachers salaries commensurate with the vital importance of their work.

Virtually every primitive society divides the children and teaches the sexes separately. Most provide the boys with dramatic initiatory rituals, needed because male lives lack distinct and dramatic stages like those found in the unfolding of female sexuality.[10] In very few cases are the boys and girls thrown together more than two years before their marriages. These divisions promote the development of a confident masculinity and of a rich and successful later sex life.

In the United States the girls and boys are expected to traffic together intimately for years before they can marry. They are subjected to intense sexual distractions and competitions during the critical stages of their educations. They are brought up in a society where sex is continuously advertised and propagandized.

The result is that American boys and girls are driven into periods of sexual experimentation and stress unparalleled in either length or intensity by any other societies. One aspect of sex is drastically downplayed, however, and that is the most important, fundamental, and sexually differentiated part —procreation. Thus the American system of coeducation vividly teaches the lesson that boys and girls are sexually similar and that sex is a matter of exchanging pleasures between them in a reciprocal way. This approach is inimical to durable love and marriage. The boys do not learn to venerate the procreative powers of woman, and the girls stunt their own consciousness of a more elaborate sexuality. Thus, in effect, masculine sexual patterns prevail throughout this educational period, even though love and marriage must usually be based on deeper and more extended female sexuality.

If you were to predict that a society teaching sex the way we do in America would face severe problems of both male and female socialization, you would be all too right. If you were to observe that its marriages would be deeply troubled, you would state the obvious. Yet unless you were extraordinarily optimistic, you would not expect the obvious to be recognized or acted upon. You would anticipate that the current trends will persist on into the sexual suicide society. The government is now on the verge of requiring coeducation in all schools that receive federal aid.

The fact is that there seems to be virtually no chance of arresting the trend toward the integration of all sexually segregated schools. Young people are being immersed, if that is the word, in the shallow currents of reciprocal sex at an ever earlier age. It seems that by denying the Holy Ghost his six inches in the schools, one dooms most of society to just that measure of sexual fulfillment.

Sex and Sports

All those women think they're men. They would
be smarter if they played like women—like I do.

Bobby Riggs

When I was a small boy, tennis was more important to me than anything else in the world. My father had won some championships in the brief days before he was killed in the Second World War. I suppose my play served as a connection with him. I practiced endlessly against barn doors; and on rainy days whenever my mother was out, I practiced inside with a shortened racket against the door to the kitchen. I had worked out an elaborate scoring system by which I could enact whole tennis tournaments, pretending to be one or another set of star players and alternating shots between them. Tony Trabert was my favorite, and I had my hair styled in a crew cut like his. I rooted against the Australians, but admired Ken Rosewall for his ground strokes. Although, as I later discovered, I myself was not very good, I won a tournament at a local club and cherished the trophy above all my other possessions. And every fall, I would take trains and subways to Forest Hills, about 150 miles away, to watch the national championships.

I would always arrive in the morning. I tried to come early enough so that I could eat breakfast at a local coffee shop. There on one occasion I sat and watched Trabert eat scrambled eggs, and on another stood in line at the cash register directly behind Ashley Cooper. Then I would saunter over to the grounds and wander among the manicured grass courts, watching one or another couple warming up: Doris Hart and someone I couldn't recognize in one court; Lew Hoad in another with Rex Hartwig; Cooper; Mo Connolly; and then, Karen Hantze. She was 16 years old at the time, with short blond hair and a pert, pretty face—freckles, bright, perfect teeth, a snub nose, and a weak serve, a long straight forehand, a slightly awkward backhand. I fell in love.

Before that I had regarded women's tennis as a boring interlude between the men's games. But from then on I followed Karen avidly. I was delighted to discover that everyone else liked her too, and applauded warmly whenever she played older players. She was so expressive, with a warm smile or a girlish pout, while her opponents were always grimly determined.

Then one day everything changed for me. Hantze was playing one of the older stars (somehow I remember Billie

Jean King but it couldn't have been). Anyway she was a tough, hard player, highly seeded, much older and less pretty, and Karen was beating her. At first I was delighted and cheered happily with the rest of the crowd from my vantage point next to the fence whenever Karen won a point, even by an error. The crowd groaned audibly when her opponent scored. Then suddenly I was shaken to see what I thought were tears in the eyes of the older woman. I began to see the match in a different way. It became clear to me who was the real underdog in the match, and in life, and I started cheering even more loudly for the older woman. I even carried some of the crowd with me. But I could not get really enthusiastic and was unhappy when Karen finally lost.

I rarely watched women's tennis after that, for I noticed that, along with all the rest of the crowd, I always rooted for the prettiest player—and somehow that wasn't what Forest Hills was about. Anyway, all the best men tennis players in the world were there, displaying every kind of tennis skill. So why should I watch the way Karen's hair flopped neatly around her bright face and the way her pert breasts rose when she served. Ultimately, Althea Gibson triumphed in the final, playing in very conventional male style: a big serve and a rush to the net. She played about as well as some high school players I used to admire in the Berkshires. Gibson was interesting, though, because she was black—a tall, gangling girl who, I was to understand, would not have been allowed on the grounds during the rest of the year except to serve drinks.

For several years after that, I didn't think much about women in athletics. I abandoned tennis after badly damaging an elbow while trying to serve like Tony Trabert one chilly fall morning, before I had warmed up. I took up football and hockey and loved them, but I was ultimately too light for football and too slow for hockey. Eventually I started long-distance running and it fully occupied that crucial role in my life previously fulfilled by tennis.

I then encountered the Press sisters. Between them they held four world records in women's track and field. Irina was a sprinter and hurdler, who could run nearly as fast as the best American high school freshman boy, while Tamara threw the 8-pound shot about 15 feet further than any Amer-

*ican woman and several feet less than men throw the 35-
pound weight. A story in the newspapers described how she
trained by doing bench presses. Neither sister resembled
Karen Hantze, but they won most of the events they entered
in the Olympics, together giving the Soviet Union more "team
points" than Bob Mathias, Tom Courtney, Glenn Davis, and
our entire championship basketball team gave the United
States. They also made the difference in the combined men's
and women's scores in two Russian-American meets. I was
disgusted. My sentiments did not change a few years later
when the Press sisters completely vanished from athletics
amid reports that they were chromosomally masculine. Later
one of Irina's successors as a world sprint record holder, a
Polish girl, was similarly disqualified. As a result women in
the Olympics now have to take what they understandably
regard as an insulting sex test. But I did not forget the Press
sisters. Years later I still cherished the image of Tamara
doing those bench presses; I could see that hulking body
arched over the bench, one bulging leg on each side, while
she shoved up the weight above her virtually invisible breasts
with a grunt—still not getting stronger than many adolescent
boys.*

*Was I wrong to conclude that the women's shot put is
a perversion of sport that has no place in the Olympic games?
Am I wrong to observe that a great many women's sports
events are boring for spectators, unless one of the girls is
pretty?*

*Ms. magazine would call me sexist and they would be
right. I would call them completely uncomprehending of the
role of sports in society and in the lives of men. The matter
is worth discussing, since it discloses the extremes to which
the feminists will go to avoid admitting differences between
the sexes.*

The feminist confusions about athletics were well expressed in an article in the January 1973 *Ms.*[1] *Ms.* attacked
discrimination against women at the Olympics and in American sports in general and attributed men's enjoyment of all-
male competition to repressed homosexuality. In a series of
articles published in late May and early June, *Sports Illustrated*

adopted a similar position and advocated approximately equal spending on physical training for boys and girls at the nation's publicly supported high schools and colleges. High officials in the Federal Department of Health, Education and Welfare indicate essential agreement. *Ms.*'s absurd position thus is not only accepted by our leading sports magazine but is also in danger of becoming official policy.[2]

The Olympics article focused on two performers, Francie Kraker, an American, and Ludmila Bragina, a Russian. Kraker broke her previous best time by a large margin, while Bragina set a new women's world 1500 meter record. Neither received any coverage in U.S. papers. An essential argument of this article was that despite the emphasis on "male musculature" in designing athletic events and despite the insistent discouragement of women, they were nonetheless closing the gap between their performances and men's. One encounters similar notions elsewhere in movement literature. Germaine Greer, for example, seems to believe that the muscular differences between the sexes are largely attributable to massive cultural influences exerted on girls in adolescence. The *Ms.* article quoted UCLA track and field coach Jim Bush to the effect that he had encountered strong resistance to including women's events in major meets. *Ms.* concluded on a hopeful note, however, envisaging a possible merger of men's and women's athletics, as the women improved, and anticipating ultimate inclusion of women on Olympic relay teams. The article erroneously maintained that only exceptional male athletes can beat the best women.

Track and field, the sport they discussed, has the useful feature of strict numerical standards covering a large variety of muscular skills. It also has the advantage of universality. Women all over the world compete. At present, the women's world records in every event are inferior to the U.S. high school freshman records of adolescent boys with relatively little training.[3] If women competed with men rather than separately, they would appear in no major meets anywhere and would be absent from the Olympics.

Women's sports currently receive an extraordinary amount of attention. Although the total number of female competitors in U.S. track and field is very small, the few who seriously train are exhibited in most of the large indoor track meets in Madison Square Garden and elsewhere. They receive an eminence that is accorded only to men who prevail in a long and elaborate series of smaller meets, collectively involving hundreds of thousands of contestants.

The women's races are a diversion. At the starting lines, there are always one or two, usually the inferior performers, who preen and wiggle to attract attention. In the race, again far more notice is paid to the feminine than to the athletic displays of the competitors. If the contest is close, there will be brief interest. But, in essence, the purpose is mildly erotic entertainment by girls in hot pants.

It will be said that these corruptions are inevitable in sexist society, where most women do not compete seriously in athletics. Most of the distractions will be attributed to the refusal of Americans to accept public sports performance as a legitimate female activity. But it is more likely, in fact, that if there were more women mingled among the men, there would be more sex emphasis and less devotion to pure athletic achievement.

Sports represent to males a realm where they can collectively test themselves against the highest ideals and standards of human performance. The boy on the Harlem playground endlessly practicing his shots envisages himself as Walt Frazier. The runner struggling up a rocky hill in Van Cortlandt Park or striding loosely through its crinkling leaves pays tribute with every step to the great stars who have preceded him there, undergone the same pangs, and enjoyed the same cool breezes, the same hope of fluid speed and final glory. The boy on the tennis court dreams of Tony Trabert . . . The fact that most of the contestants will fail to reach the standard does not change the nature of the quest; nor does it deprive them of those beatified moments in the life of every athlete when, however briefly, his usual limits are transcended and he is reborn in the image of his dream. Rabbit sees the shots arch flawlessly in the air from fingers possessed and swish repeatedly through the cords. Darling shifts directions three times, feels a tackler slip away, and finds the field open greenly 80 yards before him. The boy runs back, back in the playground outfield, stumbles around a bush, leaps desperately in the air, glove extended against the sky in the image of Willie Mays, and clumps in delectable pain to the ground against the fence with the ball clutched in his hand. He will never be closer to God.

Contrary to their currently fashionable detractors, sports embody for men a moral universe. On the team, the group learns to cooperate, learns the importance of loyalty, struggle, toughness, and self-sacrifice in pursuing a noble ideal. At a period in their lives when hormones of aggression are pouring through their bodies in unprecedented streams, boys learn that aggressiveness must be disciplined and regulated before it can be used in society. Boys learn the indispensable sensation of competition in solidarity. The twelve ruthlessly ambitious men on the Boston Celtics—six black and six white, rich and poor—become a platonic scheme of unity and sacrifice, reaching toward the fifteen green flags of previous championships hanging from the ceiling above them. They teach the crucial lesson that the more one gives, the more one wins; that the selfish star is a burden on his fellows; and that Arthur "Hambone" Williams—just four years ago an aging playground marvel on a San Diego amateur team—can make all the difference without scoring a point.

Athletics for men is an ideal of purity and truth. But when women enter everything changes. For, as *Ms.* acknowledges, most sports are designed for "male musculature." No matter how hard Mss. Bragina and Kraker train, they cannot hope to be more than somewhat distorted and inferior reflections of male performers. Their competitive exertions seem less a pursuit of a noble ideal of excellence—a physical fulfillment—than a struggle against the female proportions of their bodies. Thus the very success of their effort attracts attention to themselves as sexual objects. They run so fast or jump so high not by a realization of the natural potential of their physique but despite it. Despite her womb, her breasts, her hips, her female musculature, her lesser metabolism, Bragina, the marvel of the Olympics, can run almost as fast as a male adolescent. Her achievement is indeed prodigious. But its very essence is flawed as an athletic performance, because it is not a natural and beautiful fulfillment of the female body. It does not aspire to the platonic ideal. (It resembles in that regard, incidentally, a walking race, which is a truly perverse exhibition of physical repression and distortion as bad as the woman's shot put).

The *Ms.* article remarks that males do not play with the same abandon and resolve against a female athlete as they do against a male, even when the women are as good. Observing the fanatic, sweaty, abandoned struggle between men, *Ms.* envisages repressed homosexuality. The feminists, in fact, often convey an image of a world full of repressed homosexuals tensely awaiting emancipation by the movement.

The reason men do not compete so intensely against females, however, is different. It is that women destroy the illusion of the ideal. A man struggling to overcome his girl friend in the third set cannot easily envisage himself as Rod Laver. Therefore the man cannot allow himself to be honestly beaten by her. He must always keep something in reserve, so he can rationalize his defeat, and preserve the ritual role of sport in his life.

The woman reduces the game from a religious male rite to a mere physical exercise, with some treacherous danger of psychic damage. Mixed doubles, incidentally, do not have this effect because the women can be envisaged as accessories. But most male competitions are gravely compromised by serious female participation. They may still be fun and recreational—particularly for mature men and women. But their ritual nature, their moral purpose, their symbolic aspiration are all vaguely weakened or destroyed, especially for boys. The feminist threat to sport thus is no minor matter.

What is at stake, for example, in the *Ms.* proposal for a qualified merger of male and female athletics in the high schools is nothing less than the integrity of a vital remaining process of male socialization. Patricia Cayo Sexton, among countless other observers, has described the vast importance of sports in the lives of many boys. "Fish like to swim, and boys like to play games," she writes. Speaking of Sioux Indian youths, she quotes an observer: "The unselfconscious devotion and ardor with which many of these young men play games must be witnessed to be appreciated even mildly." [4] Sports are possibly the single most important male rite in modern society.

The entrance of a large number of teen-aged girls, at a time in high school and junior high when they tend to be larger than boys, would be disastrous for all the slow developers. Leaders in Outward Bound physical programs for ghetto children find that the best athletes perform as well—if in a different spirit—with females present. The smaller, shyer, and less developed boys, however, are completely daunted by the girls and refuse to make a resolute effort. In addition, all the lessons of group morality that boys can learn from playing games together are lost when girls are participating. The successful boys, those who work with and encourage the others in all-male groups, simply show off for the females in mixed assemblages. Nor do the girls benefit. Some of them do quite well, but their performances seem directed more toward the boys than to the real values of the undertaking.

Once again the girls would subvert the masculinity of the weaker or slow-developing boys without gaining significant athletic reward themselves. The girls who could actually play on a high school team would be exceedingly rare. But the girls, nonetheless, would disrupt and deform the most precious rituals of young boys. Again the feminists would impose on the socialization of American males burdens men have experienced nowhere else on earth.

Lionel Tiger and other anthropologists who emphasize the hunting origins of male *homo sapiens*—their many millions of years of evolution on the African savannas—offer plausible explanations for most of the specialized faculties of the male body. Its running and throwing skills, its ability to reach a pitch of violent activity for brief periods, all derive from experience of the chase. The tendency to bond with other males in intensely purposeful and dangerous activity is said to come from the collective demands of pursuing large animals. The female body, on the other hand, more closely resembles the body of nonhunting primates. A woman throws, for example, very like a male chimpanzee. She cannot run as well as men. But she has more long-range stamina and durability, and perhaps in compensation for limitations in pure strength, she has attained greater grace and beauty. Because her musculature is more internal, she can perform prodigious physical feats without breaking the esthetic lines of her body with corrugations of bulging muscles. When she doesn't strain and struggle against her being to fulfill the standards of male physicality, she reaches greater kinesthetic perfection. She can achieve triumphs of her own at least the equal of male athletic exploits.

Consider the last several Olympics, winter and summer. Which, among all the competitors, made the most vivid impression, touching most deeply the minds and hearts of spectators, male and female, all over the world? Was it Mark Spitz, leaping sleekly into the water seven times and thrashing turbulently to a gold mine and a Hollywood contract? Was it Jean-Claude Killy, peering coldly through the mists down three Alpine courses—past a wreckage of eminent failures before him—and three times catching the slithering microseconds of victory in the treacherous snows? Was it Abebe Bikila running 26 miles, 385 yards through the cobbled streets of Rome—barefoot—and winning with a smile? Was it Bob Beamon sprinting down the runway in Mexico City, springing off into the thin air, hanging as if suspended for an unbelievable time, and landing over 29 feet away, more than two whole feet farther than anyone had jumped before? Perhaps it was one of these, or the 1960 U.S. Olympic hockey team, or Billy Mills or Bob Hayes or Al Oerter or one of the other magical names.

But probably not. The performance that evoked the greatest response on ABC-TV and in the minds of most viewers came from a 14-year-old Russian girl in women's gymnastics, a sport obscure in the United States but universal in its appeal. Olga Korbut and her almost equally inspiring associates achieved a synthesis of grace, agility, humor, beauty, and, yes, strength and stamina too that transcended all the other Olympic performances and reached a level of sinuous poetry. Her dives and leaps and spins and somersaults all fused in a continuous calisthenic stream (in the true sense of the term—*kalos* and *sthenis*—beautiful strength). When she was finished, her achievement had attained the unimpeachable quality of art; there was nothing one would change, and any numbers applied by the judges seemed irrelevant.

After that, one watched the men with some disappointment. They might leap higher, suspend themselves longer, and whirl faster. But they could not touch the dazzling artistic integrity of the female performances. Their bodies seemed less flexible and somehow excessively muscled; their effort was too visible; and though they may have done more, as often happens in aesthetics, even in athletics, more is less. In a pursuit of calisthenic grace, the men found themselves in a predicament suggestive of the female miler. They were working counter to their physical endowment. And when they assumed a pose of elegance, it often seemed narcissistic. All that male musculature burdened the terms of the art.

Like gymnasts, female divers and figure skaters have no apologies to make to the men in their fields—let alone to high school freshmen in Keokuk. These women also have lent a feminine aesthetic dimension to their performances that makes them invulnerable to male emulation. The female body, when trained calisthenically, attains a flexuous grace, a perfection of sensuous form and movement that finds no male counterpart.

Outside of the serious competitive arena, women can bring this kind of grace and style to a great many recreational sports. Skiing is particularly attractive and women often seem better than men, even when moving more slowly. In any case, most of the activities that seem unfeminine when carried to the extremes of international competition are embellished by women who don't attempt to reproduce the styles and techniques most appropriate to male musculature. Abby Rockefeller and other Cambridge feminists have even shown that karate, a sport displaying great strength and violence, can be transformed into a strangely moving choreography by women who do it well. In general, women will do best by transforming athletics into calisthenics—by finding the aesthetic dimensions of a physical art and, by dint of the integrity of their performance, establishing it on their own terms. By creating and fulfilling an equal and complementary role, women can enrich the physical and athletic experiences of the entire species rather than occupying an auxiliary position in the realm of men.

In this sense athletics offer a metaphor of the entire dilemma of liberation. Mss. Bragina and Kraker and the

Press sisters enter the athletic realm on male terms. While often performing impressive feats—for women—and sometimes defeating a few lesser male competitors, they cannot fulfill the Olympian ideal of sport. In fact, when intruding on the male athletic arena, women may serve only to detract from its symbolic and ritual content and thus its value in male socialization. The sad irony, however, is that, for all their effort, they gain not liberation but bondage to the male conditions of the activity. By submitting to male values, they symbolically affirm male superiority and betray the higher possibilities of their sex.

It is athletes like Korbut who are truly liberated by their sport, who have created an impregnable athletic realm beyond the world of men. And in fulfilling the highest possibilities of her sex, she extends the aesthetic and physical experience of all mankind.

The Perils of Androgyny

Nobody, any longer, may hope to entertain an
angel unawares or to meet Sir Lancelot any longer on
a moonlit road.

Kenneth Grahame
Wind in the Willows

The conventional feminist view holds that both sexes are androgynous while American culture is sexually polarized. Sexual anxiety and frustration are ascribed to the restiveness and guilt of human beings who do not fit the cultural definitions of their roles. A spurious sexual duality is said not only to discomfit sexually aggressive or careerist women but also to thwart more passive and nurturant males.

Such men manifestly exist. But their existence does not dictate creation of a more androgynous culture. American society is already hospitable to passive and effeminate males. What they need is affirmation as men so that their existing androgyny does not lead to sexual suicide: to impotence and homosexuality. Contrary to the feminist view, the latitude available to the two sexes is not the same. While women can venture into the masculine sphere without grave damage and can even indulge in occasional lesbianism, the greater sexual insecurity of males makes it more difficult and unsettling for them to engage in female roles. Homosexuality, moreover, can inflict permanent damage on their sexual identities. Because males must bear the burdens of initiation and performance in sexual activity, a homosexual fixation is often permanent. A man cannot be easily rescued by an aggressive woman.

While there are many people who accept the romantic propaganda about male homosexual existence, the life of tricks and trades is in fact agonizing for most of its practitioners. Lasting relationships are few and sour. The usual circuit of gay bars, returning servicemen, forlorn personal advertisements, and street cruises affords gratifications so brief and squalid that the society should do everything it can to prevent the spread of the disease. This emphatically does not mean harassing or imprisoning homosexuals. In fact, the worst perversion occasioned by homosexuality is the police practice of entrapment. But at the same time it is crucial to affirm precarious males in their heterosexuality. Natural compassion for men who are already homosexual—and our recognition that some have adjusted happily—should not lead us to praise or affirm the homosexual alternative or to acquiesce in its propaganda.

Beyond the relatively few congenital inverts, there are

millions of males who under the wrong conditions are open to homosexuality. A frequent catalyst is self-abasement. Failure in love or work may so deject a man that he feels incapable of rising to a relationship with a woman. He finds he lacks the confidence for the rudimentary acts of self-assertion —even the rudimentary selfhood—needed for any heterosexual exchange.

Intercourse remorselessly sets the bounds of androgyny: to have a woman, a male must to some extent feel himself a man. A male who does not feel like a man may seek to have a man. Men who feel abased may enjoy the idea of a specific enactment and affirmation of their abasement. Men incapable of deep sexuality may be relieved to find a deep throat—to pursue sexual activity without the burden of initiative or personality or human ties. The chief attraction of homosexual activity is that it does not require confidence or male identity or a face-to-face self-exposure. It can even be performed without an erection. It is thus an inviting escape for the fallen male.

Nonetheless, actual homosexuality is by no means inevitable in such cases. A man can recover from his dejection, restore his confidence, and return to full heterosexuality. This is the usual course of events. It is tragic, therefore, if the cultural ambience provides more easily for homosexuality than for recovery of normal patterns.

In many parts of urban America this tragedy is a way of life. The precarious male is surrounded by homosexual stimuli. If he goes to a pornography shop—a frequent resort of despair—he will find homosexual literature and devices as prominent as heterosexual ones. In some sections of town he will meet homosexuals on every street corner, their genitalia pressed like vultures against their jeans. In fashionable literature, he will frequently encounter the argument that homosexuality is not a disease but merely an alternative form of sexual expression toward which all civilized men should be tolerant. He will even hear that in a time of overpopulation such nonprocreative sexuality is a positive good. In addition, he is sure to run into the grope-stat—originating in a Mattachine Society distortion of the Kinsey Report, repeated in *The New York Times,* and thenceforth attributed to *The Times*—

alleging that one in five Americans is a practicing homo-sexual.[1] The fact that people believe such nonsense says a lot about our current predicament.

Under such conditions, a man's erotic confusion may deepen, and homosexual activity may begin its infection. Once this happens, the addiction may be very hard to break. The homosexual will seek to affirm his choice by finding others to join him in it. He promotes Gay Liberation, and allies himself when he can with female inverts. A society thus creates an undertow of degradation that can reach millions.

It is ironic that a movement advocating the interests of women should encourage a movement based on misogyny: the fear and hatred of women. But that is the dead end of the liberationist myth of the androgynous male. The fact is he is not oppressed by a sexist society; it is the world of bipolar sexuality that makes it possible for him to indulge feminine impulses. Removing the structure of sexual identity leaves him vulnerable to sexual self-destruction.

Recognizing the perils of androgyny for males, Mrs. Sexton, that most original and interesting of the feminists—in that she apparently loves and understands men—presents a much more plausible theory of our social problem.[2] The arresting authority of her diagnosis and the charm of her style, however, should not blind us to the flaws of her conclusion, which is androgyny for females—a movement of the entire sexual spectrum toward the masculine end.

In Mrs. Sexton's view, the society is not too masculine, but rather too feminizing (careful not to say truly feminine); and she knows that *The Feminized Male,* as she entitles her book, is a source of violence and social unrest. She believes he is the product of homes dominated by the mother, schools dominated by women, and by technology that emasculates work. She stresses particularly the feminine character of edu-cation: schools that focus on such virtues as obedience, regu-larity, passivity, submission, and verbal skills at a time when boys' bodies are raging with testosterone and their minds are preoccupied with sports and mechanics. She elaborately and convincingly documents the differences between the sexes in learning patterns and tendencies and shows that feminine propensities are universally rewarded.[3]

In the first grade, for example, when many of the boys are a full nine months behind the girls in digital coordination, the emphasis is on penmanship.[4] She believes that the striking aversion to writing shown by so many boys throughout their education may stem from their frustrations as six-year-olds when their hands are physically unready to write.[5] She contends that such patterns continue through the educational process. Mechanical and technical interests and skills, predominantly masculine, are downplayed in favor of the feminine realms of writing and high culture. The educational utility of the boys' preoccupation with sports is universally neglected. The boys are not shown how to compute batting averages or taught the physical principles involved in the curve ball or told about the musculature of Joe Namath's knee. Instead school consists almost exclusively of sitting down quietly for long periods, at the behest of a female teacher— and reading and writing materials of little interest to most adolescent boys.

The result, according to Mrs. Sexton, who assembled reams of testing data to prove it, is that the most feminine boys prevail in school and tend to go on to college and into the best jobs. Meanwhile the most aggressive and masculine —the ones who cannot sit in one place for more than ten minutes without severe nervous strain, relieved only by dreams of cars and football games—these boys tend to drop out and take the lowest-paying work. Yet it is Mrs. Sexton's plausible contention that the mechanical interests that lead many of these boys to putter endlessly with automobiles and other technology represent no lesser intellectuality than the more verbal orientation of the others. But potentially valuable technical skills are lost because the educational system does not know how to deal with masculinity.[6]

The selection for feminity in the schools is duplicated in the bureaucracies. Here again, sedentary fastidiousness and opportune blandishment are the lubricants of upward mobility. As a consequence, the entire society becomes a difficult and hostile place for the most masculine men. Some of them can be found at construction sites, whistling "oppressively" at upper-class feminist women as they amble by, their breasts jouncing loosely in their shirts. "Gee whiz, these brutes are treating us as *sex objects!*" say the feminists in their books and magazines, pamphlets and speeches. But it is difficult to see how a working man—doomed to a lifetime of tough and relatively unremunerative labor in support of his family—is the oppressor of women who seem to embody everything the world has denied to him: options, money, style, easy sex, freedom. Anyway, the girls pass by and on to their own frustrations; after a while only the hats and work of the men are hard.

Nonetheless, the men who prevail in the educational system are victims as well. Alienated from their sexual natures —and from technical experience—they become excessively concerned with ideas and symbols. As Mrs. Sexton writes, "In academic life, words are enshrined to the point that many feel all wars are settled, and all deeds accomplished, through arguments and speechmaking. The academy is often merely a repository of disembodied words . . . but there is hardly an act, deed or object in sight. That students should get restless about this condition and that they should be grossly inept at linking words with deeds should not startle us." [7]

The consequences are more serious than student riots, however, for "if we block normal outlets of aggression, we may turn it inward. When we pacified the bopping gang of a decade ago, its members turned to narcotics and self-mutilation. And middle-class hippies (also without aggressive outlets) followed in the same path, adding their own variations." [8]

"We have much to overcome and destroy," Mrs. Sexton continues, "injustice, inequality, poverty, disease, death, hatred, unhappiness, boredom and apathy, floods and famine, illiteracy, anomie, unrewarding work, abuses of power, obsolete social institutions, the imminence of nuclear war. With so many enemies, we need a great deal of fighting spirit. It would seem wiser, both inside and outside our schools, to permit as much aggression as possible, but to direct it away from street fights and into combat with the real enemies of man." [9]

Well, Mrs. Sexton is full of words and fighting spirit too, and she has much of importance to say. But her essential answer to all those awesome problems—women's liberation and, in a sense, a male-oriented androgyny—has its limitations as well. She wants to get the women out of the home and elementary school classroom and into the executive suite; and she wants to summon the men up from construction sites, out from under malfunctioning automobiles, and into the classrooms. Here she urges a new emphasis on scientific and technical studies. She wants to transform mechanical curiosity into technological expertise, in a school environment where the natural rambunctiousness of young boys is channeled into valuable learning experiences. "Lots o' luck," you might say. But such a response—like any brief summary—underestimates the sophistication of her argument.

Philip Slater's popular book, *The Pursuit of Loneliness*,[10] makes a similar case for the liberation of women and the active affirmation of cross-sexual impulses. Like many feminists and other observers, he believes that the isolation of highly educated and ambitious females in surburban households with small children is inherently unnatural. The mothers invest in their children all the energies they might otherwise devote to career activity. The connection between mother and child becomes overloaded with all the emotions and frustrations and hopes of the woman. Meanwhile, the man is off at work for most of the day and in many cases scarcely sees his children at all. The result, according to Slater, is restive and dissatisfied women and excessively mothered children who think the world owes them a living. The boys, in particular, can be impelled toward serious sexual disorientation. Their "feminization" as Sexton calls it, is reaffirmed in school, and ultimately produces a volatile pattern of compensatory bitterness and violence, together with tendencies toward homosexuality. Like Sexton, Slater prescribes women's liberation. Slater also places a great emphasis on getting the men back into the home.

But this analysis is out of date. Sociologists, it seems, resemble generals; they always want to refight the last war. That generation of possessively mothered and ablatively fathered children, who gave Slater so much trouble at Brandeis (and the FBI so much trouble afterwards),[11] has now grown up. Their problems—and thus the current predicaments of upperclass society—are completely different from the problems of their parents. The women are not excessively preoccupied

with motherhood. Instead many of the younger ones are so
alienated from their procreative natures that they deny even
the existence of a distinctive female sexuality. The men are
not obsessively absorbed in their careers. All too many of
them are finding great difficulty in committing themselves to
anything—job or marriage or a distinct pattern of male responsibility. The result is an emerging society very different
from the one depicted in Slater's scheme.

The feminized males, whom Mrs. Sexton so artfully
pinioned, have contributed to an equally serious sexual deformation of women. Although the numbers may at present
seem small, there is a growing and influential trend toward a
masculinized female. Because sexuality is normally fulfilled in
complementary relationship to the opposite sex, this generation of "human beings" has deep trouble achieving the deep
sexual connections on which human identity and male socialization depend. Partly because of economic trends, the male,
once an obsessive provider who gave everything but himself,
is losing his career orientation. Partly because of the change
in the male, partly because of new ideas and technologies, the
obsessive mother is giving way to the obsolescent mother. The
future of love and family is in the balance.

Many of Sexton's and Slater's proposals are good. It is
eminently desirable to get more men teachers into the schools
at earlier levels. It is urgent to give work and training to
teen-age boys in male environments that they like and respect.
It is important to break down the isolation—relatively rare
and transitory though it is—of suburban mothers, and to free
the few obsessive ones of the illusion that total absorption in
their children is desirable. It is crucial to give women a consciousness not only of their own sexuality but also of the
possibilities for diverse and rewarding experience outside the
home (as well as in it, incidentally). And women should become even more conscious of the home as it reaches into the
community, in which they, but not working men, truly live.

Although far worse could happen, there is little danger,
however, that the present generation will repeat the maternal
excesses of the last. Nor is there much danger that most
women will incarcerate themselves in kitchen and nursery,
unconscious of the possibilities of jobs and enjoyable sex.

Most fathers have learned the importance of loving and fostering their children; most couples have learned sex technique; most men have learned foreplay and most women have learned orgasm; the society has overcome the terrible toils of puritanism. A new panoply of family tactics has emerged. We all know about tolerance, flexibility, growth, and individual autonomy.

It seems that recent generations have achieved a sufficient quantum of enlightenment to assure, as much as mere knowledge can, against repetition of both puritanism and momism. Our tactical repertory has expanded. The problem is that we may be winning skirmishes all over the place but forgetting the very nature of the game. While we may know everything we wanted to know about sex, we forgot to ask what it was for. While learning to open marriage, we may have emptied it. While watching for the pitfalls of family, we may have overlooked its purposes. While multiplying and dividing the woman's role, we may have virtually destroyed it, and the man's role as well. The new affirmation of "human beings" succeeds only in subverting males and females and exalting the sexual eccentric—the androgyne.

In order to strengthen the relationships between men and women, we must reaffirm the sexual differences that transcend physiology. Even if one denies such spiritual differences exist in themselves, there remains a sense in which anatomy *is* destiny. Even if a woman "thinks like a man," when she thinks of her body she is destined to have different thoughts. Over a lifetime, these thoughts accumulate. They assume a collective shape as distinctively feminine as the curve of her breasts. And when she goes to bed with a man, she cannot escape the shadow of her mind. It entwines with its male counterpart as profoundly as their bodies. If for some reason this consciousness of sexuality is aborted or twisted, the experience may be damaged as much as by a physical deformity.

Our current tendencies toward androgyny may stem to a great extent from the enormous distractive power of modern technology. As Margaret Mead has observed, it intrudes on the very earliest connection of mother and baby. Writing in 1948, she described the infant experiences of the generation that grew up to seek liberation in the world of objects and reciprocalities.[12] The mother went for childbirth to a temple of technology: the modern hospital. The baby was born on a delivery table to facilitate the work of the obstetrician. Its first cry was not even heard by the anesthetized mother. Its first experience of the world was a wrapping of soft cloth. When it was ultimately fed, no bodily contact was allowed beyond access to a sterilized breast. Soon afterwards, even the breast was exchanged for a bottle.

Thus, writes Mead, "For the primary learning experience that is the physical prototype of the sex relationship—a complementary relation between the body of the mother and the body of the child—is substituted a relationship between the child and an object . . . and deep structural differences between the masculine and feminine roles are lost." This relationship of taking objects from the mother is easily transformed into a reciprocal game. "I give you something and you give me something is not necessarily cross-sexed when it is based on bottles and zwieback rather than upon the deeply specific experience of the breast." [13] Mead goes on to show how such suppression of specific sexual experience continues throughout early childhood.

This phase is followed by nearly two decades of essentially undifferentiated education. There is a continued high density of technological, reciprocal, and objective relationships. Men and women accumulate huge amounts of information in their schooling together. They are bombarded by huge quantities of common stimuli from the artificial world of machines. They are taught always to focus outward, to respond to objective facts, and put them in logical systems usually identical for males and females. There is no male or female math or science; there is no male or female way to understand French or fix a radio. It may be that all these external messages—all this technological static—has crowded out the quiet interior transmissions of our bodies. The men and women who study the "body languages" of others for superficial messages seem incapable of interpreting the code of their own sexuality. They become feminized males and masculinized women. Then for some reason they are surprised when their bodies and minds diverge in intercourse and they are incapable of the most important communications of all.

The fashion of androgyny is influential around the world. A possible measure of its effect is the widespread decline of breast feeding. In many areas the breasts are increasingly seen as sexual ornaments, of an almost phallic character—or copulatory cushions for men—rather than crucial organs of maternity and nurturance and symbols of the larger dimensions of female eroticism. In affluent countries, the damage inflicted by this attitude is chiefly psychological. But elsewhere the result offers more visible evidence of the power of ideas.

Beyond the psychological and sexual gratifications for both mother and child, breast feeding confers a variety of nutritional, economic, and prophylactic benefits that can be approached by bottle feeding and medical treatment only for a minority of affluent and informed parents. As recent studies by the World Bank, the World Health Organization, and Brookings Institution have demonstrated, natural milk creates resistance to malaria, polio, and other bacteria or viruses. It counteracts rickets, anemia, intestinal infection, and allergies. It is crucial during the first months when early brain development occurs.[14] In addition, it evokes hormonal and psychological changes in the mother that promote maternal behavior. Thus it can benefit the mental health of the child for a lifetime (and probably the health of the woman as well).

Yet encouraged by the androgynist spirit—by modernist doctors exalting male science over female physiology, and by "feminists" exalting jobs over maternity—breast feeding is declining everywhere. During the last ten years the number of American mothers suckling their children when they left the hospital dropped by 50 percent. Only among some affluent mothers and hippies does the practice remain in style. Among the poor the continuing high level of infant mortality, mental retardation, and other deficiencies is believed by experts to be in part attributable to the widespread abandonment of this unique form of infant nourishment.

In the underdeveloped world the effect is nothing less than disastrous. The total economic losses are estimated to run into the billions annually—far greater than all current U.S. foreign aid—at a time when many of these countries are on the verge of famine. Infant and child mortality are greater almost everywhere among bottle-fed children. Nevertheless the abandonment of breast feeding also stimulates population growth. In the suckling mother, ovulation may be delayed from ten weeks to as long as 26 months. Alan Berg of the World Bank reports that in Taiwan extended suckling is estimated to reduce births by 20 percent. In India the same ratio would mean prevention of approximately five million births a year.

Stating a growing consensus of health experts around the world, Berg concludes: "Whoever is to blame for the dramatic decline of breast feeding . . . it represents a staggering loss . . . both in high mortality and morbidity rates and in outright economic cost. For the vulnerable infant and young child, a reversal of the current trend could be of greater significance than any other form of nutrition intervention." [15]

The shift to inadequate artificial substitutes is only partly a product of fashion and convenience. Although at least 85 percent of all mothers have the physical capacity to nurse for six months or longer, many women are developing psychological blocks against suckling their babies.[16] Reducing themselves to the limits of male sexuality—becoming sex objects for men—these women seem embarrassed by their greater erotic possibilities and give up what are described as among the richest and most important sensual experiences.

A return to breast feeding would be a significant move against androgyny. Margaret Mead has written of the crucial value of this practice in giving the infant a sense of complementary sexual roles, a sense of the importance of the mother and of all sexual differences. Breast feeding also gives women a further direct experience of their sexual superiority over men. Recent studies show that mothers who have nursed are most likely to believe that women have a more satisfying time in life than men.[17] The woman feeding her child dramatizes the most insuperable barrier to androgyny: women can do almost everything that men can do but men can never equal women sexually.

Male propaganda may suggest that copulation is the most exalted human experience and that sex is an exercise of male domination. But the woman with her child knows otherwise. And all men, consciously or unconsciously, recognize the supremacy of this maternal coupling in civilized society. The women who call for androgyny thus are not only attacking the foundations of male identity; they are also subverting female sexuality.

Robin Fox and Lionel Tiger in their book, *The Imperial Animal*,[18] go beyond sexual differences to assert that most human behavior of all kinds is ultimately shaped by chromosomal information, selected and assembled during the millions of years we spent hunting on the African savannas. They draw an analogy to the recent theories of linguists. Linguists speculate that all speech formation is ruled by certain principles inherent in the human brain. Thus, even though possibilities for varied expression are immense, they all must follow certain patterns, and whole lost languages may be deduced from a few surviving particles. Tiger and Fox contend that human behavior is similarly systematic and governed by what they call "biogrammar." Just as attempts to contrive languages that do not accord with the universal principles will fail—producing gibberish—so modes of human behavior that violate our deepest natures will produce "behavioral gibberish." Social disintegration will result.

When reforming the roles of men and women, we must always be careful to avoid behavioral gibberish—patterns of activity that so violate the inner constitution of the species that they cannot be integrated with our irreducible human natures. The problem of many of the sweeping new concepts of women's liberation is that, for all their technological feasibility, all their political appeal, they are sexually unconstitutional. The androgynous society is behavioral gibberish. But to understand its full costs one must understand the woman's role in civilization, and feminists do not.

The Woman's Role

We're very biological animals. We always tend to
think that if one is in a violent state of emotional need,
it is our unique emotional need or state, when in
fact it is probably just the emotions of a young woman
whose body is demanding that she have children . . . Anna and
Molly [Communist heroines of *The Golden Notebook*]
are women who are conditioned to be one way and are trying to
be another. I know lots of girls who don't want to
get married or have children. And very vocal they are about
it. Well, they're trying to cheat on their biology . . .

Doris Lessing
Harper's, *June 1973*

The average American woman who looks into the media
—that vivid trick mirror of her society—finds a cluster of
negative images. Gloria Steinem has memorably declared her,
in essence, a "prostitute." [1] Germaine Greer thinks she is "a
female eunuch," not even being paid.[2] After depicting her as
a hapless victim of history, Kate Millett defined the problem
as Norman Mailer, Henry Miller, and D. H. Lawrence, and
the solution as Genet; [3] she then came helpfully out of the
closet herself.[4] Betty Friedan envisages woman as a vain gull
of male exploitation, frittering away her talents in boredom
and drudgery.[5] Ellen Peck sees her remorselessly trapped by
babies.[6] Susan Brownmiller sees her relentlessly tweaked by
goosers (no kidding, almost everywhere, all the time).[7]

The beat goes on. John and Yoko scream, "Woman is
the Nigger of the World." Others more delicately describe
her as the permanent proletariat. Esther Vilar, supposedly
antifeminist, finds the average woman a "parasite." [8] Greer,
in debate with her, shrewdly agrees.[9] Popular singers find
woman in a state of alternating and converging sexual pain
and desire. Natalie Gittelson finds her in a state of continuous
sexual frustration and incipient or active promiscuity.[10] Philip
Roth in *Portnoy's Complaint* vividly depicts that style of
maternal "oppression" which has produced by far the most
successful single group of Americans. [11]

Meanwhile, having grandly urged, in *Ms.*, that women
dispense with underwear, Germaine Greer returns to the fray
in *Harper's* to depict Gloria Steinem and all the other women
at the Democratic convention as being "screwed" by Frank
Mankiewicz and the Democratic establishment.[12] (Greer,
however, narrowly escaped a similar fate at the hands of a
panty-raiding movie star.) [13] In case anything was unclear in
the *Harper's* piece, she continued to undress her *weltanschau-
ung* afterwards in *Playboy*—$3,000 being $3,000—maintaining that almost all heterosexual screwing is rape.[14] Thus she
added to her pejorative edge on Gloria Steinem's unhappy
hookings and Susan Brownmiller's prickly heat, but still
lagged behind, in polemical pith, the Cambridge view of
sex as a "debilitating and counterrevolutionary" distraction.

Ingrid Bengis, who can write, finds woman hateful and
angry; [15] Phyllis Chesler finds her psychopathic but curable

by the creation of artificial wombs.[16] Greer puts it more intricately: Women are sick, but only when the society deems them healthy, or when they are dull and happy and impotent, if you get it.[17] A thousand writers find them hopeless puppets of Madison Avenue, hapless victims of sexism, reluctant prisoners of suburbia. And many of these negatives, widely propagated by the media, influence the self-image of millions of women, pursuing good and constructive lives under difficult conditions. They are distracted and confused, moreover, by the corollary illusions of "liberation." [18]

Most of the proponents are graduate students, assistant professors, journalists, and various lumpen litterateurs; products of distended education and stinted experience, permissive sex and cynical love; or else they are wives and mothers manqué, having their revenge on the world of men. An indefatigable few are lesbians or dildotage activists.

But mostly they are young and intellectual, suffering from the simultaneous contraction of opportunity and inflation of prestige affecting most of their age and profession. Spoiled by doting parents during the postwar binge of pretentious motherhood, beneficiaries of a steadily ascending familial affluence, taught to expect too much of life, educated to believe that qualifications decide, and qualified as no previous female generation—these women simply have no idea how most people live, or why. Their catalogue of pejoratives neatly replaces their elders' social snobbism (which they regard as utterly despicable) with a new idiom of intellectual snobbism, conveniently directed toward many of the very same people: those same poor, status-seeking, materialistic, insensitive, dull inhabitants of America's suburbs. But it is no use asking these poor suburbanites about their lives. Why, they *must* be unhappy—they're not like *us*. And if they aren't unhappy, they must be sick (i.e., suffering from false or "lowered consciousness").

Okay. Enough for the *ad feminam* approach. Midge Decter has done it much better. The essential point is that for the liberationists, their two subjects, America and sex, are great *terra incognita*. They think sex is some kind of pleasurable massage and sexual differences an invention of "sexists"; and they think the United States is some kind of protofascist society, for which problems of scarcity and growth should no longer be of concern. They also think motherhood is a secondary role because of the population explosion (which has inflicted as much brain damage as ecological strain). Thus they cannot understand the American woman, who like the American man, is in the largest sense a sexual rather than an ideological being, who devotes a large proportion of her energies to maternal roles, who senses that sex is a product of crucial differences, and who still relentlessly lives in a world of scarcity.

Take that American suburban housewife, for example. She has been closely studied, in the general context of her suburban environment, by Herbert J. Gans,[19] and in 573 close and specific personal interviews by Helen Znaniecki Lopata.[20] They conclude, like many other observers, that people deeply enjoy suburban living, most particularly women, and that suburbanites tend to be among the happiest Americans. In addition, the sociologists show, the suburbs are particularly notable for the lack of isolation of women there. The city dweller and the farmer tend to be far more devoid of social aid and involvement. A few newcomers and misfits, often intellectual, are lonely and dissident, and they are all too often allowed to speak for the rest. Some women give the impression they would not venture forth under any conditions.

But in general, Lopata and Gans both depict a panorama of social engagement, community concern, cooperative activity and even, in many cases, cultural and intellectual animation: a realm of options that substantially exceeds those of either men or working women. Mrs. Lopata, for instance, found that suburban housewives, by a significant margin, were more likely than working women to be using their education in their lives, to be reading widely and curiously, to be maintaining close and varied friendships, and to be involved in community affairs. "The role of housewife provides her a base for building a many faceted life, an opportunity few other vocational roles allow, because they are tied down to single organizational structures and goals." [21] Working women normally looked forward to leaving their jobs. Gans found that only 10 percent of suburban women reported frequent loneliness or boredom.[22]

That such observations may be viewed as surprising suggests the unreality of the notions of so many of the fashionably intellectual. It is really absurd to suppose that American women, educated extensively and in many cases more successfully than men, would move massively to the suburbs and then sit there and do nothing. It takes a really peculiarly mercenary or elite perspective to suppose that the workaday world of business and bureaucracy, where individuals tend to be fungible units, is more challenging and important than the realm of the home. The disparagement of the role of wife, mother, and homemaker—and the celebration of careers—is in fact the single most reprehensible aspect of the so-called women's movement. It is chiefly a way by which the new generation of the privileged—often in perfect innocence, like the upper-class woman who asks a poorer acquaintance where she went to college—displays the often spurious advantages of wealth and education. The insult is not changed in essence by attaching it to an ideology of liberation that can be fulfilled, and then often unhappily, only by an elite. The fact is that the role of the housewife is more important than any other broad category of work in the society, certainly more important than the combination of academic maneuvering and morbid radical politics much favored by the movement.

Of course, one should not replace the eunuch image with one of suburban eudaemonia. Life is tough all over. Jessie Bernard has found a pattern of nervous strain more serious among American housewives with children than among married men or single women. Only single men, by every measure the most afflicted Americans, show mental stresses substantially more acute.[23] One should differentiate between those two distressed groups, however, in social terms. The single men are in trouble because their lives violate the sexual constitution; they are failures in the most important realm of manhood in civilized society, the maintenance of a family. By contrast, the substantially lesser but still serious problem of the mothers reflects the inherent difficulty of a role that is fully positive but that modern conditions, including liberationist propaganda, have made more demanding.

The changes have often been remarked. In the past a mother role may have evolved naturally from one's experience in an extended family. One's entire education and range of expectations prepared one for it. As Midge Decter has observed, motherhood was regarded as inevitable; one didn't choose it; one accepted it.[24] Thus the strain was less. Modernity, moreover, has expanded the dimensions of maternal work. In the past, sickness, mortality, slow-learning, and other childhood afflictions were taken for granted as part of life. Today the mother is expected to control them. To the difficult tasks of physical support are now added burdens of medical diagnosis, psychological analysis, and early education.

Although new technology aids to some degree in performing the perfunctory work of the household, the woman's overall responsibilities are not suspended during the early stages of child-rearing. The mother is still expected to maintain an aesthetically pleasing home for child and husband, to prepare most meals, to maintain social connections, and to continue her own private education and development. Women's lib might call it "shitwork," and it certainly is hard work. But in a sense it is the best and most important work of the society.

There is no question at all that too many husbands have neglected their own role in this process. But feminists do not help matters by claiming complete procreative control of their bodies and praising women who raise children without fathers (all the while incongruously demanding that husbands assume new child care responsibilities like changing diapers). Nevertheless fathers are taking their parental role more seriously and will continue to do so as the workweek shortens for many jobholders in coming years. Airline pilots, for example, one of our most leisured working groups, with supremely masculine jobs (the number-one choice of teen-agers), are notably attentive fathers.[25] More support from husbands and from the society, perhaps in the form of child and maternity allowances, would be of significant help in relieving the burdens of motherhood.

But it is foolish to imagine that the complex roles and relationships sustained by the housewife can be abolished or assumed by outside agencies. Her role is nothing less than the central activity of the human community. All the other work— the business and politics and entertainment and service performed in the society—finds its ultimate test in the quality of the home. The home is where we finally and privately live, where we express our individuality, where we display our aesthetic choices, where we make and enjoy love, and where we cultivate our children as individuals. All very pedestrian, perhaps, but there is not very much more in civilized life.

The central position of the woman in the home parallels her central position in all civilized society. Both derive from her necessary role in procreation and from the most primary and inviolable of human ties, the one between mother and child. In those extraordinary circumstances when this tie is broken—as with some disintegrating tribes—broken as well is the human identity of the group. Most of the characteristics we define as humane and individual originate in the mother's love for her children.

Deriving from this love are the other civilizing concerns of maternity: the desire for male protection and support, the hope for a stable community life, and the aspiration for a better future. The success or failure of civilized society depends on how well the women can transmit these values to the men, to whom they come less naturally. The woman's sexual life and how she manages it is crucial to this process of male socialization. The males have no ties to women and children—or to long-term human community—so deep or tenacious as the mother's to her child. That is primary in society; all else is contingent and derivative.

This essential female role has become much more sophisticated and refined in the modern world. But its essence is the same. The woman assumes charge of what may be described as the domestic values of the community; its moral, aesthetic, religious, nurturant, social, and sexual concerns. In these values consist the ultimate goals of human life: all those matters that we consider of such supreme importance that we do not ascribe a financial worth to them. Paramount is the worth of the human individual, enshrined in the home, and in the connection between a woman and child. These values transcend the marketplace. In fact, to enter them in commercial traffic is considered a major evil in civilized society. Whether one proposes to sell a baby or a body or a religious blessing, one is conscious of a deep moral perversion.

The woman's place in this scheme is deeply individual.

She is valued for her uniqueness. Only a specific woman can bear a specific child, and her tie to it is personal and infrangible. When she raises the child she imparts in privacy her own individual values. She can create children who transcend consensus and prefigure the future: children of private singularity rather than "child development policy."

Even the husband ultimately validates his individual worth through the woman. He chooses her for her special qualities and she chooses him to submit his marketplace reward to her—and to her individual values. A man in courtship offers not chiefly his work but his individuality to the woman. In his entire adult life, it may be only his wife who receives him as a whole human being.

One of the roles of the woman as arbiter, therefore, is to cultivate herself: to fulfill her moral, aesthetic, and expressive being as an individual. There is no standard beyond her. She is the vessel of the ultimate values of the society. The society is what she is and what she demands in men. She does her work because it is of primary rather than instrumental value. The woman in the home with her child is the last bastion against the technocratic marketplace.

The man's role is indispensable as well. But it is relatively fungible and derivative. He is in charge of the instrumental realm: the world of work and the marketplace. Here, individuality is much less in demand. Just as any particular hunter might kill an animal, so within obvious bounds any workman can be trained to do most jobs. The marketplace is the realm of utility, adaptability, and convertibility—of money. It is also the realm of objective power, where the organization of individuals by others with special knowledge or vision can lead to increased production of utility to the entire society. But ultimately not the man himself but the marketplace defines the value of the work.

Jobs rarely afford room for the whole man. Even highly paid work often creates what Ortega y Gasset called "barbarians of specialization." One may become a scientist, doctor, or lawyer, for example, chiefly by narrowing the mind, by excluding personal idiosyncrasies and visions in order to master the disciplines and technicalities of one's trade. This process does not fulfill the individual in any profound way. Nor does it usually make him interesting or whole. In fact, he is likely to succeed precisely to the extent he is willing to subordinate himself to the narrow impersonal categories of his specialty, precisely to the extent he foregoes the distractions and impulses of the integral personality.

Among men, the term dilettante may be a pejorative. Yet, because the range of human knowledge and experience is so broad, the best that most people can ever achieve if they respond as whole persons to their lives, is the curiosity, openness, and eclectic knowledge of the dilettante at her best. Most men have to forego this form of individual fulfillment. They have to limit themselves, at great psychological cost, in order to fit the functions of the economic division of labor. Most of them endure their submission to the marketplace chiefly in order to make enough money to sustain a home, to earn a place in the household, to be needed by women.

"Women's liberation" entails a profound dislocation. Women, uniquely in charge of the central activities of human life, are exalting instead the peripheral values—values that have meaning only in relation to the role they would disparage or abandon. Through the women's movement, moreover, the society is being asked to dispense with most of the devices and conventions by which it was ensured that women perform their indispensable work and by which men have been induced to support it. Among those devices and conventions is the system the feminists call sexism, which in fact, is based on the exaltation of women, acknowledgment of the supremacy of domestic values, and the necessity of inducing men to support them in civilized society.

In effect, the system of discrimination, which the movement is perfectly right in finding nearly ubiquitous, tells women that if they enter the marketplace they will often receive less pay than a man, not because they could do the job less well but because they have an alternative role of incomparable value to the society as a whole. The man, on the other hand, is paid more not because of special virtue but because of the key importance of socializing his naturally disruptive energies. In addition, his possession of a margin of financial superiority endows his role as provider or social and sexual initiator.

In practice, this system has not imposed any very grievous hardship on many women who desire to work. It has merely given them a mild burden of proof: to show their work is financially indispensable to themselves and their families; or to show that it is essentially devoted to domestic rather than marketplace values; or to show that it is of such unique quality or productivity that it justifies compromise of other responsibilities. These criteria mean that women are mildly discouraged from taking fungible jobs of an ascribed masculine character, with primary incentives of pay and status. These values are more important to the provider and initiator males. But women are encouraged to make unique contributions in the realm of aesthetics, literature, art, and entertainment, and are paid just as much as men when they do. They can conduct enterpreneurial activity when they have a marketplace idea that will enrich the community. They are also assigned a variety of nurturant and service jobs for which they are judged to have special competence.

Needless to say, moreover, women are not excluded from the work that might be described as essentially masculine. If their motivation and skill are sufficient, they can overcome almost any of the barriers the society has rather fecklessly erected against them. Females in virtually every arena of economic and social activity confute the stupid feminist charges of carefully cultivated impotence and ineptitude. Again the key test is an especially intense motivation, an exceptionally strong talent, an extraordinary resolve. These qualities are amply found in American women.

Nonetheless, the woman's place *is* in the home, and she does her best when she can get the man there too. That, she cannot easily do alone. The society has to provide a role for him, usually as provider, that connects him to the family in a masculine way. But if social conditions are right, the woman can induce the man to submit most human activity to the domestic values of civilization.

Thus in a sense she also brings the home into the society. The radiance of the values the home embodies can give meaning and illumination not only to male sexuality but also to all other masculine enterprises. Male work is most valuable when it is imbued with long-term love and communal concern of femininity, when it is brought back to the home. Otherwise masculine activity is apt to degenerate quickly to the level of a game, and unless closely regulated, games have a way of deteriorating into the vain pursuit of power. Male games are kept in socially affirmative modes by the judgment of women. Men come to learn that their activity will be best received if it partakes of the value of the home. If they think the work itself is unworthy, they try to conceal it and bring home the money alone. Like the legendary Mafiosi, they try to please their women by elaborate submission to domestic values in the home, while scrupulously keeping the women out of the male realm of work. But in almost every instance, they pay tribute to the moral superiority of women.

The feminist answer to such arguments is usually a flip question: If the woman's role is so great, why don't men want it? One answer is that in a sense men unconsciously do want it. Their desire is shown in the character of primitive male initiation rites, in which all the processes of childbirth are simulated; it is shown in the ritual of couvade, in which men actually undergo labor; [26] it is shown perhaps in the tendency of men, more than women, to turn transvestite; it is shown in love, focused on the procreative and nurturant formations of the woman's body and mind. But nevertheless it is, unimpeachably, the woman's role, and males have to be taught by women even its derivative values. In addition, when men too intimately emulate the woman's role, they endanger their masculinity. The aggressiveness and extroversion of males is most useful to the society when it is submitted to, but not absorbed by, female sexual values. The transvestite is at best a barren parody.

The fact is that there is no way that women can escape their supreme responsibilities in civilized society without endangering civilization itself. The most chilling portent of our current crises, therefore, is the conjuncture of a movement of female abdication with a new biochemistry, which shines direct and deadly beams of technocratic light on the very crux of human identity, the tie between the mother and her child.

With the possible creation of clones and artificial wombs, human reproduction is on the not-so-distant verge of becoming a branch of laboratory husbandry. It is the ultimate scandal of the women's movement that it doesn't seem to care. In fact,

Shulamith Firestone of the New York Liberationists joins the Central Committee of the Chinese Communist Party in hailing the impending technology as "a happy day for women." [27] Ms. Firestone and the Chinese have long been concerned by the number of working days lost through pregnancy and childbirth.

But forgetting the Chinese, perhaps the women's movement might be more concerned if they understood that what is happening can be accurately described as the effort of a small group of male scientists to achieve the sexual nullification of women. The statement might seem extreme. Yet to "separate, for once and for all," as Edward Grossman puts it, "intercourse and reproduction" [28]—to perfect *in vitro* fertilization, artificial wombs, cloning, and other biomedical techniques of human manufacture—is to destroy the meaning and utility of much of the female body. (If you don't know what the biomedical terms mean—or if you think they merely comprise a panoply of inviting new options—you illustrate the extent of the threat). It is a concerted attack on the physical constitution of women. Female psychology could not help but suffer grave strains as a result.

Except in the case of cloning, the limited sexual circuits of males are less affected. Masturbation will still be a convenient way to collect semen. But, of course, the destruction of female sexuality would mean also the destruction of its male counterpart in all its significant dimensions. The sexual suicide of the human race would be a *fait accompli*. If we underestimate the danger and fail to act, merely because it is only future generations that will be directly affected, we may by omission commit an act of genocide that dwarfs any in human history. Perhaps that should be considered an evil—in the view of political woman—comparable even to sexism.

The Sexual Suicide Technocracy

The family . . . is the native soil on which performance
of moral duty is made easy through natural affection so that
within a small circle a basis of moral practice is created,
and then is widened to include human relationships in general.

I Ching

Whether man will in fact take the irreversible steps of sexual suicide remains part of the essential mystery of human life. Is human sexuality so deeply imprinted that we would disdain to use the new devices and so inexorable that they could not profoundly change us if we did? Or are we in essence a genetic *tabula rasa,* on which can be inscribed any formula for eternal happiness that scientists and politicians design?

Of course, there are other possibilities. There is the view that sexual differences are of little fundamental importance in human life, that we are all primarily loving and cooperative human beings distracted by the superstitions surrounding our reproductive systems. If women can be relieved of the bondage of childbirth, they can accede to their full humanity. And we all can escape the crucible of family, in which originates our hatred and fear of outsiders, our racism, nationalism, and sexism. We can at long last join the great planetary family of human beings with which we are objectively and rationally one, but from which we are subjectively and superstitiously separated.

But it seems the problem is more complicated. We have produced a sexual culture that sustains civilized life. That sexual culture and its related constitution partake both of deep human propensities, such as the mother-child connection, and of valuable social inventions deriving from it, such as the submission of male to female sexuality in love. The deep human propensities can be weakened and the sexual culture destroyed, leaving us as sexual primitives in a world of advanced technology. The men would lack the commitment to the future, to extended time, that women confer. The women would retain only a lingering nostalgia for the patterns of human individuality that were elaborated from their love of the specific children they bore in their wombs and nurtured at their breasts. Morally vacant, these humans would have to be technocratically controlled. An external constitution of force and pharmacology would replace the internal constitution of sexuality.

In any case, one can no longer dismiss such issues of human nature as mere distractions of intellectuals who can no longer hear the beating of their own hearts. It is a tribute to the nature of the new biomedical technology that it lends an immediate and inescapable heartbeat to the immemorial games of the philosophers. For it removes our frail haven of human biology, whatever it is. We cannot shrug any longer and return to the dense realm of our immediate physical existence as human beings in society. This realm is precisely what the technology would transform.

The nature and moral implications of the new biomedical technology have been powerfully and eloquently discussed by Leon R. Kass,[1] a doctor who thinks like the best of lawyers and writes like the best of writers. In a more literary mode, Edward Grossman's essay "The Obsolescent Mother"[2] has elegiacally captured the impact of the new techniques on the long, historic saga of childbirth in mystery and tumult. Several books have been written on the subject, ranging from the cogently premonitory to the fatuously Panglossian (the idiom of the "now" theologians who have decided the grail is a test tube).[3]

The best analyses face the real portent of these developments—the impending abolition of historical and sexual man and a new stage in evolution, such as was intimated at the end of the movie *2001*. But it may happen before then, for technological ventures into the space of woman, though less cinematically spectacular, are both far more advanced and far more apocalyptic than any prospective adventures of astronauts. We are very close to a small step for man—a giant leap for mankind—over a genetic precipice.

The three approaches about which most is known are *in vitro* or test-tube fertilization; extracorporeal gestation (the artificial womb); and cloning, the exact reproduction or "xeroxing" of human genotypes. Cloning poses the most obvious threat to human individuality, but the other two related techniques have implications scarcely less far-reaching.

A clone is created by implanting the nucleus of a human cell, from any part of the body, into the enucleated cell of a female egg. This process, which can be repeated as often as eggs and wombs are available, creates genetic copies of the donor of the nucleus, identical twins in every way except age. It has the additional fillip of making possible the abolition of males, since the three necessary elements—a cell nucleus, an enucleated egg, and a womb—can all be provided by a woman.[4] Successful cloning has already been done with frogs, salamanders, and fruit flies. At present it appears that the first mammal clone will be an English rat.

The date when cloning becomes feasible partly depends on progress with *in vitro* fertilization. One potential obstacle to large-scale experimentation with humans—the acquisition of sufficient numbers of eggs—has been overcome by a surgical technique called laparoscopy, which allows scientists to acquire several ova at a time, and by new freezing and storing techniques. Laboratory fertilization itself has already been accomplished by doctors around the world. The problem comes in transmitting the blastocyte or fertilized egg to the uterine wall. In order for an embryo to form, this delicate operation must occur at the correct moment both in the menstrual cycle and in the development of the blastocyte. Although achieved many times in animals by a relatively random process, the refinements that would make it systematically applicable to humans were still uncertain at last report. Everyone agrees it is just a matter of time, and many doctors are ready to proceed with their own patients as soon as the research scientists specify the exact timing and alleviate fears of mutations and other mishaps.

The next step after *in vitro* fertilization—extracorporeal gestation and ectogenesis—is more complicated. It entails in essence the creation of artificial wombs. The problems are being approached from both ends: the saving of increasingly premature babies and the extension of the life of blastocytes into the embryonic stages. The obstacles remain formidable. The claim of an Italian scientist to have cultivated a fertilized egg into an embryo has been largely discredited.[5] Impressive successes have been obtained with rats, however, and biologists believe humans will be just a matter of time.

After reading the intelligible literature, the impression of an apprehensive layman is that it will be quite a long time before artificial wombs can be manufactured in sufficient quantities to replace natural ones. Nonetheless, the creation of even a small number of elaborate and expensive devices would be portentous because it would relieve the scientists of the tiresome task of finding and managing available women. Clones, chimeras (human-animal hybrids), and other experimental "sports" could be generated and flushed at will.

Even scientists can only guess the likely chronology of new developments. Nobel Prize-winner James D. Watson, the discoverer of DNA structure, has told Congress his fear that cloning will probably be perfected for humans "within the next twenty to fifty years" if research proceeds at its present rate— "and conceivably even sooner if some nation actively promotes the venture." [6] With *in vitro* fertilization essentially a *fait accompli* and the artificial womb contingent only on a careful re-creation of amniotic biochemistry, the precipice seems dangerously close.

For example, *in vitro* fertilization may seem a relatively limited step beyond the use of artificial insemination. That widely accepted practice has already given a few hundred medical students technical paternity over several hundred thousand children, while bringing happiness to large numbers of men and women.[7] Laboratory fertilization merely seems to extend relief to certain childless women that was previously available only if the sterility was in their husbands. The relief is decidedly better, moreover, since it allows the woman to retain full genetic maternity of her children.

Yet this seemingly innocent practice—the least of the new developments—has far-reaching implications. Since it means that virtually any couple can have a biologically related child, the value of other children is diminished. Adoption, for example, becomes significantly less attractive. Abortion becomes significantly more inviting. To have a child of one's own flesh and blood becomes seen as a virtual right, to be enforced by technicians, rather than as a miraculous blessing. Whether the change is significant depends in part on your attitude toward adoption, orphanages, and various modes of state child care. But it also depends on your attitude toward sex.

Like artificial insemination, *in vitro* fertilization circumvents the act of love. It is another rather small step in dismantling that complex of crucial connections embodied in sexual intercourse. Intercourse is demoted from its pinnacle as both the paramount act of love and the only act of procreation. The trend toward regarding it as just another mode of transmitting and receiving pleasure is thereby somewhat reinforced. The connection of the man to the psychologically potent realm of procreation is attenuated.

Of course, it can be said that this technique would be used only by otherwise sterile couples. Thus laboratory fertilization is alleged to be a gain for the role of procreation in their lives. But as Kass emphasizes, most of the women who can be helped by this technique also could be aided by surgery on their oviducts.[8] This operation, he feels, could be made more effective if it were promoted as strongly as the fertilization projects. He contends that the doctors who tell their patients, in seeking access to their ova, that this is their only hope for children, are virtually lying. For *in vitro* fertilization is no hope for anyone yet, while an oviduct operation is feasible now. In addition, fertilization does not cure sterility. It merely circumvents it, while the operation could achieve a permanent cure.

In any case the emphasis on the plight of the sterile couple is to some extent a pretext for a far more ambitious line of research heavily funded by the foundations.[9] For on the success of *in vitro* fertilization depends the success of cloning and ectogenesis. And since in pure research terms, all these experiments could be more easily and fruitfully conducted on monkeys, the insistence on immediate human involvement raises serious questions about the real motives of the enterprise.

In vitro fertilization itself affords human uses far beyond the circumvention of sterility. It makes possible a further disconnection of motherhood and pregnancy. The fertilized ovum does not have to be placed in the womb of the real "mother." Any womb will do: the womb of a sister, of a professional "mother," of a single friend, of a lesbian. Thus the very role of mother and the profound biological tie with her child—enacted in the most intense experience of human life—become optional. New, more attenuated and partial forms of motherhood become available. This development, for which strong pressures may arise from busy, preoccupied or liberated women, threatens to diminish further the sanctity of the family, diminish further the perceived and felt authority of the fundamental connections of human life.

Laboratory fertilization, though, is just a first and indispensable step toward greater leaps against mankind. The most formidable is cloning. It should not be necessary to reiterate the arguments against such an attack on human individuality, sexuality, and identity. The ability to make unlimited copies of any human reduces the uniqueness and sanctity of the individual. Apart from all the psychological complications of having an exact replica as a parent or child, the social benefits of this practice redound chiefly to the technocratic state. The state would have to decide which genotypes were most worthy of reproduction. This power is too great to invest in any human authority. It is power not merely over the immediate arrangements of human life but also over all future generations.

If the further advance, ectogenesis, is also achieved, the state could assume control over all reproduction. True child-development centers could be established and women would never have to concern themselves again with the burdens of motherhood. All the children would become the possession and responsibility of the society as a whole. This arrangement may appeal to one's idealistic visions. It might be seen as diffusing equally through the whole community the now concentrated boons and burdens of maternal love. But one should also consider the likelihood that maternal love is itself a product of sexuality—of intercourse, pregnancy, labor, nurture, and the genetic tie.

Here begins to emerge the real menace of women's liberation. By reducing the realm of the sexual constitution, one does not create a new realm of groovy communal love. One creates a vacuum in the lives of the people. Individuals no longer so closely tied to mother, family, and sexuality become more open to a totalitarian state—a state with powers, moreover, unapproached by any government in all human history.

Kass quotes C. S. Lewis's powerful tract, *The Abolition of Man:* "If any one age really attains, by eugenics and scientific education, the power to make its descendants what it pleases, all men who live after it are patients of that power. They are weaker, not stronger. . . . The real picture is that of one dominant age . . . which resists all previous ages most successfully and dominates all subsequent ages most irresistibly, and thus is the real master of the human species. But even within this master generation (itself an infinitesimal minority of the species) the power will be exercised by a minority smaller still. Man's conquest of nature, if the dreams of the scientific planners are realized, means the rule of a few hundreds of men over billions upon billions of men. There neither is nor can there be any simple increase in power on man's side. Each new power won *by* man is a power *over* man as well." [10]

Another way of putting it, however, is to say that each new power won by man in the guise of technocracy is a power over women. Ultimately even the womb becomes obsolete. Not only is the female body rendered a strange combination of otiose spaces and appendages, not only is the concept of woman in the society thus degraded, not only does man become the exemplary, utilitarian physique, but the power of women is destroyed. First, as time passes, her sexual powers will decrease. For when we break the tie between sexual intercourse and procreation, destroy the childhood memory of the nurturing and omnipotent mother, banish the mystique of the breasts and the womb and of the female curves and softnesses, we will remove as well much of the special attraction of heterosexual love. We will liberate the man to celebrate, like the ancient Spartans, a violent, misogynistic, and narcissistic eroticism. We will open the way for the ultimate patriarchy in which the technocratic state—itself a distended monster of male power—makes possible the maintenance of order and sustenance without submission to female sexuality. We would also enable the elimination of the female's most important principle: the uniqueness and sanctity of the individual human life. This principle gains its emotional authority and conviction from the realm of women, the home and family, and ultimately from the tie between mother and child.

Millions of American men know something about the spirit and feasibility of such a masculine society. The ones who have been to war can write about combat. Otherwise the epitome of male liberation is Marine Corps boot camp, twelve weeks without a moment of liberty, all devoted chiefly to the extirpation of feminine ties and sentiments in the assembled young men. From the moment one arrives, the drill instructors begin a torrent of misogynistic and anti-individualist abuse. The good things are manly and collective; the despicable are feminine and individual. Virtually every sentence, every description, every lesson embodies this sexual duality, and the female anatomy provides a rich field of metaphor for every degradation.

When you want to create a solidary group of male killers, that is what you do, you kill the women in them. That is the lesson of the Marines. And it works. Artfully exploiting the internal pressures of the group, the instructors manage to evoke a fanatical commitment from almost every recruit. They arrive as various and rebellious boys, swearing under their breath what they will do to any drill instructor who lays a hand on them. They end up, after twelve weeks of man-handling, often including violent physical abuse, gladly and voluntarily making large financial gifts to the instructors. It is the closest thing to an act of love that happens at Parris Island.

Most of those who have experienced these sentiments would testify that they are not exactly homosexual. They do not represent a shift to males of sentiments conventionally directed toward females. They represent rather a distinctive bonding process that corresponds very closely to the kind of male tie that Lionel Tiger has controversially envisaged. It has its uses in protecting a society from its enemies or in abetting the performance of crucial group activities. But it is deadly to individuality and civilization. It is deadly to the sentiments that women evoke from men: love, creativity, nurturance, commitment to the future. Above all, it is perfectly barren (in the etymological sense, from the old French word *bar,* meaning man).[11] The male group, separated from women, is the sterile solidarity. There is no real love, no individuality, and no procreative instinct.

When the group leaves the Island and is once again exposed to the female body, it treats it, needless to say, as what is called a sexual object. Women are initially regarded as desirable only in the circuit of tension and release which is the most essential form of male erotic experience. Pornographic movies near military centers tend to consist of violent attacks on women, and one of the favorite stories told on the return to the base from liberty is of the violent abuse of a whore.

The attraction of women can ultimately prevail, however, and the women can transform it into a procreative drive.

Then the sterile solidarity gives way to sexual complements. The man's desire for progeny, even if unconscious at first, induces love and a concern for the future. The woman becomes an individual, and a potential source of unaccustomed long-term meaning for his otherwise brief and barren sexuality. Thus she confers individuality on him as well.

At this point the new world of the man, to the extent it reaches into the future, becomes dependent on the woman's love for him. He relies on her for sexual identity in a way in which she, who already has a sexual identity, never has to rely on him. She can bear a child whether he stays or not, while he loses his child if she departs. His tie to the future—and thus his engagement in civilized society—passes through her womb.

When considering the implications of the new technology of reproduction, it is usual to mention the liberation of women. Nothing could be more profoundly wrong. It assures the bondage of women to male technocracy and the liberation of males from the civilizing bondage of the womb. They are freed to pursue their own sexual cycles in uncivilized groups, while the technocracy sustains the community.

The question arises why the women do not run the technocracy under these conditions. The reason is that women succumb to male sexual cycles. Having lost their erotic power over men, they become a subordinate class. The male's physique, inferior to the woman's in a sexual society, becomes superior in a sexual suicide society where the state manages procreation. The male body becomes the physical ideal and lends symbolic authority to his command of other instruments of power. The male pattern of insecurity, dominance, and group aggression will prevail over domestic and individual values. The technocracy, a dominantly male creation in the first place (some 90 percent of scientists are men),[12] remains in the hands of a male minority.

In the sexual suicide society, the only winner is the state. Increasingly in control of childbirth and "child development," the state will usurp the last bastion of human privacy and individuality: the home. Children can be homogenized and all troublesome defects and idiosyncrasies removed. Perhaps even sexism could be eliminated. But it is likely that the "vestigial procreative deformities" of women would become objects of derision. Perhaps the breasts could be removed, as Ms. Chesler finds in the myth of some Amazon tribes. In any case, the women would at last be liberated from the "baby trap" and from the oppressions of marriage and family. This is the ultimate destination of "feminism": female inferiority and familial disintegration under the auspices of the Sexual Suicide State.

Such is the ultimate destination of the current alliance of women's liberation and technocracy. What are the chances of preventing it? Here arise again the key philosophical questions about the nature of man. But it is most useful to pose them in different terms. The question is not whether mankind is good or bad, aggressive or cooperative, elaborately imprinted with a specific "biogrammar" or blankly receptive to external organization. The question is not whether sexuality is so profound that women and men would disdain the use of the machinery. The question is whether male or female sexual principles will prevail.

That question is completely different from the question of whether men or women will dominate. In civilized society, ironically enough, individual men are more dependent than women on the maintenance of female sexual dominance. For their whole socialization—their entire pattern of life—depends on a willful and cultural submission of their own rudimentary sexuality to long-term female principles. Female sexuality and identity, on the other hand, are more natural and inevitable and thus less immediately vulnerable to social change. This is why public opinion polls tend to show males as more conservative toward the new technology than females. Males know that their lives and their civilized sexuality are vulnerable; that there is an alternative for them, which they specifically rejected in their youth. Women tend not to understand this. Sexuality seems so inevitable to them that they often cannot see its precarious foundations.

The best way to assay the prospects for the new technology, therefore, is to consider whether that complex of interests and commitments, sexual drives and transcendences —whether that system of female order and principle within which males have the power and burden of initiative—whether the home and family can endure. These institutions are the chief obstacle to the technocratic state. If they endure, the realm of the state and the development and use of the technology can be limited, while the maintenance of human individuality can be assured. If the family expires, then the world of artificial wombs, clones, and child development centers can become a reality. Norman Mailer was thus most profound when he defined the movement of women's liberation as the fifth column of the technocracy. He might have added that it is also the fifth column of true patriarchy: the sterile solidarity.

The question thus becomes: Will the scientists and women's liberationists be able to unleash on the world a generation of kinless children to serve as the Red Guards of a totalitarian state? Will we try to reproduce the Nazi experiment, when illegitimacy was promoted by the provision of lavish nursing homes and the state usurped the provider male. Or will we manage to maintain our most indispensable condition of civilization—and obstacle to totalitarian usurpation —the human marriage and family.

Notes

Introduction

1. Phyllis Chesler, *Women and Madness*. Garden City, N.Y.: Doubleday, 1972.

2. Ibid., pp. 299, 304.

3. Sidney Abbott and Barbara Love, *Sappho Was a Right-On Woman: A Liberated View of Lesbianism*. New York: Stein & Day, 1972.

4. *New York Times Book Review*, February 25, 1973: 39, 40.

5. Philip Nobile, "What's the New Impotence and Who's Got It?" *Esquire*, October 1972: 95 ff.; see also, Joseph Adelson, "Is Women's Lib a Passing Phase?" *The New York Times Magazine*, March 19, 1972: 26 ff.

6. The overwhelming preponderance of males among criminals is summarized by Edwin H. Sutherland and Donald R. Cressy, *Principles of Criminology*, Philadelphia: Lippincott, 1966, p. 138: "The crime rate for men is greatly in excess of the crime rate for women—in all nations, all communities within a nation, all age groups, all periods of history for which statistics are available, and for all types of crime except those peculiar to women, such as infanticide and abortion." Edwin M. Schur points out that there are 20 times as many men as women in major prisons and reformatories and 15 times as many men in local jails (*Our Criminal Society, The Social and Legal Sources of Crime in America*, Englewood Cliffs, N.J.: Prentice-Hall, 1969, p. 41). Later statistics indicate a ratio of 25 to 1 for federal and state prisons in 1970 (*The American Almanac, The U.S. Book of Statistics and Information*, New York: Grosset and Dunlap, 1973, from The Statistical Abstract of the U.S. prepared by the Department of the Census, U.S. Department of Commerce, issued September 1972, current to September 1973, p. 160).

7. Arrest statistics by sex and category may be found in *American Almanac*, op. cit., p. 151.

8. Jessie Bernard, *The Future of Marriage*, New York: World, 1972, Table 20 (page 341 in Bantam Books edition). About twice as many single women as single men held professional jobs (ibid.), and single men are almost eight times as likely as single women to show severe neurotic symptoms and about 60 percent more likely to suffer from depression and various psychopathic conditions (ibid., Tables 18, 19).

Bachelors are 21 times as likely as married men to be incarcerated in correctional or mental institutions. Hugh Carter and Paul C. Glick, *Marriage and Divorce: A Social and Economic Study*, Cambridge, Mass.: Harvard University Press, 1970, p. 410.

9. Nora Ephron, "Women," *Esquire*, July 1972: 42.

10. Ellen Goodman, "Occupation Housewife," *Boston Globe*, June 5, 1973. This account of the Radcliffe class of 1963 discloses the impact

of the women's movement on elite women. The 400 parents involved had produced only 224 children; the housewives felt defensive; and the achievers felt frustrated. "The anxieties of achieving women . . . hang out all over the pages."

Chapter 1—The Balance of Potency

1. Elizabeth Janeway, Participant in forum discussion, "Women on Women," *American Scholar* 41 (Autumn 1972): 608. Mrs. Janeway's theories are fully developed in *Man's World, Woman's Place: A Study in Social Mythology*. New York: Morrow, 1971.

2. Kate Millett, *Sexual Politics*. Garden City, N.Y.: Doubleday, 1969.

3. Midge Decter, *The New Chastity and Other Arguments Against Women's Liberation*. New York: Coward, McCann & Geoghegan, 1972.

4. Susan Brownmiller, "On Goosing," *The Village Voice*, April 15, 1971: 5.

5. A crosscultural study of 554 of the world's societies indicated that in one-quarter of them the father is only an occasional visitor with his children. George P. Murdock, "World Ethnographic Sample," *American Anthropologist*, 1957 (vol. 59). Perhaps the most famous society where physiological paternity is not recognized is the Trobriand Island tribe studied by Bronislaw Malinowski, in *The Sexual Life of Savages in North Western Melanesia*, 2 vols. New York: Harcourt Brace Jovanovich, 1929; and in *The Father in Primitive Psychology*, New York: Norton, 1927; Norton Library paperback, 1966.

6. Ashley Montagu, *Touching: The Human Significance of the Skin*. New York: Columbia University Press, 1971, pp. 181–182.

7. Karen Horney, *Feminine Psychology*. New York: Norton, 1967; Karen Horney, *New Ways in Psychoanalysis*. New York: Norton, 1939.

8. Erik H. Erikson, *Identity: Youth and Crisis*. New York: Norton, 1968, pp. 261–294.

9. Judith Hole and Ellen Levine, *Rebirth of Feminism*. New York: Quadrangle, 1971, p. 306. (A quote from Carol Burris and Wilma Scott Heide, *Critique of Reports*, White House Conference on Children: Cluster on Individuality, December 1970, unpaginated.)

10. Seymour Fisher, *Understanding the Female Orgasm*. New York: Basic Books, 1973, p. 187. (This book is a condensation of *The Female Orgasm: Psychology, Physiology, Fantasy*. New York: Basic Books, 1973).

11. Nancy Chodorow, "Being and Doing: A Cross-Cultural Examination of the Socialization of Males and Females." In Vivian Gornick and Barbara K. Moran (eds.), *Women in Sexist Society: Studies in*

Power and Powerlessness. New York: Basic Books, 1971, pp. 173–198, passim, and p. 197; Signet paperback edition, pp. 259–287, passim, and p. 286.

12. Mary Jane Sherfey, *The Nature and Evolution of Female Sexuality.* New York: Random House, 1972.

13. Robert Musil, *The Man Without Qualities.* New York: Putnam, 1965.

14. Midge Decter, *New Chastity,* op. cit., p. 93; also pp. 61–105, passim.

15. Fisher, *Female Orgasm,* op. cit., p. 195. Fisher maintained that "the greater a woman's feeling that love objects are not dependable (that they are easily lost or will disappear) the less likely she is to attain orgasm." In Fisher's survey, a dependable childhood relationship with a strong and authoritative father was the factor most often correlated with full orgasmic capability. He also says that some women can in time become so accustomed to insecurity that they reach a high level of orgasmic success without the sense that the lover is reliable. But in general the key factors are an authoritative father and a reliable lover.

16. Quoted in Cynthia Proulx, "Sex as Athletics," *Saturday Review of the Society,* May 1973: 66.

17. Clellan S. Ford and Frank A. Beach, *Patterns of Sexual Behavior.* New York: Harper & Row, 1951. This cross-cultural study, covering some 190 different societies, indicates that the male is universally more responsive to visual stimuli (p. 95), more prone to masturbation (p. 257), and more likely to indulge in homosexuality (p. 257). In addition "The practice of concealing the women's genital region with some type of clothing is far more common than is covering the male sexual organs. . . . There are no peoples who insist on the man covering his genitals and at the same time permit the woman to expose her genital region" (p. 95).

"In all animal species . . . males exhibit far more [initiatory foreplay] than do females" (p. 259). In many societies, the man has to give a gift to the woman (p. 98).

18. Steven Goldberg, *The Inevitability of Patriarchy.* New York: Morrow, 1973, pp. 51–73. Corrine Hutt, *Males and Females.* Harmondsworth, England: Penguin, 1972, pp. 106–131 and passim.

Although this book, *Sexual Suicide,* does not emphasize the hormonal and neurological differences between the sexes, the Goldberg and Hutt studies present conclusive evidence that the observable relative aggressiveness of males is biologically determined.

19. "Is the American Family in Danger?" *U.S. News and World Report,* April 16, 1973: 71.

Chapter 2—The Necessities of Love

1. Quoted in Helen Lawrenson, "The Feminine Mistake," *Esquire,* January 1971: 146.

2. Nora Ephron, "Women," *Esquire,* July 1972: 42.

3. Germaine Greer, *The Female Eunuch.* New York: McGraw-Hill, 1971, p. 339.

4. "All About the New Sex Therapy," *Newsweek,* November 27, 1972: 65 ff. Also like the liberationists and homosexuals, Masters and Johnson disdain the "missionary" position, though they acknowledge it is the most frequently employed. ("Ten Sex Myths Exploded," *The Sensuous Society,* Chicago: Playboy Press, 1973, p. 63). Germaine Greer is more vehement. She says that "the missionary position is about the least interesting . . . it can be a bloody bore." (Interview, ibid.: 164).

5. Norman Mailer, *The Prisoner of Sex.* Boston: Little, Brown, 1971. This book expatiates on the Mailer reverence for procreative sex evident in nearly all his works and interviews since *Advertisements for Myself.*

6. Lionel Tiger and Robin Fox, *The Imperial Animal.* New York: Holt, Rinehart, and Winston, 1971; Delta paperback, 1972, pp. 76–77.

Chapter 3—The Myths of Open Marriage

1. Nena O'Neill and George O'Neill, *Open Marriage: A New Life Style for Couples.* New York: M. Evans, 1972; Avon paperback, 1973.

2. Ibid., p. 267.

3. Robert Francoeur, *Eve's New Rib: Twenty Faces of Sex, Marriage and Family.* New York: Harcourt Brace Jovanovich, 1972.

4. O'Neill and O'Neill, *Open Marriage,* op. cit., p. 259.

5. Ibid., p. 258.

6. Ibid., p. 17.

7. Ibid., p. 27.

8. Ibid., p. 145.

9. Ibid., pp. 195, 196.

10. Edith de Rham, *The Love Fraud: A Direct Attack on the Staggering Waste of Education and Talent Among American Women.* New York: Pegasus, 1965, pp. 116–117.

11. O'Neill and O'Neill, *Open Marriage,* op. cit., p. 195.

12. Ibid., p. 197

13. Ibid., p. 197.

14. Lionel Tiger and Robin Fox, *The Imperial Animal.* New York: Holt, Rinehart and Winston, 1971, pp. 57–58; Delta paperback, 1972.

15. O'Neill and O'Neill, *Open Marriage*, op. cit., pp. 147–148.

16. Margaret Mead, *Sex and Temperament in Three Primitive Societies*. New York: Morrow, 1935; New York: Dell, 1968.

17. Margaret Mead, *Male and Female: A Study of the Sexes in a Changing World*. New York: Morrow, 1949; New York: Dell, 1968.

18. Ibid., pp. 116–117.

19. Ibid., pp. 114–115.

20. Ibid., p. 89.

21. O'Neill and O'Neill, *Open Marriage*, op. cit., p. 24.

22. Robert Briffault and Bronislaw Malinowski, *Marriage: Past and Present*. Boston: Porter Sargent, 1956, p. 50.

23. Mead, *Male and Female*, op. cit., p. 195.

24. Briffault and Malinowski, *Marriage*, op. cit., p. 79.

25. O'Neill and O'Neill, *Open Marriage*, op. cit., p. 145.

26. Mead, *Male and Female*, op. cit., p. 173.

Chapter 4—Multiple Mirage

1. "Is the American Family in Danger?" *U.S. News and World Report*, April 16, 1973: 71.

2. Alvin Toffler, *Future Shock*. New York: Random House, 1970.

3. Ibid., p. 222.

4. Ibid., p. 226.

5. "Is the American Family in Danger?" *U.S. News*, op. cit.: 71.

6. Hugh Carter and Paul C. Glick, *Marriage and Divorce: A Social and Economic Study*. Cambridge, Mass.: Harvard University Press, 1970, pp. 236–237.

7. Ibid., pp. 54–57.

8. Ibid., p. 400.

9. "Is the American Family in Danger?" *U.S. News*, op. cit.: 71.

10. Carter and Glick, *Marriage and Divorce*, op. cit., p. 255.

11. R. Rapoport and R. Rapoport, "Family Roles and Work Roles," in Michael Anderson (ed.), *Sociology of the Family*. Baltimore: Penguin, 1971, p. 282.

12. Jessie Bernard, *The Future of Marriage*. New York: World, 1972.

13. Louise Kapp Howe (ed.), *The Future of the Family*. New York: Simon & Schuster, 1972.

14. Bernard, *Future of Marriage*, op. cit., pp. 3–58.

15. Caroline Bird, "The Case Against Marriage," in Howe, *Future of Family*, op. cit., p. 341.

16. Bernard, *Future of Marriage,* op. cit.

17. *The Gallup Poll,* vol. 3, 1959–1971. New York: Random House, 1972, p. 2261; Louis Harris, Poll on Women for Virginia Slims, reported in *Time,* March 20, 1972: 26; Margaret Mead, *Male and Female: A Study of the Sexes in a Changing World.* New York: Morrow, 1949, p. 92; Dell, 1968, p. 110.

18. Jan Dizard, "The Price of Success." In Howe, *Future of Family,* op. cit., p. 192.

19. Ibid.

20. Carter and Glick, *Marriage and Divorce,* op. cit., pp. 313–320, 403.

21. Pitirim A. Sorokin, *The Crisis of Our Age: The Social and Cultural Outlook.* New York: Dutton, 1941, pp. 167–169.

22. Ibid., pp. 176–204.

23. Robert Ardrey, *African Genesis.* London: Collins, 1961.

24. Midge Decter, *The New Chastity and Other Arguments Against Women's Liberation.* New York: Coward, McCann & Geoghegan, 1972.

Chapter 5—After the Hunt

1. Lionel Tiger, *Men in Groups.* New York: Random House, 1969, pp. 3–24.

2. Elizabeth Gould Davis, *The First Sex.* New York: Putnam, 1971.

3. The Hobbesian concept is not accepted as an historical reality by all conservatives, of course. It is also seen as a prophetic reality, the likely result of a collapse of the social order.

4. Steven Goldberg, *The Inevitability of Patriarchy.* New York: Morrow, 1973. Goldberg closely examines the data on every society for which matriarchal claims have been offered, and he shows that in every instance the key positions of political power or prestige are dominated by men.

Robin Fox, *Kinship and Marriage.* Baltimore: Penguin Books, 1967, p. 31 and passim. Fox maintains that no marriage system can endure with a male presence unless the men exercise control.

5. Niko Tinbergen, *Social Behavior in Animals.* New York: Wiley, 1953.

6. Robert Ardrey, *African Genesis.* London: Collins, 1961; *The Territorial Imperative.* New York: Atheneum, 1966; *The Social Contract.* New York: Atheneum, 1970.

7. Desmond Morris, *The Naked Ape.* New York: Dell, 1969; *The Human Zoo.* New York: McGraw-Hill, 1970.

8. Konrad Lorenz, *On Aggression.* New York: Harcourt Brace Jovanovich, 1966.

9. Desmond Morris, *Patterns of Reproductive Behavior*, New York: McGraw-Hill, 1971.

10. Naomi Weisstein, "Psychology Constructs the Female," in Vivian Gornick and Barbara K. Moran (eds.), *Woman in Sexist Society.* New York: Basic Books, 1971, pp. 207–224.

11. Elaine Morgan, *The Descent of Woman.* New York: Stein & Day, 1972.

12. Margaret Mead, *Male and Female: A Study of the Sexes in a Changing World.* New York: Morrow, 1949, pp. 190–206; Dell paperback, 1968.

13. Tiger, *Men in Groups,* op. cit., 59.

14. Nancy Chodorow, "Being and Doing: A Cross-Cultural Examination of the Socialization of Males and Females," in Gornick and Moran, *Sexist Society,* op. cit., pp. 259–287.

Also: Colin Turnbull, *The Mountain People.* New York: Simon & Schuster, 1972, pp. 24–26.

15. Margaret Mead, *Male and Female,* op. cit., pp. 114–119.

Baldwin Spencer and F. J. Gillen, *The Arunta.* New York: Humanities Press, 1966, vol. 1, pp. 175–303.

16. David Pilbeam, "The fashionable view of man as a naked ape is: 1. An insult to apes; 2. Simplistic; 3. Male-oriented; 4. Rubbish." *New York Times Magazine,* September 3, 1972: 30: "Among Bushmen who are still hunters, sex roles are far from rigid, and in childhood the two sexes have a very similar upbringing. However, among those Bushmen who have adopted a sedentary life devoted to herding or agriculture, sex roles are much more rigid. Men devote their energies to one set of tasks and women to another, mutually exclusive set. Little boys learn only 'male' tasks and little girls exclusively 'female' ones." In other words, the less rational is sex segregation of roles, the more the men insist on it.

17. Ruby Leavitt, "Women in Other Cultures," in Gornick and Moran, *Sexist Society,* op. cit., pp. 393–425 passim.

18. E. A. Wrigley, *Population and History.* New York: McGraw-Hill, 1969, pp. 76–77.

19. Ibid., p. 116.

20. Ibid., p. 13.

21. Ibid., pp. 116–127.

Chapter 6—Men and Work

1. Max Ways, "The Postwar Advance of the Five Hundred Million" (*Fortune,* August 1964) compares early postwar predictions with the actual subsequent growth of the capitalist countries.

The catastrophist position is exemplified by the computer projections of MIT Professor Jay Forrester and his colleagues (Donella and Dennis Meadows, Jorgen Randers, William W. Behrens III, *The Limits of Growth*, New York: Universe Books, 1972).

The Forrester study is brilliantly refuted by Robert M. Solow, "Is the End of the World at Hand?" *Challenge*, March–April 1973: 39–50. Solow reports that the Forrester computer program, given a population of Adam and Eve in Eden Garden, predicted total economic collapse and resource exhaustion in 500 years.

2. A good exposition of the case for economic growth is found in Peter Passell and Leonard Ross, *Retreat From Riches: Affluence and Its Enemies*. New York: Random House, 1973.

3. Margarita Donnelly, "Alternate-Culture Mirror America," in Louise Kapp Howe (ed.), *The Future of the Family*. New York: Simon & Schuster, 1972, p. 67.

4. The mother secretes prolactin, which both stimulates lactation and causes restlessness and anxiety that is relieved by breast feeding. She also secretes oxytocin, a tranquillizing hormone, that both induces the release of the milk and brings a sense of relaxation and peace. (Karen Pryor, *Nursing Your Baby*, new revised edition. New York: Pocket Books, 1973, p. 70). See also Lionel Tiger and Robin Fox, *The Imperial Animal*. New York: Holt, Rinehart and Winston, 1971, p. 65; Delta paperback, 1972, pp. 61–62.

5. Caroline Bird, "Money Is the Root of All Freedom?" *Ms.*, December 1972. A comparative salary and wage chart for men and women appears on pages 84 and 85.

6. Lester C. Thurow, "Education and Economic Equality," *Public Interest*, Summer 1972. Thurow offers a powerful case against the theory that increasing education and credentials engender more productive workers or account for our economic growth. Motivation and on-the-job training are most crucial to real worker productivity.

7. Quoted in Karl Bednarik, *The Male in Crisis*. New York: Knopf, 1970, p. 84.

8. Marjorie Galenson, *Women and Work: An International Comparison*. Ithaca, N.Y.: New York State School of Industrial and Labor Relations, Cornell University, 1973, pp. 87–88. Women comprise 80 percent of all physicians but men dominate surgery and medical administration. The pay and status of physicians are much lower in the Soviet Union than in the U.S. As the statistics in Chapter 6 of Galenson's book powerfully demonstrate, the Soviet Union, far from abolishing sexism, merely forces women to work harder both in the home and on the menial worksite. Because of the loss of 25 million men in World War II, the country had a working-age population dominated by women. Daycare centers and other facilities were created so that this labor resource could be more effectively exploited. But now that the

male population is approaching parity, the proportion of women among university students is dropping rapidly—from 53 percent in 1950 to 44 percent in 1965. Women comprise only 8.3 percent of Soviet professors and other high level academicians, while they supply over 60 percent of the manual labor. The pattern in other Communist countries is even less favorable to women. Galenson concludes (p. 105): "The fairly common belief in the U.S. that women are better off in Sweden or Finland—or any other country for that matter—is mistaken."

9. Reported by Sharon C. Wilsnack in "Femininity by the Bottle," *Psychology Today*, April 1973.

10. Rollo May, *Power and Innocence*. New York: Norton, 1972, p. 23 and passim.

11. Virginia Woolf's *A Room of One's Own* (Harbinger paperback, New York: Harcourt Brace Jovanovich, 1957) remains the most eloquent of feminist books. But the privacy and independence it asks for women as a condition of artistic achievement are today more available to them than to men.

12. Margaret Mead in a televised discussion of the "An American Family" series, N.E.T., April 5, 1973.

13. Thomas Pettigrew, *Profile of the Negro American*. New York: Van Nostrand Reinhold, 1964.

Chapter 7—The Ghetto "Liberation"

1. Ben J. Wattenberg and Richard Scammon, "Black Progress and Liberal Rhetoric," *Commentary*, April 1973: 35–44. "The rate of violent crimes among blacks is about ten times the rate among whites" (p. 40).

2. Herbert Hendin, *Black Suicide*. New York: Basic Books, 1969; Harper Colophon paperback, 1971, pp. 151, 153, and passim.

3. Wattenberg and Scammon, "Black Progress," op. cit.: 40.

4. The original Labor Department version is reproduced in Lee Rainwater and William L. Yancey, *The Moynihan Report and the Politics of Controversy*. Cambridge, Mass.: MIT Press, 1967, pp. 45–93.

5. Wattenberg and Scammon, "Black Progress," op. cit.: 35–44.

6. Christopher Jencks et al., *Inequality*. New York: Basic Books, 1972, pp. 97–110.

7. Andrew Billingsley, *Black Families in White America*. Englewood Cliffs, N.J.: Prentice-Hall, 1968, p. 171.

8. Kenneth B. Clark, *Dark Ghetto*. New York: Harper & Row, 1965.

9. Claude Brown, *Manchild in the Promised Land*. New York: Macmillan, 1967.

10. Malcolm X, *Autobiography*. New York: Grove Press, 1964; paperback, 1966.

11. Edward C. Banfield, *The Unheavenly City, The Nature and Future of Our Urban Crisis.* Boston: Little, Brown, 1968, pp. 210–237.

12. Wattenberg and Scammon, "Black Progress," op. cit., pp. 35–44. See also Daniel Patrick Moynihan, "The Schism in Black America," *The Public Interest,* Spring 1972, pp. 10–11.

13. Herbert Hendin, *Black Suicide,* op. cit., p. 151.

14. Thomas Pettigrew, *A Profile of the Negro American.* New York: Van Nostrand Reinhold, 1964, pp. 18, 20 (chart). Pettigrew adduces a wealth of psychological studies indicating that a key problem of ghetto males is sex-role insecurity originating in fatherless families. But some of the femininity indices ("singing ambition") are probably false for blacks.

15. Ibid., p. 16.

16. Norman Podhoretz, *Making It.* New York: Random House, 1968.

17. The drive to eliminate sex discrimination in employment may affect the black man far more than the white despite the black's already weaker position. Even the 20 percent income advantage of black males over black women is 94 percent attributable to sex discrimination, according to a recent study. By comparison the advantage of white males over white women was found to be only 64 percent attributable to bias. (Ronald L. Oaxaca, "Male-Female Wage Differentials in Urban Labor Markets," Working Paper No. 23, Industrial Relations Section, Princeton University, 1971, as quoted in Eli Ginzberg and Alice M. Yohalem, eds., *Corporate Lib, Women's Challenge to Management,* Policy Studies in Employment and Welfare Number 17. Baltimore: Johns Hopkins University Press, 1973, p. 77). Of course, such statistics are excessively dependent on appraisals of education, credentials, and experience rather than on actual job performance and competitive mobility, initiative, and aggressiveness in exploiting job market opportunities. The black women's educational advantage over black men thus skews the figures to show more sex discrimination. Nonetheless, Oaxaca's analysis suggests that the already grossly inadequate income advantage of black males over black females is extraordinarily vulnerable to the campaign against sex discrimination, which necessarily focuses on "credentials."

Chapter 8—Women vs. Blacks

1. E. Franklin Frazier, *The Negro Family in the United States,* Revised and Abridged Edition, with a new foreword by Nathan Glazer. Chicago: University of Chicago Press, 1966.

2. Kenneth B. Clark, *Dark Ghetto.* New York: Harper & Row, 1965.

3. See Lee Rainwater and William L. Yancey, *The Moynihan Report and the Politics of Controversy.* Cambridge, Mass.: MIT Press, 1967.

4. Kate Millett, "Prostitution: A Quartet for Female Voices," in

Vivian Gornick and Barbara K. Moran, eds., *Women in Sexist Society, Studies in Power and Powerlessness.* New York: Basic Books, 1971; Signet paperback, 1972, pp. 60–125. Millett's concern with rape is a motif of her book *Sexual Politics* (Garden City, N.Y.: Doubleday, 1970).

5. Susan Brownmiller is reported to be working on a book on rape. Sara Davidson, "Forewomen," *Esquire,* July 1973: 160.

6. Germaine Greer has expressed her preoccupation with rape widely. In *The Sensuous Society* (Chicago: Playboy Press, 1973, pp. 157–172) her current views are vividly expressed.

7. Gail Sheehy, *Hustling.* New York: Delacorte, 1973.

8. Germaine Greer, *The Female Eunuch.* New York: McGraw-Hill, 1971; Bantam paperback, 1972, p. 339.

9. "The right of women in poverty to secure job training . . . on equal terms with men" is asserted in Article VII of the National Organization for Women's Bill of Rights (1968), a "historical document" of feminism (reprinted in Judith Hole and Ellen Levine, *Rebirth of Feminism.* New York: Quadrangle, 1972, p. 442). The feminists have succeeded in eliciting a government campaign in favor of affirmative action in behalf of women in all educational institutions when what is needed is affirmative action in favor of black males. Since black females do decidedly better in high school than males, a neutral policy favors women.

10. C. Eric Lincoln, *The Black Muslims in America,* revised edition. Boston: Beacon Press, 1973, pp. 131–135.

11. Mary White Harder et al., "The Jesus People: Sexism Revived," *Psychology Today,* December 1972.

12. Andrew Billingsley, *Black Families in White America.* Englewood Cliffs, N.J.: Prentice-Hall, 1968, pp. 117–121.

13. Ibid., p. 118.

14. James Baldwin, as quoted in Jessie Bernard, *Marriage and Family among Negroes.* Englewood Cliffs, N.J.: Prentice-Hall, 1966, p. 128.

15. Bernard, *Marriage and Family,* op. cit., p. 129.

16. See Paul Seabury, "HEW and the Universities," *Commentary,* February 1972: 38–44.

17. Elliot Liebow, *Tally's Corner.* Boston: Little, Brown, 1967, pp. 55, 62, 86, 116–119, and passim. Liebow quotes Albert K. Cohen, *Delinquent Boys* (New York: Free Press, 1955, p. 138): ". . . people do not simply want to excel; they want to excel as a man or as a woman, that is to say, in those respects which, in their culture, are symbolic of their respective sex roles. . . . Even when they adopt behavior which is considered disreputable by conventional standards, the tendency is to be disreputable in ways that are characteristically masculine and feminine."

Chapter 9—The Sexual Sources of Demagoguery

1. Such opposition to abortion is confirmed in national public opinion polls (see *The Gallup Poll,* vol. 3, 1959–1971. New York: Random House, 1972, pp. 2225–2226). But advocates of abortion still purport to be a majority. An article in the *Ripon Forum* (April 1973: 11) depicted the anti-abortion forces as a "loud . . . well-financed . . . minority" that won in Michigan by being "well organized and politically astute."

2. Gallup (*Poll,* op. cit.) indicates that the less one's education, the more likely one will oppose abortion, and that 7 percent more women than men oppose it.

3. Phrase quoted by Eugene Fontinell, "Marriage, Morality and the Church," *Commonweal,* November 10, 1972: 126.

4. Gallup, *Poll,* op. cit., p. 1966.

5. Ibid., p. 1990.

6. Ibid., p. 2239.

7. Ibid., pp. 2328–2329 (busing); p. 2177 (welfare); p. 2271 (marijuana). On all these issues public opinion is opposed to elite opinion by at least a 70 to 30 percent margin.

8. Quoted in Christopher Booker, *The Neophiliacs.* Boston: Gambit, 1970, p. xi.

9. Lionel Tiger, *Men in Groups.* New York: Random House, 1969; Vintage paperback, 1970, p. 60.

10. Norman Mailer, *St. George and the Godfather.* New York: NAL/ World, 1972, pp. 56–61.

11. Jessie Bernard, *The Future of Marriage.* New York: World, 1972, pp. 336, 338, 339.

12. See Daniel Bell, *The Post Industrial Society.* New York: Basic Books, 1973. See also: Bell, "Relevant Aspects of the Social Scene," in Eveline M. Burns, ed., *Children's Allowances and the Welfare of Children.* New York: Citizens Committee for Children of New York. Bell concludes (p. 171): "So a post-industrial society comes to focus on children, if only for utilitarian reasons, because the whole progress of a large-scale society depends so much on this resource and its use. If children become, in a sense, a nation's most crucial resource, then one has to pay much more attention to what happens to children and to families with children, and where and why a society loses its [human] resources." Bell believes that as a society becomes more advanced it demands increasingly well-developed and educated personnel. One might add that it also needs better socialized males.

Chapter 10—The Moderate Extremists

1. The National Organization for Women's Bill of Rights, as promulgated in 1968 and summarized by NOW, called for:

I   Equal Rights Constitutional Amendment
II   Enforce Law Banning Sex Discrimination in Employment
III Maternity Leave Rights in Employment and in Social Security Benefits
IV   Tax Deduction for Home and Child Care Expenses for Working Parents
V   Child Care Centers
VI   Equal and Unsegregated Education
VII Equal Job Training Opportunities and Allowances for Women in Poverty
VIII The Right of Women to Control Their Reproductive Lives.

2. The Bill of Rights is reprinted in full among the "historical documents" of feminism in the appendix of *Rebirth of Feminism,* by Judith Hole and Ellen Levine (New York: Quadrangle, 1972, p. 441).

3. NOW proposals endorsed by both houses of Congress and/or both political parties in their national platforms include: the Equal Rights Amendment, antidiscrimination enforcement, and child-care centers. The Supreme Court has ruled in favor of abortion. The Department of Health, Education and Welfare requires all educational institutions receiving federal aid—with the exception of religious and military schools—to adopt a plan for coeducation, to be phased in completely, with sex-blind admissions, within seven years. HEW also demands an end to discrimination in athletics, although the meaning of this requirement remains unclear. Tax deductions for home and child-care expenses are now the law of the land.

4. Suzannah Lessard pointed out this feminist contradiction in an excellent review of *Ms.* magazine and two antifeminist books in *Washington Monthly,* January 1973: 35.

5. Hole and Levine, *Rebirth of Feminism,* op. cit., pp. 35–40.

6. Ibid., p. 42.

7. An excellent summary of HEW harassment of universities is found in Paul Seabury, *Commentary,* February 1972: 38–44, and in subsequent letters columns in that magazine.

8. NOW's president, Dr. Anne Scott, reaffirmed the organization's view that coeducation is constitutionally required in an appearance on William F. Buckley's *Firing Line,* WNET-TV, New York, April 15, 1973.

9. Unpublished report to the Democratic National Committee by Cecil Poole.

10. Helen Z. Lopata, *Occupation Housewife.* New York: Oxford University Press, 1972.

11. *The Gallup Poll,* Vol. 3, 1959–1971. New York: Random House, 1972, pp. 1646–1647, 1696, 1747, 1896, 2180, 2229, 2276–2277, 2339. Although Golda Meir was most admired in 1971 and 1972, Pat

Nixon's chief American competitors over the years have been Mamie Eisenhower and the Kennedy wives.

Chapter 11—The Child Care State

1. George Gilder, "The Case Against Universal Day Care," *The New Leader*, April 3, 1972: 11; reprinted in the Washington *Sunday Star*, April 23, 1972: C-2.

2. Ibid.

3. Even this program is not sufficiently upper-class oriented for many of the feminists, who complain about the income ceiling. See Phyllis A. Wallace, "Sex Discrimination: Some Societal Constraints on Upward Mobility for Women Executives," in Eli Ginzberg and Alice M. Yohalem, eds., *Corporate Lib, Women's Challenge to Management*, Policy Studies in Employment and Welfare Number 17. Baltimore: Johns Hopkins University Press, 1973, p. 78.

4. John K. Iglehart, "Report on Child Care Legislation," *National Journal*, vol. 4, no. 30, July 22, 1972: 1203. $373 million out of the $682 million total goes to Headstart. The alleged 800,000 spaces include part-time and summer programs and do not represent a serious child-care effort.

5. Gilder, "Case Against Day Care," op. cit.: 13. A more detailed examination of the travesty of day care as an accessory of welfare crackdowns under the WIN (Work Incentive program) appears in Sheila M. Rothman, "Other People's Children: The Day Care Experience in America," *The Public Interest*, Winter 1973: 23–24. She maintains that the chief effect of WIN–day care–workfare is to frighten away potential relief applicants.

6. See Patricia Gerald Bourne, "What Day Care Ought To Be," *New Republic*, February 12, 1972: 18–23, for analysis of Title 4 and other programs.

7. Ibid.: 20–21.

8. For a summary of recent findings, see Sara Stein and Carter Smith, "Return to Mom," *Saturday Review of Education*, April 1973: 37.

9. These gains are dubious. See Jerome Kagan interview, *Saturday Review of Education*, April 1973: 41. Kagan observed Guatemalan children who were isolated in semidark rooms until age 2. The mothers did not talk to them or otherwise interact, though they nursed them on demand and held them warmly. The ostensible "retardation" of the children had completely vanished by age 11 and they equaled or excelled American contemporaries in "reasoning, memory, inference, deduction, and perception." Other studies confirm that consistent maternal attention is more important during the early stages than any specifically intellectual stimulation. See Ashley Montagu, *Touching*. New York: Columbia University Press, 1971. The result, as Dr. John

Bowlby has put it, is that "children thrive better in bad homes than in good institutions." Bowlby's famous study for the World Health Organization in 1952, as reassessed in 1962, presents powerful arguments against institutional child care (*Maternal Care and Mental Health* and *Deprivation of Maternal Care,* two volumes in one, New York: Schocken Books, 1966). See also Bowlby, *Child Care and the Growth of Love,* new enlarged edition. Baltimore: Penguin, 1966. Bowlby concludes, "It cannot be too strongly emphasized that with the best will in the world a residential nursery cannot provide a satisfactory emotional environment for infants and young children. This is not merely an idea that comes from theories, it is the considered opinion of prominent practical workers in many different countries. . . . So many helpers were necessary if their infants were to receive the continuous care of a permanent mother-substitute, which their observations showed to be essential, that it would be better for each helper to take a couple of children home and close the nursery" (p. 160). For an empirical study of the effects of maternal deprivation, see René Spitz, *The First Year of Life.* New York: International Universities Press, 1965, pp. 267–292. The *kibbutzim* in Israel are often cited as evidence against these findings. But in fact, the communal children are early nursed by their mothers, receive daily concentrated attention from them, and are given consistent care from mother-substitutes (all women) the rest of the time. As they grow up, moreover, they maintain close ties with an unchanging group of peers. In a mobile, industrial society, such peer ties are hard to sustain; and the consistent attention of mother-substitutes with day-long responsibility for only a few other children is very costly to provide on a public basis. The *kibbutzim* offer a case for select, ideological, agricultural communes, for people who want them, but not a case for child development centers or sex-role changes (sex roles remain essentially separate). See Melford E. Spiro, *Kibbutz: Venture in Utopia.* Cambridge, Mass.: Harvard University Press, 1956.

10. Estimate by Mary D. Keyserling, author of a 1972 study of the day-care problem for the National Council of Jewish Women. It is a very rough guess. (*The Advocates,* "Should the Federal Government Finance a Comprehensive Daycare Program?" National Educational Television, May 23, 1972).

11. Carol Khosrovi, the extremely able former Deputy Director of the Office of Economic Opportunity. Personal communication.

12. Ibid.

13. Berna Gorenstein, "Statement from New York Ripon," *Ripon Forum,* February 1972. This argument also has been made by Bella Abzug, NOW, and others.

14. Personal communication.

15. NOW Bill of Rights, reprinted in Judith Hole and Ellen Levine, *Rebirth of Feminism.* New York: Quadrangle, 1972, p. 441.

16. Marjorie Hunter, "Senate Modifies a Child-Care Bill," *New York Times,* June 21, 1972. Also, Iglehart, "Child Care Legislation," op. cit.: 1202–1205.

17. Bourne, "What Day Care Ought To Be," op. cit.: 18–23. She maintains that $3,500 or more is really needed.

18. Ibid., 18–19.

19. Selma Mushkin, quoted in Gilder, "Case Against Day Care," op. cit.: 11.

20. Gilder, "Case Against Day Care," op. cit.: 11.

21. It should be emphasized that such programs are what can be expected from the day-care coalition, which, as Bourne observed in *The New Republic* ("What Day Care Ought To Be," op. cit.) is "based on the needs of [working] women . . . not . . . on the needs of children."

22. The enormous difficulty of raising or finding money for major new social programs is demonstrated in Charles L. Schultze, Alice M. Rivlin, et al., *Setting National Priorities, The 1973 Budget.* Washington, D.C.: Brookings Institution, 1972, pp. 252–290 (chapter on childcare).

23. Stein and Smith, "Return to Mom," op. cit.

24. Rothman, "Other People's Children," op. cit.: 23–24.

25. The most heralded crackdowns occurred in California, Connecticut, and New York, but almost every state was forced to cut back.

26. Dr. Mary Rowe on *The Advocates,* op. cit.

27. Irving Kristol, *On the Democratic Idea in America.* New York: Harper & Row, 1972, p. ix.

28. Marjorie Galenson, *Women and Work: An International Comparison.* Ithaca, N.Y.: Cornell University Press, 1973, pp. 80–84.

29. Dr. Dale Meers, "On Daycare Under the Communists," *Human Events,* April 15, 1972.

30. Marjorie Galenson, *Women and Work,* op. cit.: 59–60. Sweden is another case where American feminists have accepted government day-care rhetoric for performance. According to Claude Servan-Schreiber, *Ms.,* February 1973: 88 ff., there are now 45,000 places, enough to accommodate only 20 per cent of the working parents. See also Birgitta Linnér, *Sex and Society in Sweden,* revised edition. New York: Harper Colophon, 1972, pp. 43–44; and Edmond Dahlström, ed., *The Changing Roles of Men and Women,* containing *The Status of Women in Sweden: Report to the United Nations 1968.* New York: United Nations, 1968. On the basis of these studies one concludes that the position of women in Sweden is little different from their position in the United States, except that in Sweden they are more likely to be single and proportionately less likely to hold high positions in the universities or acquire legal abortions. Nonetheless, Swedish

government officials have vociferously adopted the feminist ideology, quotas have been set for women on Social Democratic party tickets on the local level (one-third), and with every gain the women's liberationists escalate their bitter complaints. Dissatisfaction and disorder in Sweden have been increasing in recent years—as in the United States— and it is possible that Sweden will be the first consummated Sexual Suicide Society in law and ideology. One would expect a right-wing revulsion to result.

31. See Bourne, "What Day Care Ought To Be," op. cit. A major theme of the day-care advocates is the edifying effects that "professional" care can have for children. Mary Keyserling maintained on *The Advocates*, op. cit., that most children would benefit. One assumes that she means most children would benefit from peer-group interchange for a few hours daily under professional guidance. But the likely prospect under any financially feasible program, oriented toward working mothers, is ten hours a day in an underfinanced center with inadequate supervision.

Chapter 12—Supporting Families

1. Quoted in *The Negro Family, A Case for National Action*, as reprinted in Lee Rainwater and William Yancey, *The Moynihan Report and the Politics of Controversy*. Cambridge, Mass.: MIT Press, 1967, p. 63.

2. Robert Theobald, *Guaranteed Income: Next Step in Economic Evolution*. Garden City, N.Y.: Doubleday, 1965.

3. George Romney, *The Mission and the Dream*. New York: Putnam, 1968 (printed in galleys but withdrawn by publisher when Romney withdrew from Presidential race).

4. The most comprehensive analysis of existing programs and their U.S. relevance can be found in Eveline M. Burns, ed., *Children's Allowances and the Economic Welfare of Children*, The Report of a Conference. New York: Citizens Committee for Children of New York.

5. Nicole Questiaux, "Family Allowances in France," in Burns, *Children's Allowances*, op. cit., p. 78.

6. Vincent H. Whitney, "Fertility Trends and Children's Allowance Programs," in Burns, *Children's Allowances*, op. cit., pp. 123–139. Whitney finds no evidence anywhere that a program of family allowances has significantly increased population, even when adopted for that purpose. In Eastern European countries the birth rate even declined after the program was established. Alvin L. Schorr, "Income Maintenance and the Birth Rate" (*Social Security Bulletin*, vol. 28, no. 12, December 1965: 22–30) supports the Whitney conclusions.

7. Francis Fox Piven and Richard A. Cloward, *Regulating the Poor: The Functions of Public Welfare*. New York: Pantheon, 1971.

8. Jodie Allen, "How to Save Welfare Reform," *Ripon Forum,* June 1972: 6–10. See also, "A Funny Thing Happened to Welfare on the Way to Reform," Washington: Urban Institute, 1972.

9. Daniel Patrick Moynihan, "The Urgency of FAP," an interview in *Ripon Forum,* November 1971: 4–7.

10. Henry Aaron, "Why is Welfare so Hard to Reform?" Brookings Institution, Washington, D.C., 1973. Aaron demonstrates that the problem of work incentives is nearly insuperable as long as the government provides a number of programs for the poor, based on means or income tests.

11. Samuel A. Sherer, "The Voucher Experiment," *Ripon Forum,* June 1972: 25–27.

12. Moynihan, "Urgency of FAP," op. cit., 4–5.

13. C. Eric Lincoln, *The Black Muslims in America,* revised edition. Boston: Beacon Press, 1973.

14. Ben J. Wattenberg and Richard Scammon, "Black Progress and Liberal Rhetoric," *Commentary,* April 1973: 35–44. See also, Daniel Patrick Moynihan, "The Schism in Black America," *The Public Interest,* Spring 1972: 10–11.

15. Harvey Brazer, "Tax Policy and Children's Allowances," in Burns, *Children's Allowances,* op. cit., pp. 140–149.

16. Whitney, "Fertility Trends," op. cit.

Chapter 13—The Liberated Job Disaster

1. Margaret Mead, *Male and Female: A Study of the Sexes in a Changing World.* New York: Morrow, 1949, pp. 103–104; Dell, 1968, p. 118–120.

2. Margaret Mead, *Male and Female,* op. cit., Morrow, pp. 92–104, passim; Dell, pp. 110–120, passim. See also Mead's *Sex and Temperament in Three Primitive Societies.* New York: Morrow, 1935; New York: Dell, 1968, pp. 83–88, 176–177. Baldwin Spencer and F. J. Gillen, *The Arunta,* vol. 1. New York: Humanities Press, 1966, pp. 175–303. Theodore Reik, *Ritual.* New York: International Universities Press, 1946 (see especially treatment of *couvade,* pp. 27–90).

3. At the time of writing, Frank Reissman was author of several books, editor of *Social Policy* magazine, and professor of sociology at New York University (*Transaction/Society,* November/December 1972: 124).

4. Michael Korda, *Male Chauvinism.* New York: Random House, 1973.

5. John Kenneth Galbraith, Edwin Kuh, Lester C. Thurow, "The Galbraith Plan to Promote the Minorities," *New York Times Maga-*

zine, August 22, 1971. Galbraith advocated that women be placed by quota in executive jobs in proportion to their labor force participation.

6. Bertram Gross and Stanley Moses, "Measuring the Real Work Force: 25 Million Unemployed," *Social Policy,* September/October 1972: 5–10.

7. Ibid., p. 8.

8. Ibid., pp. 5–10.

9. Eli Ginzberg, "The Outlook for Educated Manpower," *The Public Interest,* Winter 1972: 100–111.

10. Peter F. Drucker, "The Surprising Seventies," *Harper's,* July 1971: 37–38.

11. Ginzberg, "Educated Manpower," op. cit.: 106–108.

12. Carolyn Shaw Bell, "Implications for Women," *Social Policy,* September/October 1972: 11–15; "Age, Sex, Marriage, and Jobs," *The Public Interest,* Winter 1973: 76–87.

13. Colin Turnbull, *The Mountain People.* New York: Simon & Schuster, 1972.

14. Ibid., pp. 290, 291, 294, 295.

Chapter 14—The Male Imperative

1. An excellent study of the impact of modern society on male sexuality is Kurt Bednarik, *The Male in Crisis.* New York: Knopf, 1970.

2. William Irwin Thompson, "The Individual as Institution," *Harper's,* September 1972: 48 ff.

3. Charles Mingus, *Beneath the Underdog.* New York: Knopf, 1972.

4. Richard Sennett and Jonathan Cobb, *The Hidden Wounds of Class.* New York: Knopf, 1972. See also, Sennett and Cobb, "Working Class Lives," *Social Policy,* September/October 1972: 39–47.

5. Patricia Cayo Sexton, *The Feminized Male, White Collars and the Decline of Manliness.* New York: Random House, 1969; Vintage paperback, 1970.

6. Geoffrey Faux and Arthur I. Blaustein, *The Star Spangled Hustle.* Garden City, N.Y.: Doubleday, 1972.

7. Marilyn Gittell, "Putting Merit Back in the Merit System," *Social Policy,* September/October, 1972: 23–26.

8. Edward B. Shils, "Small Business: Prospects and Problems," *Current History,* July 1965. Discussed in George F. Gilder and Bruce K. Chapman, *The Party That Lost Its Head.* New York: Knopf, 1966, p. 308.

9. John Fischer, "The Easy Chair," *Harper's,* May 1973.

10. John McClaughry, *Expanded Ownership.* Cambridge, Mass.: The Sabre Foundation. Summarized in *Ripon Forum,* August 1972: 10–14.

11. Sennett and Cobb, op. cit.

12. McClaughry, *Expanded Ownership*, op. cit.

13. Juan de Onis, "Honor Killing Fought in Beirut," *New York Times,* March 4, 1973: 8. The Lebanese penal code and those of other Arab countries permit a man to kill a member of his family who "dishonors" the family by sexual misconduct.

14. Ibid.

15. See, Margaret Mead, *Coming of Age in Samoa: A Psychological Study of Primitive Youth for Western Civilization.* New York: Morrow, 1930. Also see Bronislaw Malinowski, *The Sexual Life of Savages in North-Western Melanesia.* New York: Harcourt Brace Jovanovich, 1929.

Chapter 15—Six Inches for the Holy Ghost

1. Thomas Leahy, personal communication.

2. Patricia Cayo Sexton, *The Feminized Male, White Collars and the Decline of Manliness.* New York: Random House, 1969; Vintage paperback, 1970, pp. 125–132.

3. Margaret Mead, *Male and Female: A Study of the Sexes in a Changing World.* New York: Morrow, 1949; Dell paperback, 1968, p. 273. *Coming of Age in Samoa: A Psychological Study of Primitive Youth for Western Civilization.* New York: Morrow, 1930; Dell paperback, 1968, p. 155.

4. Sexton, *Feminized Male,* op. cit., p. 105.

5. Mead, *Male and Female,* op. cit., p. 273; *Coming of Age,* op. cit., p. 155. Bronislaw Malinowski, *The Sexual Lives of Savages in North-Western Melanesia.* 2 vols. New York: Harcourt Brace Jovanovich, 1929. Although in *Coming of Age,* Mead acknowledged the good Samoan sexual adjustment, she believes it occurs at the expense of emotional intensity and individuation. She supports coeducation on the usual grounds: It subordinates sex to individuality. It is hard to understand, however, why in an advanced and complex society rather than a primitive one, association with one's own sex in school prevents individuality. Observation suggests that girls are more individual and expressive without boys in the classroom.

6. Sexton, *Feminized Male,* op. cit., pp. 104–108.

7. Ibid., pp. 108–114.

8. Ibid., p. 8.

9. "Teachers Take Aim at Sex Stereotypes," *Detroit Free Press,* November 23, 1972: 10.

10. Mead, *Male and Female,* op. cit., pp. 154–172.

Chapter 16—Sex and Sports

1. Lucinda Franks, "See Jane Run," *Ms.*, January 1973.

2. Bil Gilbert and Nancy Williamson, three-part series on "Women in Sport," *Sports Illustrated,* May 28, June 4 and 11, 1973. These simple-minded articles ascribed to irrational bias the unequal spending on male and female sports in high schools and colleges and the unequal pay and attention given to female athletes. In fact, female athletes attract far more attention than similarly mediocre male performers. It is discrimination in favor of female athletes in most sports that lets us hear about any of them at all. And as a letter to *Sports Illustrated* from Jeff Strathmeyer pointed out, women "are no worse off than 99 per cent of the men who also get no scholarships, cannot use the gym when 'the team' is practicing, and whose lack of physical strength, speed of reflexes, etc., is also a mere accident of birth." Nonetheless, the *Sports Illustrated* series predicted a revolution in athletics, promoted by officials in HEW ordering nondiscrimination by publicly supported schools. No one anywhere seems to have heard of the inexorable discrimination of hormones.

3. *High School Yearbook 1973* (Los Altos, Calif.: Track and Field News) lists records for every age group. Most world-leading female performances approximate U.S. 14-year-old male records.

4. Patricia Cayo Sexton, *The Feminized Male, White Collars and the Decline of Manliness.* New York: Random House, 1969; Vintage paperback, 1970, p. 116.

Chapter 17—The Perils of Androgyny

1. Alfred C. Kinsey, W. B. Pomeroy, and C. E. Martin, *Sexual Behavior in the Human Male.* Philadelphia: Saunders, 1948. Kinsey concluded that 37 percent of adult males had had at least one homosexual experience, but a significant portion of his sample came from prisons. He estimated 4 percent of white males are practicing homosexuals. But even this figure may be high. See, "Playboy Panel: Homosexuality," *The Sensuous Society.* Chicago: Playboy Press, 1973, p. 85. Kinsey associate William Simon, now of the University of Chicago, cited a study of 550 white homosexual males that indicates the transitory character of most homosexual experience: "About one-half reported that 60 percent or more of their sexual partners were persons with whom they had sex only one time. Between 10 and 20 percent reported that they often picked up their partners in public toilets. An even larger proportion reported similar contacts in other public or semi-public locations. Between a quarter and a third reported being robbed by a sexual partner. . . . For two-fifths . . . the longest affair lasted less than one year." (Ibid., p. 89).

2. Patricia Cayo Sexton, *The Feminized Male, White Collars and the Decline of Manliness*. New York: Random House, 1969; Vintage paperback, 1970.

3. Ibid., pp. 29–39.

4. Arnold Gesell et al., *The First Five Years of Life*. New York: Harper & Row, 1940, pp. 142, 154. See also Jeanette Jansky and Katrina de Hirsch, *Preventing Reading Failure, Prediction, Diagnosis, Intervention*. New York: Harper & Row, 1972, p. 4. Chapter One summarizes recent research indicating a significant male lag in reading and writing skills.

5. Sexton, *Feminized Male*, op. cit., p. 105.

6. Ibid., p. 131.

7. Ibid.

8. Ibid., p. 130.

9. Ibid.

10. Philip Slater, *The Pursuit of Loneliness: American Culture at the Breaking Point*. Boston: Beacon Press, 1970, pp. 53–80.

11. At one point three Brandeis alumni appeared on the FBI's most-wanted list—presumably an N.C.A.A. record.

12. Margaret Mead, *Male and Female: A Study of the Sexes in a Changing World*. New York: Morrow, 1949, pp. 268–269; Dell paperback, 1968, pp. 261–262.

13. Ibid., Morrow, pp. 270, 273; Dell, pp. 263, 265.

14. These studies are summarized in Alan Berg, *The Nutrition Factor*, Washington, D.C.: Brookings Institution, 1973. See Berg, "The Economics of Breast Feeding," *Saturday Review of Science*, May 1973.

15. Ibid., p. 32. See also Derrick B. Jelliffe, M.D., "Mother's Milk and Other Home Foods" (World Health Organization, April 7, 1973): "The increasing lack of mother's milk . . . represents one of the major nutritional problems in the world today. Not only is breast milk unique and impossible to imitate—despite manufacturers' claims—but the cost of cow's milk remains beyond the means of the average family in the developing world. . . . What the artificially fed baby gets is a very dilute, contaminated feed. . . . If breast feeding continues to decline steeply, a time must come when it will be necessary to consider alternatives." If all the world's women ceased breast feeding, Jelliffe's figures indicate an additional 250 million cattle would be needed to make up the loss.

16. Karen Pryor, *Nursing Your Baby*, new revised edition. New York: Pocket Books, 1973, pp. 139–141. For a somewhat more problematical view of breast feeding and a summary of psychological and anthropo-

logical data, see Sylvia Brody, *Patterns of Mothering, Maternal Influence During Infancy,* with an introduction by René Spitz. New York: International Universities Press, 1956, pp. 41–54 and passim. For a comparative examination of the role of breast feeding in psychological differentiation of the sexes in primitive tribes and the U.S., see Mead, *Male and Female,* op. cit., pp. 155–163, 261–263 and passim.

17. A summary of recent studies appears in Niles Newton, "Breast Feeding," *Psychology Today,* June 1968.

18. Lionel Tiger and Robin Fox, *The Imperial Animal.* New York: Holt, Rinehart and Winston, 1971; Delta paperback, 1972, p. 7 and passim.

Chapter 18—The Woman's Role

1. Leonard Levitt, "She," *Esquire,* October 1971: 210.

2. Germaine Greer, *The Female Eunuch.* New York: McGraw-Hill, 1971.

3. Kate Millett, *Sexual Politics.* Garden City, N.Y.: Doubleday, 1969.

4. *Time,* cover story, August 31, 1970.

5. Betty Friedan, *The Feminine Mystique.* New York: Norton, 1963.

6. Ellen Peck, *The Baby Trap.* New York: Bernard Geis, 1971.

7. Susan Brownmiller, "On Goosing," *The Village Voice,* April 15, 1971: 5.

8. Esther Vilar, *The Manipulated Male.* New York: Farrar, Straus and Giroux, 1972.

9. Greer, *Female Eunuch,* op. cit.

10. Natalie Gittelson, *The Erotic Life of the American Wife.* New York: Delacorte, 1972.

11. Philip Roth, *Portnoy's Complaint.* New York: Random House, 1969.

12. Greer, "Down with Panties," *Ms.,* July 1972: 8; "At the Democratic National Convention," *Harper's,* October 1972.

13. Greer, "Democratic Convention," op. cit.

14. Greer, "On Rape," *Playboy,* January 1973.

15. Ingrid Bengis, *Combat in the Erogenous Zone.* New York: Knopf, 1973.

16. Phyllis Chesler, *Women and Madness.* Garden City, N.Y.: Doubleday, 1972.

17. Greer, *Female Eunuch,* op. cit.

18. Helen Lopata, *Occupation Housewife.* New York: Oxford University Press, 1971, p. 376.

19. Herbert J. Gans, *The Levittowners.* New York: Pantheon, 1967.

20. Lopata, *Housewife,* op. cit.

21. Lopata, *Housewife,* op. cit., p. 373.

22. Gans, *Levittowners,* op. cit., pp. 230, 231.

23. Jessie Bernard, *The Future of Marriage.* New York: World, 1972, pp. 336, 338, 339.

24. Midge Decter, *The New Chastity and Other Arguments Against Women's Liberation.* New York: Coward, McCann and Geoghegan, 1972.

25. Harvey Swados, *A Radical's America.* Boston: Little, Brown, 1962, pp. 302–316.

26. Theodore Reik, *Ritual.* New York: International Universities Press, 1946, pp. 27–90.

27. Edward Grossman, "The Obsolescent Mother," *Atlantic,* May 1971: 39–50.

28. Ibid.

Chapter 19—The Sexual Suicide Technocracy

1. Leon R. Kass, "Making Babies—The New Biology and the 'Old' Morality," *The Public Interest,* Winter 1972: 18–56.

2. Edward Grossman, "The Obsolescent Mother," *Atlantic,* May 1971: 39–50.

3. Robert T. Francoeur, *Eve's New Rib: 20 Faces of Sex, Marriage and Family.* New York: Harcourt Brace Jovanovich, 1972.

4. Kass, "Making Babies," op. cit.: 39 ff.

5. Grossman, "Obsolescent Mother," op. cit.: 39–50.

6. Quoted in Kass, "Making Babies," op. cit.: 39.

7. Ibid.: 46.

8. Ibid.: 26, 30–32.

9. Ibid.: 21–22. The work of R. G. Edwards and his colleagues in Cambridge, England, according to Kass one of the most irresponsible scientific ventures, is supported by the Ford Foundation.

10. C. S. Lewis, *The Abolition of Man.* New York: Macmillan, 1947, p. 37.

11. A. M. Macdonald, ed., *Chambers Etymological English Dictionary,* new edition with supplement. New York: Pyramid, 1968, p. 55. This is incomparably the best small dictionary available and one of the best of any size, but this etymology for *barren* is not widely supported.

12. Marjorie Galenson, *Women and Work: An International Comparison.* Ithaca, N.Y.: New York State School of Industrial and Labor Relations, Cornell University, 1973, pp. 89, 104.

Bibliography

ABBOTT, SIDNEY, and BARBARA LOVE, *Sappho Was a Right-On Woman: A Liberated View of Lesbianism.* New York: Stein & Day, 1972.

ADELSON, JOSEPH, "Is Women's Lib a Passing Phase?" *The New York Times Magazine,* March 19, 1972.

ALLEN, JODIE, "How to Save Welfare Reform," *Ripon Forum,* June 1972.

ARDREY, ROBERT, *African Genesis.* London: Collins, 1961.

BANFIELD, EDWARD C., *The Unheavenly City: The Nature and Future of Our Urban Crisis.* Boston: Little, Brown, 1968.

BEDNARIK, KARL, *The Male in Crisis.* New York: Knopf, 1970.

BELL, CAROLYN SHAW, "Age, Sex, Marriage and Jobs," *The Public Interest,* Winter 1973.

BELL, CAROLYN SHAW, "Implications for Women," *Social Policy,* September/October 1972.

BELL, DANIEL, *The Coming of Post Industrial Society.* New York: Basic Books, 1973.

BENGIS, INGRID, *Combat in the Erogenous Zone.* New York, Knopf, 1973.

BERG, ALAN, "The Economics of Breast Feeding," *Saturday Review of Science,* June 1973.

BERG, ALAN, *The Nutrition Factor.* Washington, D.C.: Brookings Institution, 1973.

BERNARD, JESSIE, *The Future of Marriage.* New York: World, 1972.

BILLINGSLEY, ANDREW, *Black Families in White America.* Englewood Cliffs, N.J.: Prentice-Hall, 1968.

BIRD, CAROLINE, "Money Is the Root of All Freedom?" *Ms.,* December 1972.

BIRD, CAROLINE, "The Case Against Marriage," In Louise Kapp Howe (ed.), *The Future of the Family.* New York: Simon & Schuster, 1972.

BOOKER, CHRISTOPHER, *The Neophiliacs.* Boston: Gambit, 1970.

BOURNE, PATRICIA GERALD, "What Day Care Ought To Be," *New Republic,* February 12, 1972.

BOWLBY, DR. JOHN, et al., *Maternal Care and Mental Health* and *Deprivation of Maternal Care,* 2 vols. in one. New York: Schocken Books, 1966.

BOWLBY, JOHN, *Child Care and the Growth of Love,* new enlarged edition. Baltimore: Penguin, 1966.

BRIFFAULT, ROBERT, and BRONISLAW MALINOWSKI, *Marriage: Past and Present.* Boston: Porter Sargent, 1956.

BRODY, SYLVIA, *Patterns of Mothering, Maternal Influence During Infancy.* New York: International Universities Press, 1956.

BROWN, CLAUDE, *Manchild in the Promised Land.* New York: Macmillan, 1967.

BROWNMILLER, SUSAN, "On Goosing," *The Village Voice,* April 15, 1971.

BURNS, EVELINE M. (ed.), *Children's Allowances and the Welfare of Children.* New York: Citizens Committee for Children of New York, 1970.

CARTER, HUGH, and PAUL C. GLICK, *Marriage and Divorce: A Social and Economic Study.* Cambridge, Mass.: Harvard University Press, 1970.

CHESLER, PHYLLIS, *Women and Madness.* Garden City, N.Y.: Doubleday, 1972.

CHODOROW, NANCY, "Being and Doing: A Cross-Cultural Examination of the Socialization of Males and Females." In Vivian Gornick and Barbara K. Moran (eds.), *Woman in Sexist Society: Studies in Power and Powerlessness.* New York: Basic Books, 1971; Signet paperback, 1972.

CLARK, KENNETH B., *Dark Ghetto.* New York: Harper & Row, 1965.

COHEN, ALBERT K., *Delinquent Boys.* New York: Free Press, 1955.

DAVIDSON, SARA, "Forewomen," *Esquire,* July 1973.

DAVIS, ELIZABETH GOULD, *The First Sex.* New York: Putnam, 1971.

DECTER, MIDGE, *The New Chastity and Other Arguments Against Women's Liberation.* New York: Coward, McCann & Geoghegan, 1972.

DE RHAM, EDITH, *The Love Fraud: A Direct Attack on the Staggering Waste of Education and Talent Among American Women.* New York: Pegasus, 1965.

DIZARD, JAN, "The Price of Success." In Louise Kapp Howe (ed.), *The Future of the Family.* New York: Simon & Schuster, 1972.

DRUCKER, PETER F., "The Surprising Seventies," *Harper's,* July 1971.

EPHRON, NORA, "Women," *Esquire,* July 1972.

EPSTEIN, CYNTHIA FUCHS, *Woman's Place.* Berkeley: University of California Press, 1969.

EPSTEIN, CYNTHIA FUCHS, and WILLIAM GOODE (eds.), *The Other Half: Roads to Women's Equality.* Englewood Cliffs, N.J.: Prentice-Hall, 1972.

ERIKSON, ERIK H., *Identity: Youth and Crisis.* New York: Norton, 1968.

FAUX, GEOFFREY, and ARTHUR I. BLAUSTEIN, *The Star Spangled Hustle.* Garden City, N.Y.: Doubleday, 1972.

FISHER, SEYMOUR, *Understanding the Female Orgasm.* New York: Basic Books, 1973. (This book is a condensation of *The Female*

Orgasm: Psychology, Physiology, Fantasy. New York: Basic Books, 1973).

FONTINELL, EUGENE, "Marriage, Morality and the Church." *Commonweal,* November 10, 1972.

FORD, CLELLAN S., and FRANK A. BEACH, *Patterns of Sexual Behavior.* New York: Harper & Row, 1951.

FORRESTER, JAY, DONELLA and DENNIS MEADOWS, JORGEN RANDERS, and WILLIAM W. BEHRENS III, *The Limits of Growth.* New York: Universe Books, 1972.

FOX, ROBIN, *Kinship and Marriage.* Baltimore: Penguin, 1967.

FRANCOEUR, ROBERT, *Eve's New Rib: Twenty Faces of Sex, Marriage and Family.* New York: Harcourt Brace Jovanovich, 1972.

FRANKS, LUCINDA, "See Jane Run," *Ms.,* January 1973.

FRAZIER, E. FRANKLIN, *The Negro Family in the United States,* revised and abridged edition. Chicago: University of Chicago Press, 1966.

FRIEDAN, BETTY, *The Feminine Mystique.* New York: Norton, 1963.

GALBRAITH, JOHN KENNETH, EDWIN KUH, and LESTER C. THUROW, "The Galbraith Plan to Promote the Minorities," *The New York Times Magazine,* August 22, 1972.

GALENSON, MARJORIE, *Women and Work: An International Comparison.* Ithaca, N.Y.: New York State School of Industrial and Labor Relations, Cornell University, 1973.

GANS, HERBERT J., *The Levittowners.* New York: Pantheon, 1967.

GESELL, ARNOLD, et al., *The First Five Years of Life.* New York: Harper & Row, 1940.

GILBERT, BIL, and NANCY WILLIAMSON, 3-part series on "Women in Sport," *Sports Illustrated,* May 28, June 4 and 11, 1973.

GILDER, GEORGE F., "The Case Against Universal Day Care," *The New Leader,* April 3, 1972; also in *Washington Star,* April 23, 1972.

GILDER, GEORGE F., and BRUCE K. CHAPMAN, *The Party That Lost Its Head.* New York: Knopf, 1966.

GINZBERG, ELI, "The Outlook for Educated Manpower," *The Public Interest,* Winter 1972.

GINZBERG, ELI, and ALICE M. YOHALEM (eds.), *Corporate Lib, Women's Challenge to Management,* Policy Studies in Employment and Welfare Number 17. Baltimore: Johns Hopkins University Press, 1973.

GITTELL, MARILYN, "Putting Merit Back in the Merit System," *Social Policy,* September/October 1972.

GITTELSON, NATALIE, *The Erotic Life of the American Wife.* New York: Delacorte, 1972.

GOLDBERG, STEVEN, *The Inevitability of Patriarchy*. New York: Morrow, 1973.

GORNICK, VIVIAN, and BARBARA K. MORAN (eds.), *Woman in Sexist Society; Studies in Power and Powerlessness*. New York: Basic Books, 1971; Signet paperback, 1972.

GREER, GERMAINE, *The Female Eunuch*. New York: McGraw-Hill, 1971.

GREER, GERMAINE, "Down with Panties," *Ms.*, July 1972.

GREER, GERMAINE, "National Convention," *Harper's*, October 1972.

GREER, GERMAINE, "On Rape," *Playboy*, January 1973.

GROSS, BERTRAM, and STANLEY MOSES, "Measuring the Real Work Force: 25 Million Unemployed," *Social Policy*, September/October 1972.

GROSSMAN, EDWARD, "The Obsolescent Mother," *Atlantic*, May 1971.

HENDIN, HERBERT, *Black Suicide*. New York: Basic Books, 1969; Harper & Row Colophon paperback, 1971.

HOLE, JUDITH, and ELLEN LEVINE, *Rebirth of Feminism*. New York: Quadrangle, 1971.

HORNEY, KAREN, *New Ways in Psychoanalysis*. New York: Norton, 1939.

HORNEY, KAREN, *Feminine Psychology*. New York: Norton, 1967.

HOWE, LOUISE KAPP (ed.), *The Future of the Family*. New York: Simon & Schuster, 1972.

HUTT, CORRINE, *Males and Females*. Harmondsworth, England: Penguin, 1972.

IGLEHART, JOHN K., "Report on Child Care Legislation," *National Journal*, vol. 4, no. 30, July 22, 1972.

JANEWAY, ELIZABETH, "Women on Women," *American Scholar*, Autumn 1972.

JANEWAY, ELIZABETH, *Man's World, Woman's Place: A Study in Social Mythology*. New York: Morrow, 1971.

JANSKY, JEANETTE, and KATRINA DE HIRSCH, *Preventing Reading Failure, Prediction, Diagnosis, Intervention*. New York: Harper & Row, 1972.

JELLIFFE, DERRICK B., M.D., *Mother's Milk and Other Home Foods*, publication of the World Health Organization, April 7, 1973.

JENCKS, CHRISTOPHER, et al., *Inequality*. New York: Basic Books, 1972.

KARP, WALTER, "The Feminine Utopia," *Horizon*, Spring 1971.

KASS, LEON R., "Making Babies—The New Biology and the 'Old' Morality," *The Public Interest*, Winter 1972.

KINSEY, ALFRED C., W. B. POMEROY, and C. E. MARTIN, *Sexual Behavior in the Human Male*. Philadelphia: Saunders, 1948.

KORDA, MICHAEL, *Male Chauvinism*. New York: Random House, 1973.

KRISTOL, IRVING, *On the Democratic Idea in America*. New York: Harper & Row, 1972.

LAWRENSON, HELEN, "The Feminine Mistake," *Esquire*, January 1971.

LEAVITT, RUBY, "Women in Other Cultures." In Vivian Gornick and Barbara K. Moran, *Woman in Sexist Society, Studies in Power and Powerlessness*. New York: Basic Books, 1971; Signet paperback, 1972.

LEVITT, LEONARD, "She," *Esquire*, October 1971.

LEWIS, C. S., *The Abolition of Man*. New York: Macmillan, 1947.

LIEBOW, ELLIOT, *Tally's Corner*. Boston: Little, Brown, 1967.

LINCOLN, C. ERIC, *The Black Muslims in America*, revised edition. Boston: Beacon Press, 1973.

LINNÉR, BIRGITTA, *Sex and Society in Sweden*, revised edition. New York: Harper & Row Colophon paperback, 1972.

LOPATA, HELEN Z., *Occupation Housewife*. New York: Oxford University Press, 1972.

LORENZ, KONRAD, *On Aggression*. New York: Harcourt Brace Jovanovich, 1966.

McCLAUGHRY, JOHN, *Expanded Ownership*. Cambridge, Mass.: Sabre Foundation, 1972.

MAILER, NORMAN, *St. George and the Godfather*. New York: NAL/World, 1972.

MAILER, NORMAN, *The Prisoner of Sex*. Boston: Little, Brown, 1971.

MALINOWSKI, BRONISLAW, *The Father in Primitive Psychology*. New York: Norton, 1927; Norton Library paperback, 1966.

MALINOWSKI, BRONISLAW, *The Sexual Life of Savages in North Western Melanesia*, 2 vols. New York: Harcourt Brace Jovanovich, 1929.

MASTERS, WILLIAM H., and VIRGINIA E. JOHNSON, *Human Sexual Response*. Boston: Little, Brown, 1966.

MAY, ROLLO, *Power and Innocence*. New York: Norton, 1972.

MEAD, MARGARET, *Coming of Age in Samoa: A Psychological Study of Primitive Youth for Western Civilization*. New York: Morrow, 1930.

MEAD, MARGARET, *Male and Female: A Study of the Sexes in a Changing World*. New York: Morrow, 1949; New York: Dell, 1968.

MEAD, MARGARET, *New Lives for Old*. New York: Morrow, 1950; New York: Dell, 1968.

MEAD, MARGARET, *Sex and Temperament in Three Primitive Societies*. New York: Morrow, 1935; New York: Dell, 1968.

MEERS, DALE, "Daycare under the Communists," *Human Events,* April 15, 1972.

MILLETT, KATE, *Sexual Politics.* Garden City, N.Y.: Doubleday, 1969.

MILLETT, KATE, "Prostitution: A Quartet for Female Voices." In Vivian Gornick and Barbara K. Moran (eds.), *Woman in Sexist Society, Studies in Power and Powerlessness.* New York: Basic Books, 1971; Signet paperback, 1972.

MINGUS, CHARLES, *Beneath the Underdog.* New York: Knopf, 1972.

MONTAGU, ASHLEY, *Touching: The Human Significance of the Skin.* New York: Columbia University Press, 1971.

MORGAN, ELAINE, *The Descent of Woman.* New York: Stein and Day, 1972.

MORRIS, DESMOND, *The Naked Ape.* New York: Dell, 1969.

MORRIS, DESMOND, *The Human Zoo.* New York: McGraw-Hill, 1970.

MORRIS, DESMOND, *Patterns of Reproductive Behavior.* New York: McGraw-Hill, 1971.

MOYNIHAN, DANIEL PATRICK, "The Urgency of FAP," interview in *Ripon Forum,* November 1971.

MOYNIHAN, DANIEL PATRICK, "The Schism in Black America," *The Public Interest,* Spring 1972.

MURDOCK, GEORGE P., "World Sample," *American Anthropologist,* vol. 59, 1957.

NEWTON, NILES, "Breast Feeding," *Psychology Today,* June 1968.

NOBILE, PHILIP, "What's the New Impotence and Who's Got It?" *Esquire,* October 1972.

O'NEILL, NENA, and GEORGE O'NEILL, *Open Marriage: A New Life Style for Couples.* New York: M. Evans, 1972; Avon paperback, 1973.

PASSELL, PETER, and LEONARD ROSS, *Retreat From Riches: Affluence and Its Enemies.* New York: Random House, 1973.

PECK, ELLEN, *The Baby Trap.* New York: Bernard Geis, 1971.

PETTIGREW, THOMAS, *Profile of the Negro American.* New York: Van Nostrand Reinhold, 1964.

PIVEN, FRANCIS FOX, and RICHARD A. CLOWARD, *Regulating the Poor: The Functions of Public Welfare.* New York: Pantheon, 1971.

PODHORETZ, NORMAN, *Making It.* New York: Random House, 1968.

PROULX, CYNTHIA, "Sex as Athletics," *Saturday Review of the Society,* May 1973.

PRYOR, KAREN, *Nursing Your Baby,* new revised edition. New York: Pocket Books, 1973.

RAINWATER, LEE, and WILLIAM L. YANCEY, *The Moynihan Report and the Politics of Controversy.* Cambridge, Mass.: M.I.T. Press, 1967.

RAPOPORT, R., and R. RAPOPORT, "Family Roles and Work Roles." In Michael Anderson (ed.), *Sociology of the Family*. Baltimore: Penguin, 1971.

REIK, THEODORE, *Ritual*. New York: International Universities Press, 1946.

ROTH, PHILIP, *Portnoy's Complaint*. New York: Random House, 1969.

ROTHMAN, SHEILA M., "Other People's Children: The Day Care Experience in America," *The Public Interest*, Winter 1973.

SCHORR, ALVIN L., "Income Maintenance and the Birth Rate," *Social Security Bulletin*, December 1965.

SCHULTZE, CHARLES, ALICE RIVLIN et al., *Setting National Priorities, The 1973 Budget*. Washington, D.C.: Brookings Institution, 1972.

SCHUR, EDWIN M., *Our Criminal Society: The Social and Legal Sources of Crime in America*. Englewood Cliffs, N.J.: Prentice-Hall, 1969.

SEABURY, PAUL, "HEW and the Universities," *Commentary*, February 1972.

SENNETT, RICHARD, and JONATHAN COBB, "Working Class Lives," *Social Policy*, September/October 1972.

SENNETT, RICHARD, and JONATHAN COBB, *Hidden Wounds of Class*. New York: Knopf, 1972.

SEXTON, PATRICIA CAYO, *The Feminized Male: White Collars and The Decline of Manliness*. New York: Random House, 1969; Vantage paperback, 1970.

SHERER, SAMUEL A., "The Voucher Experiment," *Ripon Forum*, June 1972.

SHERFEY, MARY JANE, *The Nature and Evolution of Female Sexuality*. New York: Random House, 1972.

SHILS, EDWARD B., "Small Business: Prospects and Problems," *Current History*, July 1965.

SLATER, PHILIP, *The Pursuit of Loneliness: American Culture at the Breaking Point*. Boston: Beacon Press, 1970.

SOLOW, ROBERT M., "Is the End of the World at Hand?" *Challenge*, March/April 1973.

SOROKIN, PITIRIM A., *The Crisis of Our Age: The Social and Cultural Outlook*. New York: Dutton, 1941.

SPENCER, BALDWIN, and F. J. GILLEN, *The Arunta*. New York: Humanities Press, 1966.

SPIRO, MELFORD E., *Kibbutz: Venture in Utopia*. Cambridge, Mass.: Harvard University Press, 1956.

SPITZ, RENÉ, *The First Year of Life*. New York: International Universities Press, 1965.

STEIN, SARA, and CARTER SMITH, "Return to Mom," *Saturday Review of Education*, April 1973.

SUTHERLAND, EDWIN H., and DONALD R. CRESSY, *Principles of Criminology*. Philadelphia: Lippincott, 1966.

SWADOS, HARVEY, *A Radical's America*. Boston: Little, Brown, 1962.

THEOBOLD, ROBERT, *Guaranteed Income: Next Step in Economic Evolution*. Garden City, N.Y.: Doubleday, 1965.

THOMPSON, WILLIAM IRWIN, "The Individual as Institution," *Harper's*, September 1972.

THUROW, LESTER C., "Education and Economic Equality," *The Public Interest*, Summer 1972.

TIGER, LIONEL, *Men in Groups*. New York: Random House, 1969.

TIGER, LIONEL, and ROBIN FOX, *The Imperial Animal*. New York: Holt, Rinehart and Winston, 1971; Delta paperback, 1972.

TINBERGEN, NIKO, *Social Behavior in Animals*. New York: Wiley, 1953.

TOFFLER, ALVIN, *Future Shock*. New York: Random House, 1970.

TURNBULL, COLIN, *The Mountain People*. New York: Simon & Schuster, 1972.

VILAR, ESTHER, *The Manipulated Male*. New York: Farrar, Straus and Giroux, 1972.

WATTENBERG, BEN J., and RICHARD SCAMMON, "Black Progress and Liberal Rhetoric," *Commentary*, April 1973.

WEISSTEIN, NAOMI, "Psychology Constructs the Female." In Vivian Gornick and Barbara K. Moran (eds.), *Woman in Sexist Society: Studies in Power and Powerlessness*. New York: Basic Books, 1971; Signet paperback, 1972.

WOOLF, VIRGINIA, *A Room of One's Own*. New York: Harcourt Brace Jovanovich, 1957.

WRIGLEY, E. A., *Population and History*. New York: McGraw-Hill, 1969.

X, MALCOLM, *Autobiography*. New York: Grove Press, 1964; paperback edition, 1966.

Index